Samuel Pasfield Oliver

The True Story of the French Dispute in Madagascar

Samuel Pasfield Oliver

The True Story of the French Dispute in Madagascar

ISBN/EAN: 9783337318321

Printed in Europe, USA, Canada, Australia, Japan

Cover: Foto ©ninafisch / pixelio.de

More available books at **www.hansebooks.com**

THE TRUE STORY

OF THE

FRENCH DISPUTE,

IN

MADAGASCAR

WITH A MAP

BY
CAPTAIN S. PASFIELD OLIVER, F.S.A., F.R.G.S
ETC., LATE ROYAL ARTILLERY

3565

"*Vere scire est per causas scire*"

London
T. FISHER UNWIN
26 PATERNOSTER SQUARE
1885

NOTE.

THE unhappy differences between France and Madagascar naturally excite the anxiety and regret of all who, like ourselves, have watched with sympathy the steady progress of the Malagasy in the arts of civilization and in the knowledge and practice of Christianity. It is a great misfortune that the passions and calamities of war should have interposed to arrest the advance of a people who seemed destined soon to enter the comity of nations, and to play a useful part in the regeneration of Africa.

This view is deepened by the conviction that the proceedings of the French Government in Madagascar are largely due to a total misconception of the acts of England and of Englishmen in the island. The people of this country have no desire to secure any exclusive rights or privileges in Madagascar. Their earnest wish is that the Malagasy shall fulfil every Treaty obligation into which they have entered, but that, at the same time, they shall be at liberty to work out their destiny without any other foreign interference than that involved in the peaceful establishment among them of well-ordered religious, educational, and commercial instrumentalities.

NOTE.

The following work has been written by Captain Oliver, not only to furnish the public with a complete narrative of those events in the history of Madagascar which have culminated in the existing hostilities with France, but also to promote the peaceful settlement of the difficulty. This twofold object meets with our hearty approval; and we earnestly hope that Captain Oliver's laudable attempt to enlighten the public mind will be attended with that full measure of success which it deserves.

SHAFTESBURY.
J. W. PEASE, M.P.
WILLIAM MCARTHUR, M.P.
R. N. FOWLER, M.P.
JAMES CROPPER, M.P.
ALEXANDER MCARTHUR, M.P.
J. G. ALEXANDER.

PREFACE.

In the autumn of last year, 1884, two remarkable "Red-books" were circulated in Europe by the Government of Ranavàlona III., Queen of Madagascar, causing considerable curiosity in diplomatic circles and amongst those interested in the welfare of the great African island.

These publications, written in Malagasy and in French, are in excellent form, and indeed they can vie in their general get-up with the famous " White-books " of Imperial Germany and the "Yellow-books" of the French Republic; whilst they are far handsomer in their appearance, at all events, than our own ugly parliamentary "Blue-books."

They afford conclusive disproof of any charges of barbarism which may be brought against the Government of Madagascar, and give evidence that the Ministers of Ranavàlona III. are well skilled in the methods of civilized diplomacy.

But few copies of these books were distributed in England, and of these a single copy of each volume was forwarded to the Hon. Secretary of the Madagascar Committee. These copies were placed in the hands of the author of the following pages, in order that an abstract might be made of their contents, and a short explanatory narrative drawn up, to afford the necessary information to those who, whilst interested in the subject, have been unable to follow up closely the intricacies of the Madagascar question. It will be seen that I have by no means limited my plan to this object, but have given a careful historical view of the relations of France with Madagascar from the beginning.

It is undoubtedly a fact that, up to the present time, very few people, whether officials or laymen, have been well acquainted with the true bearings of the Franco-Malagasy complication; but the publication of the correspondence in these "Red-books" has thrown a flood of light on several points hitherto obscure. This enlightenment has had its due effect across the Channel, as is clear from a work by M. Ruben Saillens, recently published in Paris, to which M. Frédéric Passy, deputy for the department of the Seine, and a well-known publicist and economist, has written a striking preface, and advance proofs of which the present writer has, by courtesy of the author, had the advantage of perusing. It would thus appear that a section, at least, of the French public has at last awakened to a sense of the unjust and unscrupulous conduct towards an inoffensive and weaker race exhibited by their unworthy agents, the consular and colonial officials at Antananarivo, on the coast of Madagascar, and last but not least at Réunion.

Mr. Chesson, who, as representing the Madagascar Committee, was brought into close relations with the Envoys during their residence in England, has contributed a supplementary chapter on the Malagasy mission to Europe.

S. PASFIELD OLIVER.

Anglesey, Gosport,
    February 11, 1885.

TABLE OF CONTENTS.

CHAPTER I.

A Firebrand.

Introductory—M. Baudais appointed Commissioner by M. Gambetta—Policy of colonial enterprise initiated by M. Gambetta—Instructions to the Consul by M. de Freycinet—The disputes pending between France and Madagascar—M. Baudais accuses the Malagasy Government of ill-will and bad faith—The French grievances formulated—The Laborde inheritance—The *Toale* affair—The French Protectorate—Retrospective sketch of M. Laborde's connection with the Malagasy Government—His shipwreck and early career—He is engaged in the service of Ranavàlona I.—Manufactures war *matériel* for the Queen—His intrigues against his Royal Mistress —The Lambert and Laborde conspiracy—M. Lambert seeks assistance from the French and English Governments—His ambitious schemes receive no countenance—The Jesuit plot and attempted *coup d'état*—Signal failure—The banishment of the conspirators—Engagement between the Prince Rakoto and Lambert—Death of Ranavàlona.—Accession of Radama II.—Chart of Concession to the Lambert Company—Treaty between France and Madagascar—The revolution and revoking both the Chart and Treaty—An indemnity paid by the Government of Madagascar —Second Treaty concluded between France and Madagascar—Death of Laborde—The claims of property made by his heirs—The forged deeds— Repudiation by the Madagascar Government—M. Cassas leaves the capital —Captain Vallon's peaceable declaration—M. Meyer attempts to compromise the claims—Promulgation of the law 85—Arrival of M. Baudais.

pp. 1-50

CHAPTER II.

Materials for Incendiarism.

The second question in dispute—The affair of the smuggler dhow, *Toale*— Arrival of the gunboat *Décidée* at Mojangà—Reported outrage at Marambitsy—Letter of Lieutenant Buisson to the Hova Governor—Captain Vallon's inquiry—Demand for reparation by M. Meyer—Reply of the Malagasy Government—State of the dispute on arrival of M. Baudais— The sequel of the affair—The third section of the Madagascar Question —The claims of sovereignty or Protectorate over the north-west coast by France—The treaties of 1840-41 with the Sàkalàva chiefs—Insurrection at Nossi-Bé in 1849—Night attack on Tafondro in 1851—Death of Tsimandroho—Treaties of friendship made by Admiral Fleuriot de Langle

—The village of Mahagolo in Baly Bay burnt by the French in 1859— Punishment of the Sàkalàva by the French man-of-war *Labourdonnais*— The Sàkalàva acknowledge Radama II. as sovereign—Radama acknowledged sovereign of Madagascar by French Treaty in 1862—Treaty concluded by M. Garnier acknowledges Ranavàlona II. as sovereign of Madagascar in 1868—French claims dormant until the arrival of M. Baudais—M. Baudais reports to his Government the infringement of French rights in north-west Madagascar ... ... pp. 51–77

CHAPTER III.
CONFLAGRATION.

M. Baudais is authorized by his Government to concert defensive measures with the governor of Nossi-Bé—Arrival of the *Forfait* in Malagasy waters — Wrangling correspondence and stormy interviews — The meeting at the palace of Tsiazompaniry—Demand made for the removal of the national flag from the west-coast—Formal protest of the Malagasy —M. Baudais leaves the capital—Commotion at Antananarivo—Threats against the French—The tricolor hauled down, and retirement of M. Campan—Captain Le Timbre seizes the flags in Passandava Bay—An embargo placed on the *Antananarivo*, and on the *Stilman*—Landing of arms and ammunition—Gravity of the situation—Change of government in France—An embassy to Europe determined upon—Objections of M. Baudais—Squabble about the *Madagascar Times*—The Hova envoys reach Paris—The negotiations—Rupture of the conferences—Departure of the ambassadors from France ... . pp. 78–101

CHAPTER IV.
TORMENTUM BELLI.

Arrival of the Malagasy ambassadors in London—The Madagascar committee —Deputation to Lord Granville—Reception of the envoys—Difference between the French and Malagasy accounts of the causes which led to the rupture of the conferences—Offers of mediation by Her Majesty's Government—Rejection of the good offices proffered by England— Resignation of M. Duclerc—M. Fallières becomes President of Council— The policy at the Quai d'Orsay towards Madagascar unchanged—Admiral Pierre dispatched to Madagascar—Another change of government at Paris—M. Jules Ferry becomes Premier—Aggressive policy in regard to Madagascar maintained—Instructions to the Admiral—Operations in Passandava Bay—Bombardment of Mojangà—Expulsion of French residents from Antananarivo and the interior—The ultimatum—Alarming reports at Tamatave—Captain Johnstone of the *Dryad*—His prudent conduct— A committee of defence formed—An armed party landed for the protection of the consulate—Lieutenant Knowles, R.N., assistant to Mr. Pakenham —Illness of the British consul—Flight of the native inhabitants—The ultimatum rejected, and bombardment of Tamatave—The Pierre-Johnstone correspondence—The French flag hoisted on the fort—Shelling of Hivondro, Fenoarivo and Foule-point—Foreign consuls ordered to haul down their flags—The Shaw incident—Arrest and close confinement of Mr. Shaw—The *Taymouth Castle*—The British consul and staff ordered to quit Tamatave—Death of Mr. Pakenham—Captain Johnstone's conduct upheld by the British Government — Regret expressed by the French Minister—Captain Johnstone promoted for his services on this occasion.

pp. 102–130

CHAPTER V.
NEUTRAL SENTIMENTS.

Arrival of the French subjects expelled from the interior at the coast— Repulse of night attacks on the French outposts—Grave announcement by Mr. Gladstone in the House of Commons—Statement by M. Challemel-Lacour in the Chamber of Deputies—Modified instructions to M. Baudais —Admiral Pierre's ill health and retirement—Mr. Gladstone's reassuring speech at the Mansion House—Death of Admiral Pierre—Sequel of the Shaw affair—Meeting at Exeter Hall—Spontaneous offer of indemnity accepted by the British Government—Return of the Malagasy ambassadors to their country—What they had accomplished—Reception by Her Majesty—Revision of the treaty of 1865—Restriction of the liquor traffic —Speech of Ravoninahitriniarivo—The United Kingdom Alliance— The embassy in America—The ratification of a treaty with the United States—Short treaties of amity and peace with Germany and Italy—The envoys reach Antananarivo ... ... pp. 131–150

CHAPTER VI.
REGINA DEI GRATIA.

The death of Queen Ranavàlona II.—Her successor—Brief retrospect of the late sovereign's reign—The plot of Rasata frustrated by Rainilaiarivony— Change of policy—Reforms initiated—The destruction of the idols— Charity of the Queen—Political, educational, and social improvements— Governmental departments instituted—The ministers—Administration of justice—Reorganization of the army—The codification of the laws— Emancipation of the Mozambique slaves—Accession of Ranavàlona III. —The speech from the throne at Mahamasina—Notice of the Prime Minister—His character, services to his country, and the results of his policy—The return of the envoys—The natural allies of the Hovas— Address by Ravoninahitriniarivo—The correspondence between the Government of Madagascar and the French Commissioners published— Effect of the Malagasy Red-books in Europe ... ... pp. 151–168

CHAPTER VII.
OPERATIONS CIVIL AND MILITARY.

Tour of H.M.S. *Dryad* along the east coast—The British flag unknown—The *Dryad* supposed to be a French ship in disguise—The export of all food supplies forbidden—Protest of Captain Johnstone, R.N.—The Prime Minister complies with Captain Johnstone's demands—Annoyances to neutrals—Unfortunate state of affairs, owing to the French occupation— Admiral Galiber takes command—Proposal to reopen negotiations— Bombardment of Vohémar without notice—The other parts on the east coast shelled and burnt—Negotiations resumed—Fruitless results of the conferences at Ambodimanga—Mr. Graves, the new British consul, and Mr. Pickersgill, the vice-consul, reach their posts at Tamatave and

Antananarivo — H.M.S. *Tourmaline* relieves H.M.S. *Dryad* — Boat voyage of Lieutenant Hayes—French reconnaissance towards Manjakandrianombana—M. Campan visits the Hova retrenchments — Pourparlers—The fifth conference—Departure of Admiral Galiber—The interpellation by M. Lanessan in the Chamber of Deputies—Interesting debate —Speeches by M. Jules Ferry and others—The Chamber resolves to maintain all the rights of France—Special committee appointed to examine the credits asked by the government—Depositions by the witnesses—Conflicting evidence—M. Lanessan's report—Recommendations of the committee —The President of Council—The bill passed by a large majority in the Chamber, and subsequently in the Senate ... ... pp. 169–202

CHAPTER VIII.
BLOCKADE.

Admiral Miot sent from France to relieve Admiral Galiber—Cordial relations between the ships of the two European powers—British property destroyed at Andevoranto—Mr. Graves proceeds to Mojangà—Blockade of the river leading to Mahabo—Registry of British Indian subjects—Francisation of Arabs and Indians—Black labour—Admiral Miot assumes command— Blockade of Mahanoro and Fenoarivo notified—The *Orénoque* and *Capricorne*—Renewal of negotiations—The Malagasy Government willing to do everything to satisfy France except the sacrifice of the independence of their territory—Admiral Miot proclaims his instructions— The conference —The bases insisted on by France—Mr. Pickersgill's report—Kabary at Andohalo—Patriotic sentiments evoked at the assembly—All able-bodied men ordered to prepare for service—Proclamation by the Queen Ranavàlona III. in the gazette—Visit of the British Consul to Antananarivo— —Address to the Queen—The grand Kabary—The Queen's speech— Reply of the Prime Minister—Review of the troops amidst great enthusiasm—Reconnaissance by the French—Mahanoro shelled by the *Allier*— Certain points in Passandava Bay occupied by the French—Members of the "Friends' Foreign Mission Association" treated cordially by Admiral Miot—Capture of Vohémar, and successful assault on Ambaniou—Captain de Vogue arrives in Madagascar—Admiral Peyron informs the Chamber that 12,000,000 francs have been spent on the Madagascar expedition.
pp. 203–245

POSTSCRIPT ... ... p. 245

SUPPLEMENTARY CHAPTER.
The Malagasy Mission 248

APPENDIX.
Soatsimanampiovana 265
Ultimatum of 1st June, 1883 268

INDEX 273

MAP OF MADAGASCAR.

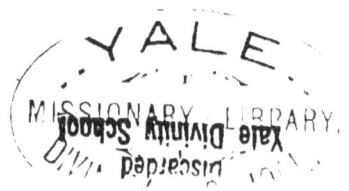

CHAPTER I.

A FIREBRAND.

IT was in August, 1881, that M. A. Baudais, the newly-appointed French Consul for Madagascar, and Commissioner of the French Government, left Paris to take over the duties of his post at the court of Antananarivo. He had just received his commission at the hands of M. Gambetta, who then directed the foreign relations of the Republic, and he was armed with special instructions to carry out vigorously an active policy in accordance with that spirit of colonial enterprise [1] which the then French

---

[1] In a recent number of the *Edinburgh Review* (No. 323, July, 1883), in reference to the action of France in distant expeditions, it is pointed out that the spirit of colonial enterprise in remote parts of the globe which has recently been manifested by the present French Government appears to the writer to be entirely fictitious; "it has no real root," he states, "in the country; and it has been prompted partly as a compensation for their diminished influence in Europe, and partly as a mode of exciting patriotic enthusiasm for the purposes usually described as 'political capital.' Not one Frenchman in ten thousand cares a rush for the great names of Dupleix, La Bourdonnaye, or Montcalm, or even knows that Napoleon sold to the United States not only Louisiana, but the finest part of the North American continent. The passion which founds colonial empires has no place in the French heart. The idea of expatriation, which is attractive to numbers of our own countrymen, is on the contrary painful and repulsive to the great majority of the French. The *amour du clocher*, as they term it, is one of the strongest and most universal sentiments of the French people. Hence, of all the states of Europe, at the present time, France is least given to foreign emigration and

Minister seems to have initiated during his tenure of power, so soon to terminate for ever.

With the arrival of the new French Commissioner at Antananarivo, where M. Baudais succeeded M. T. Meyer, an altogether different aspect with regard to the pending diplomatic discussions between the two governments appears to have been inaugurated; and from this period, therefore, it will be convenient to commence our account of the causes which ultimately led to the present hostilities between France and Madagascar.

At this date the political situation was not unclouded, but tact and conciliatory measures could undoubtedly have brought about a *modus vivendi* between the weak native and the strong European power; whilst the haughty and overbearing tactics and demeanour of the Commissioner of the Republic designedly brought about a threatening atmosphere charged with explosive materials to which it was M. Baudais' mission afterwards to apply the spark.

> " *Confound the peace establish'd, and prepare*
> *Their souls to hatred, and their hands to war.*"

Acting in accordance with the instructions confided to colonial enterprise. The stress produced by the excessive pressure of population in these islands and in some parts of the continent is unfelt in France. She has at her gates a vast territory in Northern Africa to which the migration of the French in fifty years has been extremely small. In point of fact, the impulse which has conducted the French within the last few years to Mexico, to Tunis, to Congo, to Madagascar, and to Tonquin, can be shown to take its rise in the speculations of a few adventurous individuals, who have succeeded in implicating the Government in their private affairs, and have sought to retrieve a personal disaster by a national intervention."

him by the chief of his department, the French Consul, on reaching the capital of the Hovas, found ready to his hand several comparatively minor disputes left unsettled by his predecessors, which, however, were speedily nursed into serious grievances of grave import, and only required additional stirring to furnish pretexts for exacting reparation under menace of force of arms.

Before M. Baudais had been three months in Madagascar the Ministry of M. Gambetta was defeated in the Chamber and resigned; but M. de Freycinet on his accession to office lost no time in confirming his predecessor's instructions to M. Baudais,[1] to insist on the full acknowledgment of French interests and French rights in Madagascar. Accordingly, in a somewhat roughly worded despatch addressed to the Prime Minister, Rainilaiarivony, dated 29th April, 1882, the French Commissioner expressed himself to the following effect. He stated that the French Government saw with regret that the Treaty of 1868 was unceasingly trampled on in practice, notwithstanding the protestations and pompous phrases of the Hova Government. He complained that none of the French grievances had met with any redress during the previous five years;

[1] "Our intentions," wrote M. de Freycinet, "remain still the same; we are not less solicitous to-day than we were last year to avoid, in our relations with the Government of Antananarivo, anything which could awaken in it that distrust which, however little justified, it has lately manifested: our only preoccupation is to ensure the safety of our interests and our rights, which have nothing incompatible with the independence of the Hova nation.

for instance, the liquidation of the Laborde inheritance had been treated in a spirit of bad faith by the Malagasy officials; the affair of the *Toale* dhow had not been satisfactorily settled, and, in short, the treaty impugned in many important points. Again, not content with indirectly breaking their treaty engagements with the French, the Ministers of Ranavàlona II. had not hesitated to make an open breach of the treaty by the promulgation of a law relating to property, known as Law 85 ; whilst last, but not least, M. Baudais drew the attention of the Prime Minister to a fact yet more serious than the preceding ones—the assumption of authority by the Hovas over the north-west provinces, which had been secured to France by treaties many years previously. Rainilaiarivony was informed that the presence of a French squadron off those coasts indicated the importance France attached to her rights of protectorate, and finally the Malagasy Government was solemnly warned that France had decided to exact all her rights and enforce them with the utmost rigour.

All the grievances of France against Madagascar were thus recapitulated at length in this despatch, which formed, in fact, a species of indictment against the Government of Ranavàlona II.; and we are thus enabled to formulate the French claims at this period, and investigate the foundations on which they were based.

They may be conveniently reduced under three heads, which can best be explained separately, viz.,

I. The liquidation of the Laborde inheritance, and the rights of French subjects in regard to landed property in Madagascar.

II. The affair of the smuggling dhow, the *Toale*.

III. The rights of French sovereignty or protectorate over the north-west coast of Madagascar.

I. *The Liquidation of the Laborde Inheritance.*

In order to fully understand this subject, a retrospective view must be taken of circumstances which occurred a good many years ago, and for this purpose a brief sketch of the early French trading establishments on the east coast of Madagascar may serve in some degree to explain the extraordinary position occupied by the late M. Laborde for nearly half a century in Madagascar. The disputes which arose after his death as to the ownership of the premises occupied by him for many years during his lifetime are important because they gave rise to serious alleged grievances, by which the French consular authorities sought to fasten upon the Hova Government accusations of ill-will, bad faith, obstruction, and open violation of the treaty concluded between France and Madagascar in 1868.

When Radama I. came down from his capital in the

highlands to the east coast in 1817, with a large following and an escort of some twenty-five thousand soldiers, to exercise his powers of suzerainty over the Betanimena and Betsimisaraka chiefs, he visited Tamatave, where he concluded an amicable arrangement with Jean Réné and Fiche, the two half-caste chiefs who ruled on the banks of the Hivondro. Whilst at Tamatave, Radama received cordially the congratulations of the French traders resident in that port, and at the head of them was M. Arnoux, who represented the commercial interests of the French community.

M. Arnoux was the agent of the Colonial firm "Rontaunay," of Réunion, and he formed an important sugar plantation and factory at Mahéla, on the coast south of Tamatave. This establishment seems to have flourished until after the death of Radama in 1828, when, disquieted by the reports from Imerina, M. Arnoux proceeded to Antananarivo, to invoke the protection of the new Queen Ranavàlona I., who received him graciously in March, 1829. On his return journey, M. Arnoux died, and he was succeeded in the management of his business by M. de Lastelle. Shortly after this the expedition under Commodore Gourbeyre bombarded Tamatave, and the situation of M. de Lastelle was precarious. He was engaged in putting up some water-mills which he had just received, when he was summoned to the capital by the Hova

Government; and on his attending the Court he was fortunate in securing the favour of the Queen and Andrian Mihaza, her minister. He obtained permission to erect a distillery, and besides was authorized to farm the customhouse duties at Fenoarivo, Mahanoro, and Mananzary, besides being invested with other commercial privileges. By favour of the Queen, M. de Lastelle was commissioned to proceed to Europe and purchase various goods for the court of Antananarivo, and about this time it appears that he was joined by his compatriot Laborde. The early history of M. Laborde is somewhat wrapped up in obscurity, but according to M. Francis Riaux (Secretary to the Madagascar Company), and to M. d'Escamps, it is recorded that Jean Laborde was born at Auch on the 16th October, 1805, and was the son of Jeanne Baron and Jean Laborde, the latter being master wheelwright, blacksmith, and saddle and harness maker (*Archives municipales de la Ville d'Auch*). Madame Pfeiffer states in her last book of travel that M. Laborde served several years in a cavalry regiment, but, desirous of seeing the world, he purchased a substitute after the death of his father and embarked for the East Indies. He established at Bombay several shops for the repair of steam-engines and arms, saddlery, &c., and seems to have made a small fortune. His restless spirit, however, did not allow him to remain long in one spot. He disposed of his workshops to a friend, and started in 1831 for the Indian (Mascarene?) archipelago. The vessel, which was commanded by a M. Savoie, was wrecked near Fort Dauphin, and, like the semi-mythical Robert Drury, M. Laborde not only lost his worldly goods but his liberty; "for" adds Madame Pfeiffer sarcastically, "in this hospitable country all shipwrecked sailors become slaves." From this point the accounts differ somewhat. Madame Ida Pfeiffer, who professes to have taken her romance from the lips of M. Laborde himself, says, that he (Laborde), with several of his companions, was conducted to Antananarivo to be there sold; but happily for him the Queen, hearing that he could manufacture muskets, gave him his liberty, and engaged him to serve her faithfully for five years.[1] M. Laborde accepted the offer, and established a workshop, where he manufactured all kinds of arms, even small pieces of ordnance, powder, and other articles. In spite of her hatred towards the Europeans, the Queen ended by taking him into her confidence, and at the same time constituted him her principal adviser in her important and serious undertakings. In fact, according to the narrative of Madame Pfeiffer, M. Laborde played the same part of confidential adviser to the Queen Ranavàlona I. as the French Commissioner accused Mr. Parrett of acting

---

[1] *Voyage à Madagascar par Mdme. Ida Pfeiffer.* Traduit de l'Allemand. Paris: Hachette, 1881, p. 150.

towards Queen Ranavàlona II. There is only this difference, that during the former period M. Laborde was acting as intimate adviser to the sovereign who, like Catherine II. of Russia, has been styled by French authors "the modern Messalina,"[1] whose name has been universally detested for the cruelties perpetrated under her rule, and by whom all foreigners were excluded from her dominions, for a period of a quarter of a century (twenty-six years, from 1831 to 1857), during a reign of despotic terrorism. On the other hand, Mr. Parrett's only claim to the keen dislike and jealousy on the part of the French consuls and commissioners appears to be that he has been the intimate friend of Rainilaiarivony, the minister of the late Ranavàlona II., during whose reign and ministry Madagascar has been raised from the depths of idolatry and superstitious influences to a certain standard of civilization, which can be judged of by the wonderful progress of Christianity and education, morality and humanity throughout the island, within the last fifteen years. Admitting that both these individuals have been, as it has always been alleged, the intimate advisers of their respective sovereigns, the results of their counsels are hardly in favour of the late French consul.

According to M. d'Escamps (p. 183), Messrs. Savoie and

---

[1] M. d'Escamps gives her the title of the "Female Caligula," p. 124. M. Jules Ferry spoke of her in the Chamber of Deputies in March, 1884, as "l'horrible Ranavàlona" (*Journal Officiel*, Mars 28, 1884).

Laborde, after their shipwreck, were received by M. de Lastelle, and M. Savoie married a Malagasy woman, sister of the so-called Princess Juliette Fiche, *alias* Fisatra, of the Betanimena tribe (who are blacks, and not of the lighter coloured tribes of the interior). Through the friendship of M. de Lastelle, and on his recommendation to the Queen, M. Laborde proceeded to the capital (not to be sold as a slave), as a skilled mechanician and artisan, who could instruct the Hovas in the arts of manufacturing firearms and gunpowder, &c., and, with the help of a small collection of art and science manuals (*Manuels Encyclopédiques Roret*), M. Laborde established factories of different descriptions in the vicinity of the capital.

The French histories of this period [1] attribute to M. Laborde the initiation of these factories, but they omit to mention that he found a number of native artisans who had been instructed in various manufactures by well-skilled English mechanics. That he made good use of the material he thus found ready to his hands there is no doubt, but his predecessors certainly deserve their share of credit, of which the lion's portion has been popularly ascribed to Laborde. We need only to mention some of these Englishmen whose names should not be forgotten by

[1] M. Désiré Laverdant mentions, in 1844, that M. Laborde was grand master of ceremonies and dancing master at the court of Antananarivo, and he it was who introduced the waltz into the country. (See *Colonization de Madagascar*, p. 129.)

Malagasy of the present day. Under Mr. Cameron alone, who was engaged in the construction of machinery and other public works, nearly six hundred youths were constantly employed. Under his superintendence a canal was cut between the river Ikiopa and a lake at Amparibé, which was converted into a reservoir of water for the powder-mills, which were also erected by Mr. Cameron. The labours of the artisans, Messrs. Chick, Brooks, Canham, Rowlands, and others, who taught the natives to work in carpentry, joinery, and iron, &c., were highly prized by the people; and Mr. Cameron undertook the establishment of an iron foundry, a glass manufactory, printing, leather-work, and brick-making. Mr. Cameron, from 1826 until 1835, instructed the people in building and constructed a number of houses and palaces for the Government. A Frenchman named Le Gros has also left behind him a fine specimen of his skill in the timber palace of Isonierana. In 1822 Mr. Rowlands, a weaver, introduced the English wheel and loom, and Mr. Canham, from 1824 to 1834, taught the natives tanning and leather-work. It is remarkable that M. Laborde's name does not appear as having been at the capital as long as any of the English missionaries or artisans remained. These artisans and missionaries were all desired to leave Madagascar in 1835, in which year Messrs. Cameron and Chick declined to serve any longer, as Christianity was forbidden. The last missionaries,

Messrs. Johns and Baker, left finally in July, 1836, and it must have been on the departure of all the English mechanics that M. Laborde was summoned up to the capital by Ranavàlona on the recommendation of M. de Lastelle as before mentioned.

This period of M. Laborde's career, from 1831, when he was wrecked, until 1836, when the last missionaries left Imerina, remains clouded in mystery; but at all events he was connected with M. de Lastelle during this time, and with the trade on the coast. Now the traders on the coast at this period were all more or less connected with the slave trade, for it was not until the year 1834 that the Act for the abolition of slavery in all the British dominions was promulgated; and even then the existing slave laws remained in force until 1st February, 1835, after which time apprentice labourers, so called, were employed on the plantations of Mauritius. But in the neighbouring colony of Réunion the preparation for the enfranchisement of the slaves was not legislated for until 1845, and the actual emancipation of the slaves was only carried into effect by the French Republic in 1848. Now listen to what the Reverend Wm. Ellis stated to Lord Clarendon in 1856. He wrote in reference to the French party then intriguing at Antananarivo as follows: " In mentioning the French gentlemen residing at the capital, I refer to M. Laborde, a native of Mauritius, and formerly a slave dealer, who many years ago came from Mozambique to Madagascar, where he proposed to manufacture arms for the native government. He has since been employed on several occasions by the Queen, and exercises considerable influence over a few of the chiefs" (*Life of Wm. Ellis.* Murray, London, 1873, p. 235).

On M. Laborde's arrival at Antananarivo he was installed, together with a M. Drotie, by Ranavàlona at Avaratr' Ilafy in the neighbourhood of the capital, where he constructed workshops for the Queen. He was subsequently moved by the Queen's orders to Ambodin, Andohalo, and a country residence was assigned to him at Ambohitsorohitra. While later, orders were given for the establishment of factories and industrial works at Mantasoua,[1] about twenty miles from the metropolis, where a huge royal arsenal was developed under the immediate superintendence of M. Laborde. It will be seen that these properties have been claimed by the heirs of the Laborde inheritance. Of what happened between 1836 or 1837 and 1847 there is little or no trustworthy record. During this decade the cruel despotism of Ranavàlona and her advisers Rainiharo and his brother was ruthlessly exercised throughout Madagascar; large portions of the beautiful island were ravaged by sanguinary campaigns, undertaken solely for blood and

---

[1] The large establishment here constructed was named *Soatsimanampiovana*, *i.e.*, "beauty without change." See Appendix.

plunder, whilst Imerina was sealed to all outside interference. Whilst France and England were engaged in hostilities, or rather reprisals, as they are called in these days, against Madagascar; and whilst the heads of Frenchmen and Englishmen were being exhibited on poles at Tamatave, M. Laborde was engaged in manufacturing muskets, gunpowder, and munitions of war for the use of the Hova army against his own countrymen. At the same time he appears to have acted, as already stated, in the *rôle* of skilled expert and confidential agent to the sovereign. But even as his predecessor Robin, who deserted the Malagasy cause, as he formerly had the French army, and returned again to the French under Gourbeyre in 1831, a double renegade; so M. Laborde, about 1847, commenced intrigues against his royal mistress and made overtures to the French Admiral Cécile, then commanding the French squadron in the Indian Ocean. At the instigation of M. Laborde, Rear-Admiral Cécile wrote to Prince Rakoto, the Queen's son and heir, promising him the support and approbation of France in his projects of reform, in other words, of revolution; for under Laborde's influence the idea of dethroning Ranavàlona and of placing her son on the throne had been insidiously suggested to the Prince and a few of his trusted companions. From this date the embryo conspiracy was cautiously organized which spread its ramifications through all classes of society in Imerina, and although the development was slow, after some years the adhesion of many powerful chiefs encouraged the ringleaders to commence active operations.

At this time, in 1855, M. Laborde was able to secure the services of another European, a compatriot, as unscrupulous and ambitious as himself. This was Joseph François Lambert, a Mauritius trader, who was part owner of a steamer, the *Mascareigne*, which was employed in the profitable transport [1] of free labourers (black, of course) from the Mozambique channel to Réunion. Now, these so-called free labourers, engaged for a term of years to work upon the Réunion plantations, were in real truth nothing more or less than slaves. Father de la Vaissière quotes the evidence of Father Jouen, who was eye-witness of the infamous scenes enacted by the European traders in procuring these *engagés* for the labour market in Réunion,[2]

---

[1] "Avant d'entreprendre le voyage de Madagascar, M. Lambert devait aller acheter pour la France des nègres sur les côtes de Zanzibar et de Mozambique et les transporter à l'île Bourbon. C'est une nouvelle espèce de traite mitigée, inventée par le gouvernement français et tolérée par l'Angleterre. Le nègre n'est esclave que pendant cinq ans et reçoit de son maître, indépendamment de la nourriture et du logement, deux écus par mois. Au bout de ces cinq ans, il est libre de continuer à travailler ou bien de mourir de faim s'il ne veut pas travailler. Il peut même se racheter plus tôt au prix de cinquante écus, et même retourner dans son pays s'il a pour cela l'argent nécessaire."

[2] "The recruitment of labourers," says Father Jouen, "was just commencing in Baly Bay (1859), and it attracted to these coasts a crowd of vessels by the hopes of fabulous gain. The hired labourer, (*engagé*), who could be obtained on the spot for twenty or thirty dollars, fetched at Réunion scarcely less than two hundred or two hundred and forty dollars (1,000 to 1,200 francs, £40 to £48). From this it may be judged to what a pitch the cupidity of the

which sufficiently indicates the small difference which existed then between the free labour transport and the former slave trade. They were then, and have been until recently, the same traffic under a modified name.

M. Lambert was a native of Redon (Ile et Vilaine), the son of a custom-house official, and was a French subject, although trading as a merchant of Mauritius,[1] in which colony he married a Creole wife. When he arrived in Madagascar in 1855 he was thirty-one years of age. Engaged as he was in the labour traffic, he was anxious to be on good terms with the Queen of Madagascar, and, prompted by M. de Lastelle, was enabled to perform a service by taking a cargo of rice to the Hova garrison at

---

traders was aroused. That of the Malagasy was not much less, in view of the strong liquors, the barrels of arrack and presents of all sorts which were lavished upon them. Thenceforth on the part of the Malagasy there was nothing but wars and incursions to steal men and sell them to the white people. Free or slave, they were alike carried off pitilessly, whoever was captured. How often have we ourselves seen these unfortunates fastened to a long pole, with irons on their neck and feet, squatted on the shore awaiting the hour of embarkation. These were the *voluntary* hired labourers for the Island of Réunion. What resulted from these doleful operations? It was that, once on board ship, these miserable folk, plundered, stolen, brutally torn from their country and families, only cared to escape at all hazards from such terrible slavery. The very chiefs who had sold them were the first to slyly suggest to them the idea and furnish them with the means of flight, with the infernal idea of recapturing and selling them a second time. Add to this the carelessness of the masters and crews, who more than once left their vessels almost deserted and defenceless at the mercy of these madmen: the temptation was too strong to be resisted. The first of the revolts took place on board a vessel named the *Happy*; fortunately for the captain and men, it was repressed in time; but it cost the lives of 140 Malagasy, who were killed or drowned" (*Madagascar, its Inhabitants and Missionaries.* By Father de la Vaissière, S.J., vol. i. p. 309).

[1] Lambert, Menon et Cie de Port Louis, Ile Maurice.

Mojangà[1] who were then blockaded by the surrounding Sàkalàva tribes. In return for this operation M. Laborde obtained permission for M. Lambert to ascend from the coast to Antananarivo, where he was received with great favour at the court of Ranavàlona. Introduced by Laborde to the Prince Rakoto, who was only five years junior to Lambert in age, the latter speedily ingratiated himself with Rakoto and took the oath of blood as sworn brothers according to Malagasy custom. According to M. d'Escamps and other French authors, the Crown Prince had previously made spontaneous appeals for the protection and assistance of the French, viz., in 1847, as before mentioned, to Admiral Cécile, and again in 1852 to M. Hubert Delisle, Governor of Réunion, from both of whom he received marks of sympathy; and later he is said by M. Riaux to have requested the protectorate of France from the emperor. Lambert on the occasion of his visit was well provided with presents for the Queen and her court, *objets de luxe*, Parisian knick-knacks, and last but not least French spirits, liqueurs, and sparkling wines.

It was now suggested to the Prince that M. Lambert should proceed to Europe as the confidential agent and representative of the Prince, offering in his name to place

---

[1] D'Escamps and other French authors mention Fort Dauphin, but Père Finaz in his diary gives Mojangà as the place relieved. See P. de la Vaissière, vol. i. p. 231.

the whole of Madagascar under the protection of France, and appealing to the generosity of the French emperor for assistance in arms and men of science.

MM. Laborde and Lambert drew up a deed of concession, by which the Prince promised, on his accession, the exclusive monopoly of working the agricultural and mineral wealth of the island to M. Lambert and a company to be formed under his auspices with a French protectorate. This secret document was signed by the Prince on the 28th June, 1855, and with this precious concession and letters begging the emperor to look on M. Lambert as the representative of Rakoto, M. Lambert departed for Europe at the end of 1855, and lost no time in seeking an interview with Napoleon III., who, true to his alliance with England, would not listen to any suggestions of interference in Madagascar without the co-operation of England.

M. Lambert next proceeded to London, but Lord Clarendon would not countenance the ambitious schemes of the adventurer, and moreover warned the Colonial Government of Mauritius of the plots disclosed by M. Lambert and his indiscreet proposals. At this time the Rev. Wm. Ellis had received an invitation to visit Imerina, and before proceeding thither he had an interview with Lord Clarendon, who informed him of Lambert's projects and the conspiracy which had been set on foot to dethrone the

Queen of Madagascar. Mr. Ellis on proceeding to Antananarivo in 1856 found himself in a responsible and critical position. He was under a constant and not friendly surveillance. He was credibly informed that M. Laborde had offered two hundred dollars to any one who would receive a book from the missionary, or who would give information concerning persons who had done so; and infinite pains were taken to entrap him into speech or overt act that would give offence to Ranavàlona. His sagacity and caution saved him from these snares.

Referring to one of his conversations with the Prince Rakoto at this period, Mr. Ellis wrote: "The Prince asked, 'What is best to be done? How can the country be best protected and improved? What is likely to be its future?' I replied, that the alliance and the protection or even the moral influence of England would be one of the best guarantees for its independence. He said, the Queen would enter into no treaty unless some emergency should arise; but, he added, the first thing he should do when he could act would be to seek the friendship and protection of England. 'I am glad you have come; you have seen the country, seen the state of the people, heard from themselves something of their sufferings, and of the grievous yoke they have to bear. I hope the English will sympathize with us in our troubles. The chiefs wished a few months ago to make me king; they were proceeding with their design, and would have put both Rainjohary, the Queen's paramour, and Ramboasalama to death that day, and would have set my mother aside and made her resign, but I alone prevented it; I would not be disloyal to my mother, much as I suffer: I would not consent, but threatened to disclose their plans if they did not desist. I would rather wait till God shall make me king than be a party to any evil to my mother, though no government is so bad as the government of Madagascar now is.' I told him I thought he would not regret having taken no part against his mother, and hoped that God would give him wise and faithful friends in his hour of need, for whenever the administration of the kingdom should devolve on him he would have no bed of roses." . . . Mr. Ellis proceeded: "There are but two courses open before Madagascar, either to rise to a position of strength and prosperity that shall enable it to maintain the dignity of an independent nation, or subjection and subordination to some one of the great powers of the present day. If the French assume the protection of Madagascar, it will become what Algiers and Tahiti are—a French colony—and you will act under their authority and for their advantage. On the other hand, great as the difficulties and discouragements are, they are not insurmountable. You may in a few years become sufficiently powerful with true friends to protect yourselves. But to this end you must unite the peoples of Madagascar as one community. You must try to make the Sàkalàva feel that union with you is better than vassalage to France; for the French now speak of them in the journals of Mauritius as 'our allies the Sàkalàva.'"

Mr. Ellis mentions as the companions of M. Laborde at Antananarivo a M. Hervier, *alias* Père Finaz, a Jesuit priest, in disguise as a civilian clerk, together with two other priests, P.P. Jouen and Webber, who acted as assistant apothecaries to Dr. Milhet Fontarabie. These were all associated with M. Laborde to assist in accomplishing the designs of the latter against Ranavàlona.

Mr. Ellis informed Lord Clarendon "that the Prince and some of the officers were exceedingly anxious about the result of M. Lambert's voyage to Europe, and applied to me very soon after my arrival for any information I might possess on the subject. The Prince was greatly surprised and deeply affected on becoming acquainted with the representations that had been made by M. Lambert. He said the papers taken away by that gentleman, so far as he had been made acquainted with their contents, were simply a statement of the grievances of the people. He had repeatedly represented to his mother that the sufferings and burdens of the people were too great; and during the period of M. Lambert's visit had conversed frequently with him and M. Laborde on the same subject, but had expressed no wish that any application should be made to the French Government. He further stated that he did not prepare the letters or papers taken by M. Lambert, and had no knowledge of the intention to prepare any papers of the kind until they were completed; that they were written in the French language, of which he does not understand half a dozen words, and were, he believes, drawn up by the priest, assisted by MM. Laborde and Lambert; that when the papers were presented to him M. Laborde translated verbally the pages containing a statement of the grievances of the people, and then said, 'If you think this is true, add your name to it.' That after long refusing he did at length, almost by compulsion, affix his name to the papers, but only as attesting the truth of the statement of the sufferings of his countrymen. He declared emphatically that he had never authorized any application for troops or money, or any other means of deposing the present ruler of Madagascar. On my inquiring what was the object of the statement of grievances, if not to seek redress, he replied that he thought a representation from M. Lambert and his friends to the effect that the burdens of the people were too heavy, might induce the Queen to adopt a milder rule. The Prince further stated that MM. Laborde and Lambert said they were determined that there should be a change, and that if it could not be effected by other means, they would apply to the French Government for troops, and if these were refused, they would themselves hire troops, for they had twenty-five millions of dollars to appropriate to the object. In reference to their intimation of their intention to bring troops, the Prince said he thought if they did, the native forces could arrest their progress; but he added, that he told MM. Laborde and Lambert that he would be the first to fight and shed his blood in defence of his mother.

"I deem it right to inform your Lordship that there is a party at the capital opposed to the Prince, and in favour of his rival, a son of the Queen's eldest sister. The pretensions of this rival are encouraged by the Frenchmen at the capital, and some of the secondary native officers are said to have been parties to the project of MM. Lambert and Laborde for bringing French troops to Madagascar; and when the Prince mentioned them in connection with this part of the plan, he said they owed their lives to his forbearance in not acquainting the Queen with their proceedings. The Queen's secretary also stated that the papers were signed, and a sort of oath not to divulge the secret extorted by the priest from the Prince at the close of a dinner party; and a degree of compulsion, little short of absolute force, was used to secure his signature, and that they held his hand on the Bible whilst the priest pronounced the oath. I am unable to describe the Prince's expressions of gratitude when I read to him the reply given by your Lordship to M. Lambert's proposal. He said that he prayed to the Almighty ever since M. Lambert's departure that the French troops might not come, and he added : 'I thank God for his protection.'" On Mr. Ellis's return to Mauritius he met M. Lambert at Government House, where the latter accused the Independent missionary of creating mischief at Antananarivo, and bitterly complained of his having defeated all the plans of the French party and their disinterested schemes for the good of Madagascar.

Meantime M. d'Arvoy, formerly French consul at Mauritius, had been acting as agent of M. Lambert on the west coast of Madagascar, where, at Bavatoubé, works had been established for the exportation of coal and petroleum. As Bavatoubé is but a very short distance from the French colony on the island of Nosibé, the works were judged to be safe under protection of the French flag; but Queen Ranavàlona warned M. Lambert that she would not permit M. d'Arvoy to remain, and in October, 1855, a detachment of Hova troops destroyed the works of Bavatoubé, which were defended by M. d'Arvoy, who was slain whilst resisting, and his cannon and companions captured as prisoners of war. Although this took place on a coast since alleged by the French to be under their protection, no notice was taken of this act of authority by the government either of France or of Réunion. In conformity with instructions from London, however, the Governor of Mauritius issued a proclamation forbidding any British subject or foreigner resident in the colony of Mauritius from committing any hostile act against the government of Madagascar under severe penalties.

Lambert, after a preliminary trip to the Mozambique coast regarding the supply of blacks to Réunion, in which profitable trade he still took part, arrived in Madagascar during May, 1857, and proceeded in great state, accompanied by Madame Pfeiffer, to the capital. The conspiracy was now fully matured, and all the preparations and details of the projected *coup d'état* fully organized. There was only one thing wanting, the willingness of the Prince to become a cat's-paw in the hands of the French. The eventful day and hour arrived, and the result was a *fiasco*. At daybreak the 21st June, Raharo, in charge of the troops guarding the palace, was to open the doors to the conspirators, and at a given signal the Prince was to be proclaimed king, the Prime Minister and his friends seized, and the Queen informed that her deposition was the will of the people, &c. But all along it appears that the Queen and her government were perfectly cognisant of the plot and its arrangements. The secrets of the chiefs of the projected revolution were in the hands of the Prime Minister, and it is almost certain that the Prince himself informed his mother of every step contemplated by MM. Laborde and Lambert. Raharo, at the supreme moment, failed to fulfil his engagement, either through want of courage or ability, if indeed he ever intended to carry out the projected treachery. The *coup d'état* was entirely frustrated, and the conspirators foiled in their signal perfidy. The Queen would have been justified in taking the lives of the foreigners who had instigated her son and his companions to depose her from the throne, for she would inevitably have lost her life with her crown; but it was ever the Malagasy custom, dictated by long experience, to be very cautious in shedding the blood of any foreigner; and fortunately for MM. Laborde and Lambert, they with their companions were only expelled from the country. Not only were the European adventurers given their lives, but they were also permitted to take with them all their goods and chattels; whilst all the rich presents which M. Lambert had brought from Paris for the Queen and her courtiers were returned to them. Rainiharo might have quoted the words Virgil puts in the mouth of Laocoon, " Timeo Danaos et dona ferentes." The vengeance of the Queen was wreaked upon those unhappy subjects of hers who had been deluded into joining the conspiracy, or those yet more innocent Christians who, being convicted of belonging to societies which met in secret for prayer, were looked upon as engaged in plots against the idols and against the sovereign who supported them. The persecution of the native Christians was renewed with relentless vigour in consequence of the unpardonable attempt by a crew of European adventurers to overthrow the government of an island where they had received every hospitality.

The baffled conspirators were escorted to the coast and shipped back to Réunion, where they awaited with impatience the death of the old Queen, who, however, reigned for four years more.

Naturally the premises which Laborde had occupied in Antananarivo and Ambohitsorohitra, as well as the large estate on which were situate the extensive works of Soatsimanampiovana, being Crown property, were taken possession of by the Hova government. The dwellings were dismantled, and the industrial manufactories unroofed and left deserted. M. Laborde made no claim whatever on this occasion either on the properties or for compensation: neither did he attempt to sell them. The lands, of which he was only tenant at the will of the Queen, as well as his slaves, belonged to the sovereign of Madagascar.

In August, 1861, Ranavàlona I. died, and now indeed the rich prize, the possession of Madagascar, seemed as if it would fall without hindrance into the hands of the speculators of Réunion. On the accession of Radama II., the first arrivals at Antananarivo from beyond the sea were MM. Laborde and Lambert, eager to claim the acknowledgment by the new king of the secret agreement by which he had virtually handed over to a French company the monopoly of farming the whole island and its unlimited wealth, mineral, vegetable, and animal.

Through the influence of Captain Jules Dupré, commanding the French squadron on the Indian station, and of the Governor of Réunion, M. Laborde was appointed consul for France in Madagascar, and he thereby acquired an official *status*, which seemed to stamp the approval of the French Imperial Government on the scheme of the Lambert-Laborde Company.

Under such influences it is not surprising that a more comprehensive deed of concession, based upon that of 1855, was drawn up and signed by the king on the 9th November, 1861.[1]

1881
Nov.
9th.
CHART OF CONCESSION.

WE, RADAMA II., KING OF MADAGASCAR,

Considering our deed of the 28th June, 1855, by which we have given exclusive power to our friend M. J. Lambert to constitute and direct a Company having for its object the working of the mines of Madagascar, and the cultivation of the lands situated on the coast and in the interior.

Whereas it is important to define the terms of the charter which we grant to M. J. Lambert for the services which he has rendered us, and enable him at the same time to form this

---

[1] See Ellis's *Madagascar Revisited*, pp. 159-162. "I had heard that there had been in 1861 some renewal of the engagement between the king and M. Lambert, but did not know until this occasion that the concession had been at that time so formally complete 1."

Company, which we invoke with all our heart to aid us in our projects of civilization of our country.

CHAPTER I.

We authorize M. J. Lambert to form a Company having for its object the working the mines of Madagascar, the forests and lands situated on the coasts and in the interior. The said Company shall have the right to make roads, canals, dockyards, establishments of public utility, to coin money with the king's effigy ; and, in one word, it shall be able to do all that may be judged suitable for the development of the country.

CHAPTER II.

ART. I. We grant and concede to the Company the exclusive privilege of working all the mines of Madagascar, both those which are already known and those which may be discovered hereafter.

ART. II. We grant and concede equally to the said Company, either for itself or for those whom it may admit to participation of this faculty, the privilege of selecting on all the coasts and in the interior of the country, unoccupied lands to be placed under cultivation. In consequence the Company will become proprietor of the lands which it shall choose, as soon as it shall have declared its actual possession.

ART. III. The Company shall not pay any duties on the minerals extracted, nor on the agricultural produce which it may develope.

ART. IV. The minerals produced from the mines of Madagascar, and the vegetable produce, shall enjoy the privilege of free exportation, without any export duties ; the properties shall not be liable to be charged with taxes ; that which is imported for the Company shall not pay any dues.

ART. V. We engage ourselves to favour this Company with all our power, and especially to aid it by procuring labourers.

We give over to the Company all the mines of Soatsimanampiovana, in order to continue the immediate employment of the workmen. We give as well to the Company the palace of Soaniérana, as the head-quarters seat of administration.

On its side the Company engages itself by a loyal reciprocity to aid us with all its power in our projects for the amelioration and civilization of our country, remembering that it is founded with the object of procuring the welfare and prosperity of our government.

We will that the present deed, made in good faith, in presence of God, to aid the civilization of our country, shall be a guarantee for our friend J. Lambert, at the same time, that it will bear testimony of our recognition, in short, to aid him in the formation of this Company, which we desire to see constituted as soon as possible, and that it will be a token of our royal word, from which we shall never draw back.

Antananarivo, 8 *Makarabo* 1862. (*9th November*, 1861.)
By the King. (*Signed*) RADAMA II.
Minister of Foreign Affairs, (*Signed*) RAHANIRAKA.
Commander in Chief, (*Signed*) RAINILAIARIVONY.
Minister of Justice, (*Signed*) RAINIKETAKA.

I certify the present translation agrees with the deed in Malagasy, given by H.M. Radama II. to M. Lambert on the 9th November, 1861.
Antananarivo, 13th September, 1862.
(*Signed*) Consul for France, LABORDE.

M. Lambert engages to give to H.M. RADAMA II., and his successors, 10 per cent. of the profits which accrue to the Company.
Antananarivo, 12th September, 1862.
Initialed R. R.   R. H. K.
(*Signed*) RAINILAIARIVONY.
(*Signed*) RAINIKETAKA.

I certify the truth of the additional article dated 12th September, 1862. (*Signed*) Consul for France, LABORDE.
(*Countersigned*) Chief of the French Mission, J. DUPRÉ.

Verified as to signatures of H.M. Radama II., Rainilaiarivony, Rahaniraka, Rainiketaka, his Ministers.
Antananarivo, 13th September, 1862.
(*Signed*) Consul for France, J. LABORDE.
Seen for attestation of the signature of H.M. Radama II., and of his Ministers, Rainilaiarivony, Rahaniraka, and Rainiketaka.
H.B.M's Consulate.
Antananarivo, 13th September, 1862.
(*Signed*) T. C. PAKENHAM,
H.B.M. Consul for Madagascar.

Meantime the Government of Mauritius had despatched Colonel Middleton, Royal Artillery, on a mission of congratulation to Radama, and on the 26th November, M. le baron Brossard de Corbigny was sent by the emperor from Paris to the court of Imerina, which he reached on the 8th February, 1862, accompanied by M. Clément Laborde, "a young man of twenty-eight years, the son of M. Laborde," his mother being a Malagasy (from which it would appear that M. Laborde was married to a Malagasy woman in 1832, soon after he reached the island). M. de Corbigny has given a carefully detailed account of his visit to the court of Radama II. at this period.

Now the Baron de Corbigny gives some valuable evidence with regard to the claim of the Laborde heirs to the royal works at Soatsimanampiovana. (*See letter of M. Baudais to M. Gambetta, No. 2, December* 1, 1882, *infra*, p. 37.)

Speaking of his arrival there, he speaks of the house there as a comfortable dwelling, "where M. Laborde often resided under the government of the late Queen;" and after describing the various factories and foundries, &c., M. de Corbigny expressly mentions that "these different works belonged to the State, the workmen were all Hova soldiers, who had erected close by a large military village, where they resided with their families." At the time of M. de Corbigny's visit he says that the new king had abandoned these useful establishments and the cannon foundry in order that the soldiers might be more peacefully employed in agricultural pursuits. (*See* "*Revue Maritime et Coloniale*," vol. v. 1862, pp. 565-605.)

Later in the same year, 1862, Captain Dupré, commanding the vessels of the French navy on the station, was commissioned as plenipotentiary to be present at the coronation of Radama II., and conclude a treaty between France and Madagascar. This treaty was signed by the king and the French envoy, in presence of the English Government Mission, on the 12th September, and on the same day the deed of concession granted to M. Lambert was again signed in public by the king. MM. Dupré and Lambert hastened to France with their respective documents, and the Company of Madagascar was set on foot under Imperial auspices.

The narrative of the revolution which ensued, resulting in the death of Radama II., and the repudiation of the French treaty and the Lambert concession, is too long to be inserted here. It is sufficient to recall to mind the fact that, after long negotiations, the Government of Rasoherina paid the French authorities eighty-six barrels full of silver dollars (valued at 906,184 francs, *i.e.*, £39,247 English), weighing nearly twelve tons, on the 8th October, 1865, in return for which the worthless deed signed by the unfortunate Radama was given up and publicly burnt by the Governor of Tamatave. On the death of

Rasoherina a second treaty was concluded by M. Garnier, the French Commissioner, with the Government of Ranavàlona II. on the 4th August, 1868. In this treaty Ranavàlona II. was fully recognized as Queen of Madagascar in its entirety, without reserve ; and Article IV. was couched in the following terms : " The French in Madagascar shall enjoy a complete protection of their persons and properties. They shall be able, as subjects of the most favoured nation, and in conformity with the laws and regulations of the country, to establish themselves wherever they may choose, to hire on lease or acquire all kinds of property, landed or movable, and carry on all commercial and industrial operations which are not interdicted by the laws of the country. They shall be able to take into their service any Malagasy who is neither a slave nor a soldier, and who is freed from any former engagement. Nevertheless, if the Queen require their workmen for her personal service, they can leave their service after having warned those who have engaged them."

A month after the signature of the new treaty, Ranavàlona II. was crowned in great state, and the ceremony was especially noticeable as being the first coronation in Madagascar where the idols were conspicuous by their absence, and Christian texts and emblems with a native code of laws presented publicly as the principal features of the royal function. These innovations were followed by the baptism of the Queen and her Prime Minister, and the ignominious destruction of the idols and their belongings throughout Imerina. In the following year Queen Ranavàlona was formally married to the Prime Minister.

From 1869 to 1878 the kingdom of Madagascar enjoyed a period of peace and security, during which the consolidation of the government and the improvement of the social condition of the people occupied the whole attention of the Prime Minister. The Queen made a royal progress to Betsileo, where a lasting impression for good was left upon the southern tribes. Improvements in the army and rural police were gradually introduced, and the administration of justice placed on a better footing. The work of the Prime Minister was vastly increased, and finally a government was formed on the departmental plan to relieve Rainilaiarivony from a portion of his duties, and ministers were appointed to supervise the several departments. In June, 1877, all Mozambiques (*i.e.*, African slaves) were emancipated, a bold and noble stroke of legislation, carried out with tact and skill by Rainilaiarivony.

Trade increased steadily during the first decade of the reign of Ranavàlona, and the prosperity of the country was only broken by the visitations of severe epidemics, which swept over the island.

At intervals various complaints were preferred by the foreign traders on the coast, which the Prime Minister and his government strove to redress when brought to the notice of the Council at Antananarivo ; but doubtless the conduct of many of the old Hova governors at distant stations was aggravating and obstructive. Nevertheless, as long as M. Laborde was alive no serious disputes took place between the foreign consuls and the Madagascar Government. Indeed, latterly M. Laborde was more Hova than the Hovas themselves, yet at the same time thoroughly under the influence of the Jesuit mission.

In December, 1878, M. Laborde died at Antananarivo, and with the appointment of M. Cassas as his successor commenced a series of complaints of the ill-will alleged to be shown by the Malagasy authorities against the French portion of the foreign residents. There is no doubt that the French Catholic Mission considered itself aggrieved at the preference undoubtedly exhibited, and not unnaturally, by the Prime Minister and the Queen's court for the work promoted by the London Missionary Society.

It should be borne in mind that during M. Laborde's lifetime the French and English consular authorities seem to have acted in perfect concord, and it was not until some considerable time afterwards that the relations between the consulates were slightly strained ; for it must be confessed that Mr. Pakenham's sympathies were thoroughly French, and it is much to be regretted for the sake of the Hovas that they were so pronounced.

At the end of August, 1879, Rainimaharavo, chief secretary of state for foreign affairs, resigned his office, and an able officer of the 15th Honour, Ravoninahitriniarivo, was appointed by the Malagasy Government to succeed him. In the first Red Book, the correspondence opens with the notification of this appointment to M. Cassas, who had, a few days previously, opened a correspondence with the Prime Minister relative to a property which the heirs of the late M. Laborde claimed to possess in the capital.

M. Cassas took this opportunity to declare that his government had sent him to explain to the Malagasy Cabinet the dissatisfaction it felt at the conduct exhibited towards the French by the Hovas, and that efficacious measures would be taken to secure for his countrymen the strict observance of the treaty by the active presence of a French squadron on the coast.

The commissioner for the Republic also complained that the former Minister, Rainimaharavo, had dared to address in writing the Secretary of the French Consulate as " A. Campan," without any title, an incivility which could not be overlooked. " I have been obliged," he wrote, " to send copies of the letters of Rainimaharavo not only to Paris, but also to the Governor of Réunion and to the commander-in-chief of the station, with a report in which I expose the ill-will of the Hova Government in all that concerns French claims. This ill-will, concealed under appearances of courtesy, is everywhere shown, and each day discovers to me some new trick, unmannerly enough moreover, on the part of Rainimaharavo, to hinder the observance of the treaty for which it is my mission to enforce respect in its entirety. You must therefore entirely change your conduct towards us, unless you wish to incur personally, Mr. Prime Minister, the responsibility of a rupture between the two governments."

M. Cassas demanded an interview with the Minister in order to discuss the validity of the claims made by the heirs of M. Laborde; and we may here give the French statement of the case on which these claims were founded.

" M. Laborde, Consul for France, died at Antananarivo, on the 27th December, 1878; and, by his will, he designated as his sole heirs, sharing equally, his nephews, M. Edouard Laborde and M. Campan, the latter Secretary of the Consulate at Antananarivo. All his landed property included in the inheritance was described at length in the despatch of the 4th of October, 1881. With regard to each property the title deeds are indicated, and these titles are indisputable and perfectly valid. The value of these properties has been estimated at 217,400 dollars (about £43,480), but this sum is far from representing their real value; for one of them alone, the concession of Soatsimanampiovana, would be worth more than a million (*francs*) to a company who would undertake the working of its rich mineral wealth. I should, moreover, allude to the sum of 10,200 dollars (about 51,000 francs = £2,000), the value of several other plots of ground, for which, however, the legal titles of ownership are not in the possession of the heirs. The following procedure was employed by the Hova Government to prevent the two nephews of M. Laborde from realizing any portion of their inheritance for upwards of three years. It was very careful not to dispute all at once the said inheritance. After the death of their uncle, the heirs, who possessed no fortune of their own, desired to lay out part of the property situated in Ambohitsorohitra (a suburb of Antananarivo), and to build on it a branch house of business.

"The government allowed them to proceed with the buildings for some months, after which they prohibited the continuance of the works, declaring that they had no right to build upon the land in question. At this time the right of ownership was not disputed, but for no assigned reason the building alone was forbidden. Protestation was made, but it was necessary to submit to these exigencies, and the house remained uncompleted. Moreover, molestations became so frequent, and of such a menacing character, towards M. Campan, that, fearing for the safety of his family, he was obliged to separate them from him, and send them to Réunion, where they have stayed for two years. The heirs then found a purchaser for the piece of ground situated on the Place Andohalo, at Antananarivo, as well as for the buildings standing on the premises; including the house of the consul, the office of the consulate, and various outbuildings occupied by the families Laborde and Campan. The price was 100,000 francs (£4,000), and the sale was arranged. It was the Catholic mission which became the purchaser; and it was agreed that possession of the premises should be taken on the 1st September, 1879. The Prime Minister, meantime, declared that the heirs of M. Laborde were not owners of the soil, which could not be sold. He sent to the purchaser and informed him that if he took possession of the ground he would dispute the ownership. Père Cazet, the *préfet apostolique* of the mission, comprehended the imprudence which he would commit in concluding the purchase, and the contract was rescinded by mutual consent. The Prime Minister pretending (a year after the death of M. Laborde, and for the first time) that the landed properties did not belong to the inheritance, M. Cassas, who had arrived in the meantime, offered to exhibit to him the title deeds proving the ownership." [1]

The momentous interview for the production of these documents took place at the French consulate on the 3rd of September, as the regulations of the French

[1] See despatch of M. Baudais to M. Gambetta, Yellow Book, Affairs of Madagascar, 1881-1883, No. 2.

Government do not permit the removal of such authentic, original documents from the consular office. The text of one of these documents, exhibited to Ravoninahitriniarivo, who was accompanied by Ramaniraka and Razanakombana, was as follows :—

"*Antananarivo*, the 7th Alahamady, 1864.

"Radama II., by the grace of God, King of Madagascar, and defender of the laws of the country. The ground of M. J. Laborde, Consul of France, at Ambohitsorohitra, *azy mainty molaly*. We, Ministers for Foreign Affairs, give this deed to M. J. Laborde as witnesses that this land is his *mainty molaly*.

(*Signed*) "CLEMENT LABORDE, WILLIAM MARKS,
"RAMANIRAKA, RAZANAKOMBANA."

The second of the two documents was in similar terms, merely substituting Ambodin' Andohalo for Ambohitsorohitra.

According to M. Cassas he called upon Ramaniraka and Razanakombana to verify their signatures to these documents as attesting witnesses; but Ravoninahitriniarivo states that before permitting them to answer, he expressly asked M. Cassas whether he would accept their answer as the truth; upon which he was silent.

At the very first sight of these papers, when exhibited to the Malagasy Secretary of State, he professed to be

FORGERIES?   41

greatly surprised by the figures 1864, the date of the year in which they were supposed to be written, for Radama II. died in 1863 ; and Rasoherina, his successor, commenced her reign in that year.

In fact, the minister declared them to be forgeries ; he wrote: "You must understand, Mr. Commissioner, that Radama II. being dead in 1863, could not grant these holdings in 1864. In justification of what I have just said ; during the reign of Radama II. no document was written in 1864 (with the exception of these papers, forged perhaps by certain persons), because his reign did not reach 1864 ; and even the first documents of the Government, executed by his successor, only commenced in 1863. As proofs, there can be quoted the letters written by Rasoherimanjaka to the Emperor Napoleon III., and to Queen Victoria, as well as the answer of the latter, besides other official documents. I will, therefore, beg of you to justify this date ; and if, nevertheless, you should find an admissible proof contrary to what I state, I will then produce other proofs ; but if you cannot produce any proof contradicting our assertion, it will be useless for us to exhibit other proofs."[1]

---

[1] One of these other proofs consisted of a statement in M. Laborde's own handwriting, which conclusively showed that the land was not his. He writes—

"Je déclare avoir acheté la case de Razakamanana pour la somme de 110 piastres (*dollars*), et non l'emplacement.

"En foi de quoi, &c.,

"*Antananarivo*,   (*Signé*)   "C. J. LABORDE."
"ce 2 Mars, 1835."

Ravoninahitriniarivo proceeded to explain that, even if the documents were what they pretended to be, nevertheless the terms *azy mainty molaly*, inserted in the deeds, indicated that the tenancy was merely to be held during the Crown's good pleasure.

The minister quoted the cases of many foreigners, including Englishmen, to whom premises had been granted during their residence in the island at the will of the sovereign. Amongst them he instanced Mr. Hastie, who was installed by the first Radama at Antsahavola, Mr. Chick at Amparibé, Mr. Canham at Ambohimandroso, and especially M. Legros, the French architect of the palaces, who had actually occupied the very premises afterwards occupied by M. Laborde; and it was evident that the various residences granted to M. Laborde were for the purpose of his carrying out the works of the sovereign who employed him; and that mere occupancy did not constitute a proof of ownership.

Ravoninahitriniarivo added: " I wish you to know, Mr. Commissioner, that M. Clément Laborde was entrusted by Radama II. with the seal of the Foreign Office. At the death of the latter, he did not return the seal to the Government, and when it was sent for he refused to give it up. Nor was it until a long time afterwards that in consequence of the remonstrances of the Government he gave it up. You can judge from this what M. Clément

Laborde could do with it if he wished." The minister concluded with an expression of regret that a solution of their disputes could not be arrived at, and suggested on the part of his government that the affair should be submitted to the arbitration of a third power. M. Cassas was indignant at the accusation that M. Clément Laborde had made a criminal use of the seals of the Foreign Office, scouted the idea of forgery, and argued that the deeds of ownership were signed and sealed during the lifetime of the king.

"You have fallen into a singular error," he said, "and I confess my astonishment at seeing natives of the country ignorant of things which I know perfectly. The title deeds are dated the 7th Alahamady, 1864 (26th March, 1863), that is one month and eighteen days before the death of the king, which took place on the 25th Adaoro, the second month of the Malagasy year (12th May, 1863). The Malagasy calendar, composed of twelve months of twenty-nine or thirty days, like that of the Mussulmans, that is, lunar months, is in advance of the Gregorian calendar by many days in each year, which can easily cause errors to be made by people who have an interest in making them. The treaty which you signed with England has two dates, ours and yours; the date on the English copy is 5th December, 1862; on the Malagasy version, 15th Alakaosy, 1863. If you will take this date, which perhaps you will admit is exact, as a point for reckoning from, you will arrive at the conclusion that the 7th Alahamady, 1864, comes before the 12th May, 1863. It is therefore only playing on the words when you tell me that Radama II., having died in 1863, could not execute deeds in 1864. You take the first of these dates from our calendar, and the second from your own. The surprise which you tell me you experienced in reading the date of the title deeds of ownership may thus be dismissed, Mr. Minister, and you will agree with me in appreciating the authenticity of the documents.

"After having declared the deeds to be forgeries, you enter upon a learned disquisition on the expression, *azy mainty molaly*. If the title deeds are false, what object is there in this dissertation, very learned but most obscure? Having studied the history and laws of Madagascar, I believe that this is the most sure means of acquiring full rights of ownership. The word *azy*, oblique case of the pronoun *izy*, means to say formally, *to him—belonging to him*, which expresses full ownership. The words *mainty molaly* signify *blackened by soot*, and indicate a thing to be respected, an undisputed right on account of its antiquity. If the expression *I give* does not appear in the deeds, it is precisely because the lands and buildings already belonged to M. Laborde, and these deeds merely confirm the right of ownership and add the royal sanction."

"It is incontestable," observes M. Saillens (p. 26), "that the doubt was permissible. If Radama had wished to inaugurate a new system and grant to Europeans the right of possessing in perpetuity—*a right which the Malagasy themselves did not possess*—there has been in the document above quoted an inexplicable laconism. . . . It is strange that, in the case of such a total revolution in the question of ownership, expressions more clear, more explicit, and more solemn should not have been selected." "M. Laborde," continues M. Saillens, "an intimate friend of the monarch, would not have neglected to dictate to him clear and precise terms if he had treated of a perpetual donation. But all leads to the belief that M. Laborde himself, so well acquainted with the Malagasy manners and customs, only considered himself as the usufructuary of the premises."

M. Cassas was highly indignant at the proposal that the matter in dispute should be referred to the arbitration of a neutral power. After having given the Malagasy Secretary of State a lesson in the idioms of his own language, he proceeded to read him another lecture on the conventionalities of European diplomacy :—

"Without wishing to offend, allow me to say that your strange proposal shows your manifest ignorance of diplomatic usages. I have been sent here expressly to treat directly with the Hova Government in all matters concerning the French subjects residing in Madagascar, and with full powers to terminate them according to my discretion. Should you renew your singular request, I shall be obliged to consider it as a rupture between our two governments brought about by you, since it will imply the non-recognition of my official position and the powers I derive from it."

Ravoninahitriniarivo in reply, repeated his arguments that M. Laborde had only held his land by the will of the sovereign, &c. :—

"Besides, I must tell you, Mr. Commissioner, and beg you to note it well, that, according to the laws of our kingdom, the sovereign of Madagascar is the sole lord over the land throughout the island. As to the occupied land, the sovereign can, at pleasure, turn off the tenants, should the land be required for the use of the government."

The minister explained with regard to the question of dates that, before the date of the deed in question, Radama II. had caused the Gregorian calendar to be accepted in Madagascar in place of the old Mussulman one, thus completely displacing M. Cassas' argument derived from the latter. He further regretted the dissatisfaction of the consul at the proposal to submit the whole matter to arbitration, and stated that he had no intention of ignoring the official position or powers of the Commissioners :—

"If you and I cannot agree to settle this affair between

M. Campan and our government (and indeed I sincerely desire to see it settled equitably), who shall judge between us? From what we had heard, we believed that the usage in analogous cases among civilized nations was to submit the question to the decision of a friendly neutral power. Is not this the case? or have we not understood rightly? Should you consider this as the pronunciation of a rupture between our two governments, we shall be astonished, Mr. Commissioner, for it will seem as though you did not appreciate our sincere desire to maintain a friendly understanding with a government so great and distinguished as that of France."

The correspondence continued between the government of Madagascar and M. Cassas, the latter energetically protesting against the flagrant violation of the Treaty of 1868 by the obstruction placed by the Malagasy authorities in the way of the free transmission of the Laborde property to the claimants; and the French consul, after complaining that the Prime Minister would not reply personally to his letters, as he did to those of his English and American colleagues, departed from Antananarivo in high dudgeon, and betook himself to Tamatave at the end of 1879.

According to the French Yellow Book, M. Cassas addressed on the 9th of January, 1880, an exhaustive report to M. Gambetta, fully exposing the position of French affairs in Madagascar; and M. Charles Buet states

(*Madagascar, la Reine des Iles Africaines*, p. 301) that, in consequence of the strained relations between the French consul and the Hova Government, the former official retired from Antananarivo to Tamatave; and about this time there seems to have arisen a considerable amount of tension between the French and English representatives, owing, it is said, to the negotiation by Mr. Pakenham for the sale of 8,000 muskets to Rainilaiarivony.

It was in June that M. Cassas received an answer, far different, however, to what he had expected, from the home authorities, by the arrival of a French man-of-war, *La Clochetterie*. The captain of this ship, on reaching Tamatave, lost no time in disavowing the warlike proclivities of M. Cassas, and announcing the peaceful intentions of the French Government; and at the official dinner given, according to custom, by the governor of the port, Captain Vallon declared "that all that the French Government required was the maintenance of the *status quo*, that France desired to preserve peace and the existing friendly relations at any price." M. Cassas indignantly protested, announcing in reply that so long as he should represent France in Madagascar, he should not fail to vindicate with energy all their rights as often as they appeared to him to be disregarded. Very soon afterwards M. Cassas was removed from his post and sent to Hong Kong, being replaced by M. Théodore Meyer.

M. Meyer arrived in Madagascar on the 6th April, 1881, and previous to his coming there was published at Antananarivo in a Grand Kabary, or public meeting, held on the usual Kabary ground at Andohalo, the new code of laws drawn up by the government of Ranavàlona II.

The promulgation of this code, which included the famous law, No. 85, took place on the 29th March, and the French consul subsequently insisted that the publication of this law opposite the doors of the French consulate was a studied insult to the French. As the French consulate faces Andohalo, any public gathering on the Andohalo ground must be opposite to the consulate. (See letter of M. Baudais to M. Gambetta, dated 13th December, 1881.)

M. Théodore Meyer appears to have suggested a compromise between M. Campan and the government of Rainilaiarivony, but no correspondence is published by the Malagasy Government referring to this attempt to arbitrate between the disputants, and it is probable that no official letters passed between the parties. According to the account subsequently given by M. Baudais, this tentative proposal of M. Meyer failed, because M. Campan would not abate his terms below 300,000 francs, while the Prime Minister considered that the sum of 250,000 francs would be ample compensation for a claim which he disavowed.

As from this it would appear that only a difference of 50,000 francs separated the disputants, it is remarkable that no compromise was arrived at. Anyhow, the good intentions of M. Meyer were frustrated, for he was transferred from Madagascar to Singapore in October, and was succeeded by M. Baudais, who, on his arrival, found the Laborde affair still a *lis pendens*. "M. Baudais's style," says the *Times*, "is concise, not to say peremptory; he made it clear from the outset that he was not the man to stand any prevarication or delay."

It is evident that the Laborde inheritance could at this stage have been compromised, but such a termination was far from the object of M. Baudais. It was a good grievance and formed the first of the three principal complaints which the French Commissioner preferred against the Malagasy Government. The subject of the second charge against the Ministers of Ranavàlona we will now proceed to investigate.

CHAPTER II.

MATERIALS FOR INCENDIARISM.

II. *The Affair of the Dhow "Toale."*

THE French gunboat, *La Décidée*, arrived at Mojangà in April, 1881, and the officer commanding the vessel, Lieutenant F. Buisson, hearing that a French vessel had been plundered and part of its crew massacred during the previous month at Marambitsy, at once addressed a letter to the Hova Governor of Mojangà requiring satisfaction for the outrage. This letter is important in considering the French claims of protectorate over the Sàkalàva tribes, as it plainly shows that at that date the instructions of the Government to the naval commander-in-chief of the station recognized the Hova sovereignty over the coast of the Bouéni, that is, of Iboina, including Mojangà; it is therefore given *verbatim*.

M. Buisson's complaint, addressed to the representative of the Madagascar Government, Ramasy, the governor of the district, and dated April 20, 1881, was worded as follows :

" The inhabitants of Bouéni, subjects of king Bakary, who is himself the subject of Her Majesty the Queen of

Madagascar, have assassinated the master of the dhow *Toale*, a French vessel, and have stolen the goods landed from that vessel for purposes of trade at Marambitsy. This crime has certainly been committed by the subjects of Bakary, for in addition to the information I have received, the inhabitants have taken flight on the arrival of the gunboat *Décidée* in the roadstead of Bouéni. It remains, therefore, only to make the facts known to you, and to desire you to take all requisite measures to afford the satisfaction which the commander-in-chief of the station has a right to exact. A canoe laden with goods was abandoned by the inhabitants when they caught sight of us, and I took possession of it, and now forward it to you, as it may afford you assistance in tracking the criminals, for I am satisfied that the goods found in it belonged to the *Toale*. Hitherto the *Décidée* has always been able to report the excellent relations which have existed between us, and I am convinced that, on this occasion again, you will show that you uphold the Hova flag with a high and firm hand as a sign of civilization in the Great African Island and as the enemy of all acts of brigandage and piracy. I expect that the commander-in-chief will be here within a month, and that by that time you will have arrested the offenders."

In this letter we have the unprejudiced opinion of a French naval officer that during the cruise of his vessel on the north-west coast, the Hova authorities had conducted themselves in a friendly spirit towards the French and upheld the *Hova* flag in the interests of civilization. It is necessary to emphasize the upholding of the *Hova* flag, as subsequently the hoisting of the Hova flag in this neighbourhood was made the subject of complaint by the French Commissioner, as we shall see hereafter.

M. Buisson reported the outrage to Captain Vallon and also sent notice of it to M. Meyer at Antananarivo. Immediately upon the latter communicating with the Malagasy Government, the Prime Minister sent explicit orders to the governor of Mojangà to cause an inquiry to be made forthwith, reparation exacted from, and chastisement inflicted on the convicted malefactors.

This message to the Governor of Mojangà was despatched in May, and shortly afterwards Captain Vallon, commanding the French squadron in the Indian Ocean, arrived at Mojangà and instituted an independent inquiry as to the rights of the outrage at Marambitsy. The results were communicated to the Minister of Ranavàlona II., through the commandant of Tamatave, in June; and again in August another demand for satisfaction was addressed to Ramasy at Mojangà by Captain Vallon. No reparation having been made by September, M. Meyer again addressed the Foreign Secretary on the subject. He reminded the Minister that the Malagasy Government had promised, four months previously, to punish by force the people of the Bouéni coast unless the assassins were delivered up and the plunder restored. He quoted the minister's own words to the effect that if the Governor of Mojangà had not at his disposal sufficient force to destroy the rebels (note the word rebels as implying Hova rights of sovereignty), he, Ravoninahitriniarivo, would be proud to proceed himself at the head of a force and inflict chastisement. Four months had elapsed and France had not yet obtained satisfaction, whilst the minister, said M. Meyer, knew well that the insignificant forces at the disposal of the governor were inadequate for the due punishment of the *rebels*. The Commissioner of the Republic next proceeded to demand instant reparation from the Government of Madagascar :—

"The time has now come to hold you to the promise you gave to France ; you can only redeem it by making the promised expedition. *The Sàkalàva people must be chastised* (compare this with 'our Sàkalàva allies' mentioned by French orators and authors *passim*), and in order that they may learn the value of the lives of the four French subjects, it is necessary that four [1] of the principal offenders

---

[1] M. Meyer must have studied Homer's Iliad, and was thinking of Achilles' sacrifice of captives at the funeral of Patroclus.

> "All hail, Patroclus ! let thy vengeful ghost
> Hear, and exult on Pluto's dreary coast ;
> Behold Achilles' promise fully paid,
> Twelve Trojan heroes offered to thy shade."
> (*Book* xxiii. 220, *Pope's Trans.*)

shall expiate by death the outrage perpetrated by them at Marambitsy. This is the first satisfaction which I have the right to exact in the name of the Government of the Republic for the insult offered to the flag. As to the practical object of our claim, I would have you observe, Mr. Minister, that France cannot wait indefinitely the results of an expedition which is not yet even organized. The price of blood must be paid within the shortest time. Commandant Vallon fixes it at 400 oxen in good condition. I do not wish, on account of the good relations existing between the two Governments, to increase this valuation, evidently too little, for the life of a French subject cannot be assessed at the value of a hundred oxen, as it would form a dangerous precedent. I have the honour to request by way of compensation the Government of the Queen to pay in advance into my hands the amount of this indemnity, converted into money, at the rate of fifteen dollars for each ox, their value as estimated at the custom-house, amounting to the sum of six thousand dollars (£1,500), which will be remitted through me to the widows and orphans of the poor victims. This is the second satisfaction which I claim as the price of blood shed on this occasion. Again, according to a return furnished by the commandant of Mayotte, the value of the goods plundered amounts to three thousand seven hundred and forty dollars (£748). I request the Government of the Queen to deposit this amount in my hands. By complying at once with these two requests *the Government of the Queen will prove to the civilized world that she knows how to make her authority respected as well upon the west as upon the east coast; in one word, throughout the extent of the kingdom: for, I repeat, the Queen of Madagascar should not allow that such crimes could be perpetrated within her territory.*"

What clearer admission could be made by the French Commissioner than this, that the Queen's authority throughout the island east and west was acknowledged by the French Government, in the person of the representative of the Republic?

M. Meyer went on to say: "We have not, as you know, taken it into our own hands to execute justice, nor have we undertaken any reprisals against the offending subjects of the Queen; it is her task to chastise them; but meantime it is just that pecuniary reparation should be made by her Government."

Throughout it is evident that at this period, viz., the 18th September, 1881, the French consul had no knowledge of any protectorate such as was afterwards claimed by his successor. Meanwhile the officer who had been sent down from Antananarivo to Mojangà to prosecute inquiries relating to the occurrence at Marambitsy, had returned to Imerina, but was detained sick at Ambohimanga, the summer residence of the court. When the chief officers of the state accompanied the Queen to Ambohimanga, the ministers were enabled to obtain the report of their envoy, and to hear personally from him the true circumstances of the case. The affair, as reported by the Hova Commissioner, differed *in toto* from that as represented by the French naval officers, and appeared in quite another light. Instead of the Sàkalàva being the aggressors, the Hova envoy reported that the dhow, hailing from Mayotte, was engaged in smuggling firearms into the country, and that on being called upon to desist, the foreign Arab crew had fired upon the Bouéni, who returned their fire in self-defence. It is best to give the circumstantial account of Ravoninahitriniarivo to M. Meyer :—

"On the 23rd Alakaosy, 1881, the Governor of Mojangà and the soldiers of the garrison resident in the neighbouring villages received orders to march against the Sàkalàva, and should it appear that they had really committed any crime, arrest the offenders who had committed murder, and restore the plundered goods. But, some time after the order was despatched, a letter was received from Bekirondro, dated 1st Alakaosy, 1881, followed by others of later date, saying that these Arabs had sold firearms at Andoka. The men sent by Bekirondro, in endeavouring to stop the traffic, were fired upon by the Arab-French subjects ; Jongoa, a Malagasy subject, fell dead, and then only did the comrades of Jongoa return the fire ; consequently the Governor of

Mojangà informed me of this, and the expedition was immediately put a stop to. . . . I declare, Mr. Commissioner, that I in no way seek to exculpate the Malagasy subjects, if the wrong which they have committed is shown clearly; but I inform you of this, that we may examine well into the circumstances of the affair; that is, the conduct of the Sàkalàva and of the Arabs as it is above reported; for we only seek the truth in this business. From examination of the above report it appears that: (1) The Arabs introduced merchandize at a place where the Government of Madagascar has not yet established a custom-house. (2) They sold firearms; whereas, according to our treaty, the introduction of these articles into Madagascar is prohibited; the right of doing so is reserved to the Queen of Madagascar alone. (3) The officials, despatched by Bekirondro to warn them against such acts, were received by musket-shots, by which one was slain, named Jongoa. It appears from this, that the Arabs not only violated the treaty, but were also the first to fire and cause bloodshed. . . . Notwithstanding the account given by Bekirondro, which I have quoted, and the facts thus disclosed, I have no wish to act hastily in this affair, and therefore I shall send officers who will endeavour to bring this unfortunate transaction to a happy termination."[1]

[1] The sequel may as well be inserted here. After considerable wrangling and discussion, Ravoninahitriniarivo concluded the matter by consenting to pay the indemnity required:—

Such was the state of the dispute as to the right story of the *Toale* outrage when M. Baudais succeeded M. Meyer at the capital in November, 1881.

III. *The Right of French Sovereignty.*

The third and by far the most serious section of the Madagascar question is that which deals with the French claims over the north-west coasts of Madagascar.

According to the report drawn up by M. de Lanessan, and presented to the Chamber of Deputies by the Special Committee on the 7th of July, 1884, it appears that France bases her claims over certain portions of Madagascar on several treaties.

It is stated that, on the 14th of July, 1840, Tsioumeka [1]

"Concerning the affair of the *Toale*, you said that it troubled you little whether the heads of any of the Sàkalàva were cut off, even of three hundred of them; but that you claimed only the money in reparation. I now inform you, Mr. Commissioner, that notwithstanding what we consider should be the equitable adjustment of this business; and as, in spite of what we protest, you declare that money alone can settle the *Toale* affair, such being the case, in consideration of the desire which we have to maintain friendly relations with the French Government, the sum of 9,740 dollars (about £1,948) will be paid by us." (No. 42, 13th May, 1882.)

The indemnity was duly paid in July, 1882, to M. Compristo, commanding the *Pique* gunboat at Mojangà, and thus terminated so far the affair of the *Toale*.

[1] The proclamation of Baron de Hell, Governor of Réunion, Rear-Admiral in the French Navy, by which possession is taken of the newly-annexed colonies in the Mozambique Channel, may be noticed as an indication of the spirit which animated the Orleanist party in France at that period.

" *Saint Denis, Bourbon,* 13th February, 1841.

" *In the name of the King.*—We, the Governor of the island of Bourbon and of its dependencies. Whereas by an act, dated 12th Djoumad, 1256 of the Hegira (14th July, 1840), the Queen of the Sàkalàva, Tsioumeka, with the

(the young ex-Queen of the Bouéni Sàkalàva who had taken refuge from the Hovas in Nossi-Bé at that time) ceded to Louis Philippe the islands of Nossi-Bé and Nossi-Cumba and all rights of sovereignty over the coast from Passandava Bay to Cape St. Vincent. (The text of this treaty is given by De Clerq in his *Recueil des Traités de la France*, p. 594 ; but it is said that the originals of this and other treaties about to be mentioned could not be produced to the Malagasy Envoys.)

advice of her Council, has made a cession to the King of the French of all her rights of sovereignty over the countries situated on the west coast of Madagascar (from Passandava Bay as far as Cape St. Vincent), and over the islands of Nossi-Bé and Nossi-Cumba. Having regard to the despatch of the Minister of Marine and the Colonies of the 25th September, 1840. No. 326.

" Considering that the rights of France over Madagascar and the islands dependent on it result from the priority of taking possession and of occupation of a part of that island at a period when other nations held little or no relations with that country and had no fixed establishment therein.

" That France has never renounced her rights in this respect, since she has invoked and proclaimed them every time that circumstances required.

" That, as England founds her right of sovereignty over the continent of New Holland (Australia) on the fact of the taking possession of Botany Bay, so the sovereignty of France over the whole island of Madagascar cannot be disputed, by application of the same principle and in consequence of the taking possession of and occupation by her, of several parts of the coast, notably of Fort Dauphin, Foule Pointe, Tamatave, and Antongil Bay, &c.

" It results from this that the cession made by the Queen of the Sàkalàva and the chiefs placed under her authority can only be considered as a fresh recognition of former rights of France over that part of Madagascar formerly or now occupied by the Sàkalàva tribes. Considering that it is necessary to regulate the occupation of the islands Nossi-Bé and Nossi-Cumba and to organize the discipline, &c.

" On the report of the Commissioner and Privy Council, we herewith ordain the following :

[*Here follow the administrative and military dispositions, &c.*]

" (*Signed*) BARON DE HELL,

" Rear-Admiral, Governor of the Island of Bourbon."

A SOI-DISANT KING.

Another treaty was concluded between France and Tsimiaro, the so-called king of Ankara, the northern province of Madagascar, in April, 1841. (The full text of which is given in an appendix to M. Lanessan's report.[1]) Again in 1846, Tsimandroho, ex-chief of Vohémar,

---

[1] "Treaty concluded between France and Tsimiaro, King of the Ankara country and of the isles adjacent.

"I, Tsimiaro, son of Adriansolo, King of Ankara, of Nossi-Bé, Nossi-Mitsiou, Nossi-Faly, and other islands adjoining our possessions in the mainland.

"Declare to you, in the presence of my brothers and of my chiefs, that I cede to His Majesty, King Louis Philippe I., King of the French, all my rights over the lands of Madagascar, which rights I hold from my ancestors, and that I also cede to him all the islands which surround my kingdom of Ankara.

"We request to be looked upon by His Majesty the Great King as French subjects, and to be treated as such. I am persuaded that His Majesty the Great King, to whom I have made a gift of all my states, will look upon me as his son, will protect me against every enemy, and will keep off from me every kind of evil.

"I am persuaded also that His Majesty the King of the French will be pleased to extend his benevolence over our subjects. We shall take in future the name of French, whoever shall be the enemy of the Great King shall be ours, and we will take up our arms against him; whoever shall be his ally shall be ours, and we will aid him with all the means in our power.

"If His Majesty, the King of the French, elects to unfurl his flag on any spot whatever of our states we swear by God and by the last judgment, that we will defend it until death.

"I pray His Majesty the Great King to send us soldiers to remain at Nossi-Mitsiou, and a vessel of war to protect us against the Hovas or all other enemies.

"This act has been drawn up by me, Tsimiaro, in the presence of M. Passot, officer of His Majesty the King of the French, and sent by the Governor of Réunion, of M. Jehenne, captain of the King's sloop the *Prévoyante*, and all the officers of that vessel.

"(*Signed*) TSIMIARO, PASSOT, JEHENNE, G. CLOUÉ."

"*April*, 1841."

This treaty, concluded in April, 1841, was ratified in June, the same year.

resident in Nossi-Bé, (where he had taken refuge from Ranavàlona I.) ceded to Louis Philippe his personal rights over the lands from which he had been expelled.[1]

These treaties, writes M. d'Escamps,[2] were renewed in 1848 by the Chief Tsimandroho and the Queen Panga; but no reference is given to the records of these ratifications.

[1] " Declaration of Tsimandroho to the Great King of France, Algiers, Réunion, and many other places.

" I, Tsimandroho, of the family of Gold, formerly King of Vohémar on the mainland of Madagascar, at present master of a part of Nossi-Bé and Nossi-Faly, having been conquered on the mainland by the Hovas, our cruel enemies, I am not in a state to defend myself against their attacks. Unless another king comes to our succour we are all lost.

" I have collected all my councillors and principal chiefs to deliberate as to what we should do. We recognize that the King of France is capable of conquering the Hovas, and that he will not deceive us. If he comes to our succour we shall all live as well as our families. On this account I place myself in the hands of the Great King of France. I give him my lands, my villages, and all my subjects. I pray him to aid us against the Hovas. All my countrymen desire to learn to fight like the French and to go to battle with them. I desire greatly to be the relation of the King of France, that he may be my father and I his son. I will follow the orders of the King of France and of his representatives in this country. If he tells me to remain standing, I will remain standing, if he tells me to sit down I will sit down, and if he tells me to work or to fight, I shall do what he tells me. We know *nothing*; we desire, all of us, that the King of France should send to us persons to instruct us in reading and writing and many other things " (*History of Madagascar, its Inhabitants and Missionaries*, by Father de la Vaissière, S.J. tom i. p. 111). Père Jouen adds that Tsimandroho received from the French Government a yearly subsidy of 1,200 francs (£48) ! Which subsidy appears only to have been paid for one year. See idem, p. 110.

[2] *History and Geography of Madagascar*, by Henry d'Escamps, 1884.

A resolution was passed in the Chamber of Deputies on the 5th February, 1846, to the following effect : " France does not abandon any of her rights over Madagascar, or refuse any sacrifice imposed by such grave interests, but she expects prudence on the part of her Government will prevent it engaging in distant and onerous expeditions unless there is absolute necessity " (*Moniteur*, 6th Feb., 1846).

INSURRECTION.

From subsequent events it does not appear that Tsimandroho was capable of governing those of his tribe in the island of Nossi-Bé, as in July, 1849, an insurrection broke out at Nossi-Bé (in anticipation of which Tsimandroho absented himself from the island), and the Sàkalàva inhabitants, reinforced by their countrymen from the adjacent mainland, almost succeeded in taking the island from the French. Fortunately for the latter, assistance arrived from Mayotte in time to prevent the utter destruction of the colony, but nevertheless several European lives were sacrificed and a number of Sàkalàva were slain.

An expedition was organized to make reprisals on the mainland, but it returned without having come in contact with the enemy.

Whilst Tsimandroho was unable to restrain his countrymen from attacking the French in 1849, so also the French failed to protect Tsimandroho from the vengeance of his compatriots two years subsequently. (*De la Vaissière*, tom. i. p. 157.) According to Father de la Vaissière, Tsimandroho left the French colony after the unsuccessful revolt against the French (of which he was one of the chief instigators) and formed an alliance with the Hovas, but again left these last in 1851, for some reason not stated, and returned to Nossi-Bé, where he remained for some few days at Tafondro. A band of about 150 men, Sàkalàva from the mainland (one account says Hovas), made a night attack on Tafondro on the 5th April, 1851, surprised the guard, and cut off the head of Tsimandroho. The reason for this vengeance taken by the Sàkalàva of the mainland on the unfortunate Tsimandroho was that he had submitted to the French (*De la Vaissière*, tom. ii. p. 131).

In 1859-60 Admiral Fleuriot de Langle and M. Desprez, acting in his name, concluded with certain chiefs on the west coast a series of treaties of friendship and commerce in which the ancient rights of France were strictly recognized.[1] "All these treaties were made," states M. Lanessan, "with the object of affording the tribes on the coast sufficiently powerful protection to enable them to resist effectually the frightful tyranny of the Hovas."

"Unfortunately," he adds, "France has not kept these engagements which she had made, and her *protégés* suffered treatment so much the more rigorous on the part of the Hovas because they had made such efforts to escape from their domination."

I.

[1] The first of these treaties was signed on board the *Cordelière* by Viscount de Langle in Baly Bay, where, as a preliminary, by way of reprisal for several former acts of plunder committed by the Sàkalàva tribes ruled over by Queen Outzinzou, her village of Mahogoulo was burnt.

The rights of Outzinzou over the south-west coast of Baly Bay were declared forfeited and handed over to King Tsiahouan of Ambongo, to whom the care of the whole of the west coast of the bay was committed. King Tsiahouan was further to levy a war indemnity on the subjects of Queen Outzinzou of 3,000 dollars, *i.e.*, £600; and 5,000 dollars (£1,000) damages for the loss of

It has been said that treaties are kept when their purposes are maintained, and they are violated when their privileges are supported against their ends and their objects. Now it would appear that the treaties above mentioned have not been maintained and have certainly been violated, according to the statements of M. de Lanessan.

goods plundered from the *Marie-Angélique*, besides which another 5,000 dollars were also to be claimed to make good the repairs of injury received by the vessel. Should there be any surplus it was to be handed over to the families of the people slain by the treachery of the inhabitants of Baly Bay.

Yet in addition the King Tsiahouan was engaged to collect a sum of 1,000 dollars (£200), as an indemnity due to the reverend Jesuit Fathers for loss sustained on Sunday, 13th February, when Mahagoulo was bombarded by the *Cordelière*. In all the sum of the indemnities and damages amounted to £2,800!

King Tsiahouan, recognizing the ancient rights of France, ensured to French vessels the right of trading on the coasts held by him, &c.

Art. IX. The King Tsiahouan engaged that these agreements should be accepted by his kinsfolk, the King of the Tsitampikis, Réentigna, and Andriana, chief of the Mivavis. (This last was elder brother of Raboky, father of Ontzinzou.)

Art. X. The commandant (M. de Langle), considering that from time immemorial Baly Bay had marked the limits to the kingdoms of Bouéni and Ambongo, was willing to restore the ties of relationship and alliance which formerly existed between the two great divisions of the independent Sàkalàva by inviting them to come to an understanding with him to settle their commercial relations with France.

Art. XI. M. de Langle found Saty-Ambala and Safy-lessouky (?) princesses, relations of King Angareza of the Bouéni Sàkalàva, established on the shores of Baly Bay, who were held as guarantees for the king; and the envoys of King Angareza, viz., Tofotra, Sàkalàva, Bakary, Manafy, and Tamay, with full powers to treat for him, in common accord with the above-named princesses, agreed to submit themselves to the will of France in regard to the settlement of the affairs in Baly Bay.

Art. XII. The commander-in-chief, on behalf of his sovereign H.M. Napoleon III., accepted the submission by which Angareza and the princesses

Lastly M. Lanessan appends to his report a concession made by King Laymeriza of the province of Féhérègne, with the full consent of his chiefs, of the territory, bounded on the south by the right bank of the River Angoulake, to the north by the left bank of the Belitsara, on the west by the sea, to the east by the mountains of Tahiuksuaka stretching from one river to the other. (This precious

<small>his aunts, who had been installed by their father and grandfather (Andrian Souly, last king of the Bouéni, who gave up Mayotte to France), placed themselves under the protection of France, which recognized afresh the right of protectorate.

Art. XXXIII. The commandant, considering the goodwill of the Antalote population of Marambitsy, wished also to extend the protection over the shipping of this community.

Art. XXXIV. Bona-Moussa, or any other chief indicated by the king of the Bouéni, or of Ambongo, shall give to the dhows of Marambitsy a permit of navigation which shall give the name of the dhow, the name of the master, number of crew, passengers, destination, &c.

Art. XXXV. Every vessel of Marambitsy or Baly carrying a permit will receive from the French authorities the same assistance as if she sailed from Nossi-Bé or Mayotte.

Art. XXXVI. It is to be understood that the security granted to vessels of Marambitsy or of Ambongo will not authorize the trading in blacks.

Art. XXXVII. If free people wish to take passage on the dhows to engage themselves at Mayotte or at Nossi-Bé, or to contract a longer engagement at the sugar factories, they shall be placed on the list of passengers, and the local administration will take care that the engagements of these people are in accordance with the rules drawn up by the imperial decree which regulates this business.

The foregoing convention was signed by Viscount de Fleuriot de Langle, and the Reverend Fathers, the Jesuit priests of the Baly mission, assisted at the conferences and bore witness to the signature, viz., Pierre Pira and J. Goré, missionaries.

Then follow the signatures of the chiefs.

Bakari — Manafi — Toufouzi — Tamahi—Abdallah—Massoua—Cassimou—Bona-Moussa — Ousséni — Abdallay-ben-Ally — Ally-ben-Daidi — Mamihi — Mavahazé.</small>

document was signed at Tullear Bay.) This extent of country is apparently granted from sheer goodwill, without any consideration in return, to two merchant captains, MM. Rosiers and Bellanger.

The foregoing treaties are those relied upon by the French Republic for supporting the claims of a French protectorate over the north-west coast of Madagascar, and

II.

The second treaty is a convention between Viscount de Langle and Outzinzou, queen of the Manouis, a fraction of the Ambongo Sàkalàva, dated 26th September, 1859.

The commander-in-chief reappeared in his corvette the *Cordelière* in Baly Bay in September, 1859, to take over the indemnities which he had levied the previous February after the bombardment of Mahagoulo, on which occasion he had declared that Queen Outzinzou, ruling over a tribe of the Ambongo named Manouis, had forfeited her rights for plundering French vessels and resisting the crew of the *Cordelière*.

The punishment inflicted on Outzinzou and her people, and the absolute interdiction of all commerce during seven months, had produced a salutary effect on that princess, and on the tribe of the Manouis. Accordingly the queen and her chiefs came and made their submission to M. de Langle, and declared that they only held their authority and territory by the benevolence of H.M. the Emperor of the French, whose clemency they implored.

The commandant, accordingly, in the name of his sovereign, accepted their submission and was pleased to re-establish relations with them and to relieve the queen from the blockade which he had imposed, on certain conditions; amongst these was the payment of the indemnity to the Jesuit priests in kind instead of in specie by an equivalent of 280 fat oxen within three months, fit for immediate killing. The terms of the indemnity for the *Marie-Angélique* were to remain as fixed by the convention of the 26th February. The rights of France were duly recognized. The envoys of Marambitsy, viz., Amissi-Mari, Samaï, Abdallah, and Abdallah brother of Bouéna-Moussa were made acquainted with the new clauses of the convention and gave guarantees by a note of hand, under seal, placed in the hands of the commander-in-chief.

Besides this, six children were required, as hostages, to be placed under the care of the Abbé Jouen to be educated at Nossi-Bé.

general claims over the north, north-east, and west shores of the island.

In 1861 the Queen Ranavàlona I. died, and on the accession to the throne of King Radama II. in August, 1861, all the captive Sàkalàva were made free and sent to their homes with valuable presents for their chiefs and friends, together with messages of peace and goodwill. The new king also sent the bones of the Sàkalàva chiefs who

---

The Tsitampikis people and the Magnéas, governed by Sambou-Tsiahouan and his brothers, were to have free access to French ships visiting the bay, &c.

The chiefs chosen by Queen Outzinzou, not knowing how to sign, made their crosses : Ouringui (*manantani*, or Prime Minister) ; Fananazouna (commanding the troops) ; Tsitahora, brother-in-law of the Queen ; Cazany, harbour-master.

Abbé Jouen, S.J., and two of his pupils, Marie Joseph, and Apolinaire, signed as witnesses.

III.

The third convention was passed between M. Desprez, Lieutenant, commanding the *Labourdonnais*, and Queen Narouva of Menabé, at the mouth of the River Sizoubonghi, on the 30th March, 1860. Like the former treaties, this convention was occasioned by the necessary punishment of the Menabé Sàkalàva, who had murdered the crew of the *Marie Caroline* and plundered the vessel.

M. Samat, a trader at Tsimandrafouze, acted as interpreter, and Father Pagès, a Jesuit missionary, and M. Rosiers, the captain of a trading-ship, the *Céleste et Amélie*, certified the correct translation and signed as witnesses.

The Sàkalàva who signed were Narouva, Queen ; Zabelletsi-Mananjouki ; Tsi-Fikané ; Tsi-Maloume, son of Ariari ; Citreffé ; Saïd-Meriza.

IV.

A fourth treaty was concluded at Machicora by Lieut. Desprez with Ibart and Ribiby, kings of the Mahafaly.

This last was signed by Antine, chief of the Vezo at Machichora, and envoy of King Ibart ; also by Toulondoso and Moenidoso, chiefs of Ribibi.

had died in captivity back to their ancestral tombs. In consequence, embassies under selected chiefs of the Sàkalàva were sent to Antananarivo to accept the welcome friendship, and to offer allegiance to the king and government, the tribes along the whole line of country to the north-west, with scarcely an exception, following this example. Radama received them with that frank good-nature which needed no voucher for its sincerity, and entertained them at his court with right royal hospitality. They offered to surrender their arms, but he said "Take them back with you, and if I should want your help, you will have them ready." (*Madagascar Revisited*, by William Ellis, p. 94.) The result of this treatment, so unlike anything that had ever occurred in Madagascar, surpassed all expectations, and excited universal admiration. The Sàkalàva to the west and the south reciprocated the confidence of Radama, and returned his kindness, tendered their allegiance, agreed to furnish recruits for the Hovas, and Imerina probably did not contain firmer supporters or more sincere friends than the Sàkalàva afterwards proved.

The French envoy, M. le baron de Corbigny, was one of the first to recognize the King of Madagascar on the part of the Emperor of the French, who subsequently appointed Commodore Dupré to be present at the king's coronation and to conclude a treaty with Madagascar.

The first treaty between France and Madagascar was concluded on the 12th September, 1862,[1] and no reservation as to any rights over the north-west coast of Madagascar was made by the French plenipotentiary.

This treaty was signed by the Emperor Napoleon, countersigned by MM. Drouyn de Lhuys and De Langle, on the ratification at Paris on the 11th April, 1863; but it was disavowed by the Malagasy Government after the deposition of Radama II. a month subsequently. During the reign of Rasoherina, the widow of Radama II., it was found impracticable to conclude a treaty at first on account of the difficulty with regard to the large indemnity demanded by the French for the annulment of the Lambert concession, which was finally paid in January, 1866, and next by the illness and death of the Count de Louvières who was despatched from France as plenipotentiary for the negotiation of a fresh treaty.

The Count de Louvières died on the 31st December, 1866, and was succeeded as envoy and plenipotentiary by M. Garnier, a naval officer, who arrived in Madagascar when Rasoherina was in a moribund state.

[1] M. Galos wrote in the *Revue des Deux Mondes* (October, 1863, p. 700): "This question of right is, besides, set at rest at present by the Treaty of Friendship and Commerce of the 2nd September, 1862. By that Act, in which Radama II. appears as King of Madagascar, we have recognized, *without restriction*, his sovereignty over all the island. In consequence of that recognition two consuls have been accredited to him, the one at Antananarivo, the other at Tamatave, who only exercise their functions by virtue of an *exequatur* from the real sovereign."

On the accession of Ranavàlona II., April, 1868, and after the funeral ceremonies and mourning were over, M. Garnier resumed the interrupted negotiations, and the new treaty was finally concluded and signed on the 4th August, 1868. Under this treaty France fully recognized Ranavàlona II. as Queen of Madagascar, and MM. Laborde and Soumagne were appointed consuls at Antananarivo and Tamatave respectively, as during the former reign.

It appears, moreover, that subsequently a French consular officer resided at Mojangà, at whose instance M. Laborde, the French consul, in 1874 accused the Hova custom-house officer at Ampasibitika of taking exorbitant customs dues at that port ; besides, all foreign vessels paid without demur the usual duty on their cargoes of imported goods to the Hova officials at the western and north-western ports up to a very recent date.

Admiral Gore Jones, commanding the Indian station, received instructions from the British Government to visit Antananarivo, and for this purpose he anchored his flagship, *Euryalus*, off Tamatave on the 5th June, 1881. He then accompanied Mr. Pakenham up to the capital, and was received by the Queen, and had a private conference with the Prime Minister. " The general effect of our mission," reports the Admiral, " has been excellent : everybody agreed it had thrown life and movement into the capital ; and all the Europeans were especially pleased.

The Queen was also glad, as no mission had previously been sent to compliment her during her reign ; and, judging of a reign by the acts of the monarch, it has been the greatest and most beneficial that Madagascar has ever seen. Her Majesty is a truly good and moral woman."

In his address to the Queen, Admiral Gore Jones expressed his belief that France was in accord with England in wishing to forward the prosperity of Madagascar, and to *increase the Hova influence*, especially at the seaports on the south-west coast, where recent bad acts on the part of petty chiefs had proved a strong Government was required. He especially noted the marked improvement in the Hova territory over every other part of the island he had visited.

The Queen, in her reply, requested the Admiral to tell Her Majesty that her sincere desire was for the extending of Hova influence all over the island. "I tell you," she said, "that I and my Government intend to establish military stations at some points on the west coast."

It was not until the arrival of M. Baudais in the autumn of 1881 that the claims of France to protect the Sàkalàva of the north-west coast were brought to the serious notice of the Malagasy Government ; and they were put forward under the following circumstances.

In June, 1881, Mr. Parrett, the printer of the London Missionary Society, was sent by the Prime Minister on a mission to the north-west of the island, the object of which was kept secret, but which was generally supposed to have reference to the mines situated there. He was joined at Mojangà by Mr. Pickersgill, a missionary of the same society, who had for some years been settled at that port. These two gentlemen made a short tour through the north-west coasts, and they were surprised to find that the Sàkalàva tribes were openly declared subjects of Ranavàlona II., as they had been warned that the contrary was the case. Whilst, however, the name of the Queen, and also that of Rainilaiarivony, were held in great respect, there was no lack, says Mr. Pickersgill, of complaints against the Hova officials. As has already been said, certain lands and privileges had been granted by Radama at the time of the conquest, and these the Hova governors had regularly been encroaching upon. Messrs. Parrett and Pickersgill asked the Sàkalàva why they did not complain; and the answer was, that the Hova governors refused them permission to go up to the capital, as the complaints were against their officials, and their appeals would not be listened to. Messrs. Parrett and Pickersgill then suggested that the aggrieved chiefs should accompany them to Antananarivo, and this suggestion was cheerfully accepted. The people of Ampasimena expressed their loyalty to the sovereign of Madagascar, and King Tsimiharo claimed to be one of her *ambassiandro*, and declared that Nossi-Mitsiou, the island on which he was residing, belonged to Ranavàlona.

Accepting the offer of the missionaries' escort, three of the most important among the chieftaincies despatched envoys, consisting of an adviser or councillor, and a relative of the chief. These embassies were heartily welcomed by the Malagasy Government, one of the results of their visit being an acknowledgment of their right of direct communication with and access to the Queen of Madagascar. In token of their allegiance, the Queen's Government gave the representatives of the Sàkalàva chiefs proper white flags, the Malagasy ensigns, in place of the red, or Arab, flags, which they had previously floated, to be hoisted at their chief towns and ports on the coast, and this assertion of national right on the part of the Malagasy gave umbrage to the French colonial authorities at Nossi-Bé and to the newly-arrived French Commissioner at the capital.

Old Tsimiharo, of Nossi-Mitsiou, very naturally and properly, declined to receive or hoist the Hova flag, since he was most accessible to the French authorities at Nossi-Bé, and, indeed, in receipt of an annual subsidy from the French Government of 1,200 francs. (*Diplomatic Documents*, 1881–83.)

M. Baudais, the French Commissioner of Antananarivo, accordingly wrote to M. Gambetta, Minister of Foreign Affairs, as follows :—

"*Antananarivo*, 16th November, 1881.

"Mr. Minister,—The following information has come to my knowledge.

"It appears that there have arrived in the province of Imerina certain Sàkalàva chiefs or their envoys. It is said that after long negotiations with the Sàkalàva chiefs, who are under our protectorate, at Nossi-Bé, and its dependencies, and of whom one Tsimiharo, amongst others, receives an annual subsidy from France, these chiefs have come or have sent proxies to visit the court of Ranavàlona. It is added that the Queen is about to send and take possession of the territories submitted, and there to unfurl her flag.

"As soon as this news reached me I immediately dispatched a courier to warn the commandant of Nossi-Bé of what was about to take place. I added in the letter which I addressed to him, that had I known where to find a ship of war on the station I should have hastened to make the same communication to its captain. The report was true. The Sàkalàva chiefs have come, and their interview took place at Ambohimanga, the present residence of the Queen, and a sacred village, to which the entrance of foreigners is forbidden. The Malagasy Government has not lost an instant, and to those who know their slowness in coming to a decision, it is a proof the more that all was arranged beforehand.

"On the 8th November the envoys returned (without passing through Antananarivo), accompanied by troops under arms, and carrying four Hova flags. Two of them are destined to be planted in Nossi-Faly and Nossi-Mitsiou, the two last on other points of the coast, in the vicinity, no doubt, but which have not been indicated to me exactly.

"Now we have indisputable rights over Nossi-Mitsiou and Nossi-Faly.

"In 1840, Tsimiharo, then taking refuge on the west coast, from whence he came each month to draw at Nossi-Bé the pension which the French Government allowed him, ceded to France *all his rights over Ankara* (the northern part of Madagascar) and over the islands which depend on it, Nossi-Mitsiou and Nossi-Faly included.

"The Hova Government never dared take possession of them, and in Ankara has never held but a few insignificant posts, occupied by so-called garrisons, which only exist on paper. At Vohémar there is a garrison of eight men, at Diego Suarez of six, at Marontsangana of from fifteen to twenty. That is all.

"It is only by great trouble that I have been able to procure the information which I forward to you. All means have been tried to keep the matter secret. The prolonged and unusual stay of the Queen and her court at Ambohimanga is relevant to this. Every one of whatever rank follows the Queen when she is absent, and remains with her. To keep the court away, therefore, is to deprive Antananarivo of all news. It was agreed to keep complete silence as to all these attempted acts of possession. Since the month of May these affairs have been in train, and it is only six months afterwards, on the 2nd November, that the representative of France here has been informed, and then only by personal inquiry.

" BAUDAIS."

CHAPTER III.

CONFLAGRATION.

WE have thus brought down our retrospective view of the various matters in dispute between the Governments of France and Madagascar to the period when M. de Freycinet renewed the instruction of his predecessor, M. Gambetta, to the consul for France at Antananarivo, at the commencement of 1882.

At this time, the reports of M. Baudais led the French Minister for Foreign Affairs to suppose that the Hova Government intended to contest the rights of protectorate claimed by France over the north-west coast; and if, said M. de Freycinet to his Commissioner, your views are correct, "we shall find ourselves face to face with a proceeding equivalent to an act of hostility." The reports received from Nossi-Bé and from the ships of the French squadron by Admiral Jauréguiberry, Minister of Marine and the Colonies, confirmed the reports[1] received at the

---

[1] The commandant of Nossi-Bé gathered from conversation with Sàkalàva chiefs, on their return from Antananarivo, that they had merely proceeded thither to beg of the Queen to withdraw from their coasts the garrison posts which she had established there. The French commandant warned the chiefs at Nossi-Mitsiou and Nossi-Faly against permitting the Hova flag to be hoisted at those islands.

Foreign Office, of the presence of Hova emissaries in the Ankara country; and that the chiefs of that province had been subjected to overtures on the part of Queen Ranavàlona. Nevertheless there was not sufficient evidence to warrant energetic measures being as yet taken by the French naval authorities; so the minister merely authorized M. Baudais to concert with the commandant at Nossi-Bé all the defensive measures he might judge necessary for the efficacious protection of French rights, secured by the treaties made with the Sàkalàva chiefs, over the dependencies of Nossi-Bé, and over that portion of the mainland included in the same conventions.

Captain Le Timbre shortly afterwards telegraphed from Zanzibar that he was called by the course of events to Malagasy waters; and M. de Freycinet wrote from the Quai d'Orsay, freshly affirming "the strong resolution of the Government of the Republic on no account whatsoever to suffer, directly or indirectly, any prejudice to the existing rights of France in Madagascar."

Meantime, according to M. Baudais, events of some importance appeared to be brewing on the west coast of Madagascar, to the south of Mojangà. The Hova Government, it was said, sought to establish in an effective manner, to the west and south-west, its dominion, which up till that time had been "purely fictitious." The tribes of the interior, so it was reported, knowing that this project would be ruinous to them, were collecting together in the neighbourhood of Baly Bay, to repulse the Hova aggression with which they were threatened; and these warriors formed a body more than sufficient in numbers to oppose the Hovas; that is, so long as they were united. " The reason given by the Hovas," wrote M. Baudais, " for this expedition, was a request for protection made to them by Queen Beravony of Marambitsy against the depredations of her neighbours at Souhalala. This is only a pretext. On the contrary, the Queen of Souhalala, Safy-Ambala, daughter of Andrian-Souly, declares that her niece, Beravony, cannot alienate any portion of her territory. The Sàkalàva are one of the peoples which Radama I. and his successors could never reduce under their dominion. . . . Up till now it has not been possible for the Hovas to establish more than two or three customhouses; and consequently the foreign trade is carried on with the Sàkalàva without Hova intervention, which is a serious loss to the Hova treasury. The object of the Madagascar Government, therefore, is not so much to subdue the Sàkalàva as to seize the points of the coast where the ships come to trade, to establish throughout the coast custom-house stations, and thereby supplement the cash receipts of the Queen's treasury."

In April, M. de Freycinet saw the necessity of adopting without delay active measures, calculated to arrest the

LEGITIMATE REQUIREMENTS.

execution of designs of the importance of which there was no doubt. He instructed M. Baudais in a despatch dated the 25th, as follows :—

" If when you receive this despatch the situation is not modified in a sense conforming to our legitimate requirements, you will not fail to recall the notice of the Government of Antananarivo to the position secured to us by the treaties concluded with the Sàkalàva chiefs of Ankara, and to the obligations as well as the rights which we have acquired by the engagements between those chiefs and France. . . . But if your friendly representations have no effect, you will not hesitate to declare that our fixed determination is not to suffer the slightest infringement of the rights which the Treaty of 1841, ceding Nossi-Bé, ensures to us on the coast; and that we shall use with that object all the means at our disposal. The presence in Madagascar waters of several of our ships will besides leave the Hovas in no doubt as to the interest with which we follow up the course of events, of which the north-west coast is the theatre, and on the value we attach to the maintenance of the position taken up by France on this point."

Several rather stormy interviews took place between Rainilaiarivony and M. Baudais, and the latter addressed the despatch of the 29th April, already alluded to in Chapter I., in which he recapitulated the grievances of which

France had to complain. He informed the Prime Minister of the probable eventuality when the settlement of all these questions would be taken in hand by the commandant of the squadron on the station, then at Nossi-Bé, who would quickly obtain satisfaction. The French consul observed : " The tone of the answers to my letters, a tone always disingenuous, and in no way relevant to the particular object of my communication, causes considerable obstruction in the settlement of all the questions. This must cease, and it will form the subject of a special letter which I shall address directly to the Foreign Minister.

"If this style of reply to my letters is continued, I shall be forced to communicate with your Excellency only by *notes*, which, in their character as *notes*, will necessarily be couched in a tone far more peremptory than that which I have been accustomed to employ, and will, in consequence, render the relations between our two governments far less easy."

Meantime, rumours of the French claims over Madagascar were spread in the capital, and on the 3rd May there was considerable excitement amongst the lower class of the populace. Numerous groups collected on the Kabary ground at Andohalo, opposite the French consulate, and made known their dissatisfaction with loud hootings and shouts, according to their custom.

Meantime the flag-ship, the *Forfait*, arrived at Tamatave,

where on landing, the commandant, M. Le Timbre, made a speech to the governor and his officers at the Fort on the 5th May. This speech, "very firm and dignified," wrote M. Baudais, produced a great effect at Tamatave; and as soon as the text of it reached the capital, a good deal of alarm and agitation was perceptible on account of the hostile tone of the address.

On receiving a copy of Captain Le Timbre's discourse, the French Commissioner demanded an interview, which took place at the office of the foreign department, in the palace of Tsiazompaniry, in Antananarivo, on the 16th May.

At the conclusion of this momentous interview, a letter [1] (presumably written in advance) dated from Tsiazompaniry was handed by the consul to Ravoninahitriniarivo. It concluded thus :—" The orders of my Government are imperative, Mr. Minister. I demand, therefore, of you, *Yes* or *No*, whether you are disposed to remove your flag from the territories where that of France alone has the right to wave. Your letter of the 13th May is not an answer. I require one. I have, therefore, the honour to warn you that unless within twenty-four hours, that is, by to-morrow,

---

[1] "A letter prepared beforehand at the consulate, and at the head of which had been added the words, *Palais de Tsiazompaniry*, at the moment you handed it to me in the palace," writes Ravoninahitriniarivo.

"This letter was written at the palace during the audiences; it had to be translated immediately, and its only object was to obtain a categorical answer. I was therefore obliged to give it a brief form" (M. Baudais to M. de Freycinet, 18th May).

17th May, at noon, I receive a categorical answer, I shall consider the silence as an official refusal on the part of your Government."

Having delivered this letter, M. Baudais retired. On the following day, by 11 a.m., the answer of the Malagasy Government reached the French consulate. The minister delared that his Government protested : "If these treaties with the Sàkalàva were made anterior to the treaty of 1868, they are annulled by the treaty concluded between us subsequent to theirs, and you must admit that consequently they became void. You add that my protest against the possession by you of these lands is nothing but a simple denial, and is no answer. I maintain that the opinion which I have uttered on this affair is a full answer."

M. Baudais took this as a formal refusal to remove the Hova flag from the places where it should not be hoisted, and he reported to his department at Paris that the population of Antananarivo was in a state of intense excitement, that Kabarys were held and emissaries of the Government harangued the groups of townspeople, spreading reports that France wished to take possession of the Queen's territory, and that the people would never allow it, as she was sovereign over all Madagascar. These rumours, said M. Baudais, took a threatening consistency on the 19th, and the whole night had been spent at the palace in deliberations upon the critical situation, when the most extraordinary opinions were expressed. He learnt that proposals had been made to get rid of all foreigners resident in Antananarivo. The French consul was conscious of his safety, although he perceived that he was under constant surveillance; in fact, the Prime Minister took every precaution that the person of the French representative should not be insulted. In short, the situation became so uncomfortable, that the Commissioner of the Republic determined to leave Antananarivo since his presence could be of no further use; and as discussion was at an end with the Hova Government, he considered that it did not suit the dignity of the French consul to remain any longer at the capital.

M. Baudais arrived at Tamatave on the 29th May, leaving M. Campan, the Chancelier of the Consulate, where the French flag remained flying for some time longer. But the tricolor was not destined to wave much longer in Antananarivo, for a few nights after the departure of M. Baudais, placards were posted on the walls and door of the consulate, threatening death to the French officials, and large crowds assembled making remarks upon the notices. As soon as the consul heard of the commotion at the capital, he ordered M. Campan to haul down the flag and retire to the coast, first warning the French subjects that they must consult their own safety, and if they remained must do so on their own responsibility.

On the 12th June, Captain Le Timbre informed the Commissioner at Tamatave that he had just learnt that a body of Hova troops was expected on the coast in order to embark on board the only vessel possessed by the Malagasy Government, the *Antananarivo*, in order to proceed to the west coast. Captain Le Timbre added that as the west coast was territory placed under the protection of France, this embarkation would be an act of hostility, and he requested M. Baudais, therefore, to inform the Government of Madagascar that if such an operation was persisted in, he should oppose it by force of arms. The Minister of Ranavàlona naturally expressed his astonishment and regret at such a hostile manœuvre being contemplated, but could only protest.

A few days afterwards, the Creole director of a coffee plantation owned by a French firm at Mitinandry on the east coast was murdered, but it does not appear to have been suggested that this outrage was in any way due to political disturbance, as it was the result of private animosity.

It was now determined by the French to exercise some authority, and publicly demonstrate their rights of sovereignty on the north-west coast; for this purpose M. Le Timbre took the *Forfait* round to Nossi-Bé, where he took on board the civil governor of that colony, M. Seignac-Lesseps, and thence steamed to Passandava Bay, where the flag of Ranavàlona was flying at Ampassimiena (Mahavanona), the village of Queen Binao. Here, on the 16th June, the French officers landed without opposition, hauled down the flag and took possession of it. A few ships' carpenters who accompanied the party cut down the flagstaff and chopped it into firewood, to the astonishment of the neighbouring Sàkalàva villagers.

The *Forfait* was next anchored off the mouth of the river Sambriano, up the stream of which MM. Le Timbre and Lesseps pulled in a gig, followed by a whale boat for a distance of some five miles, to within an easy range of the village Behamaranza. Here a similar operation was performed. For these two gallant exploits Captain Le Timbre was promoted to the rank of Rear-admiral by M. de Mahy.

Returning to Tamatave, after consultation with M. Baudais, Captain Le Timbre placed an embargo on the *Antananarivo*, and a few days later, when an American ship, the *Stilman*, came into the roadstead, laden with arms and ammunition, Captain Le Timbre announced that he would stop the delivery of the cargo to the consignees, the Malagasy Government.

Andriamifidy, who was at this time acting as Foreign Secretary, hastened to inform M. Baudais that the contract for arms had been concluded by his Government with an American firm before any difficulties had been raised in 1881, consequently the French consul would be held responsible if he thought proper to prevent the fulfilment of the contract.

Colonel Robinson, the United States consul at Tamatave, also insisted on the removal of a steam launch which the French naval commander had placed to watch the *Stilman;* so it was not long before the embargo was taken off, and the stores of arms and ammunition landed and taken possession of by the Hova governor.

Meanwhile, the Commissioner penned a brief despatch to Paris, informing the Minister for Foreign Affairs that the situation was becoming more and more grave, that diplomatic measures were completely exhausted, and it was an urgent case of necessity to exact complete and immediate satisfaction. The naval commander agreed with him in this opinion, and requested precise orders by telegraph to Zanzibar. M. Baudais concluded by saying, " We must have complete satisfaction or abandon Madagascar definitively."

On the same date that M. Baudais, at Tamatave, forwarded his message, the government at Antananarivo determined to send an embassy to visit the governments of the various powers which were in friendly and commercial intercourse with Madagascar, and to lay before them all the pending questions in dispute between France and themselves.

During all this time the English consul at Tamatave

had preserved a discreet silence, and it was well understood that he was on terms of intimacy with the French officials, whilst from his failing health, his increasing apathy and distaste for business, the officers of the Republic perhaps thought that they could reckon on his non-interference to some extent.

Matters, however, had now reached such a critical stage that it was necessary to inform the English Foreign Office that something unusual was happening, and Mr. Pakenham telegraphed *viâ* Zanzibar to Lord Granville that the Hova Government had protested against the seizure of the Hova flags by the French commodore at Passandava ; that a Hova embassy was about to be sent to England and other powers, and that an embargo had been put on the *Antananarivo*. This seems to be the first intimation we have that the British Government took any interest in the disputes between the French and Hova Governments. The resolve of Ranavàlona's minister to send a special embassy to Paris appears to have taken M. Baudais somewhat aback, and evidently did not please him. He was resolved to obstruct the passage of the Hova envoys as long as possible.

The letter from Ravoninahitriniarivo announcing the forthcoming mission of envoys to Europe reached M. Baudais on the 7th July, on which date he forwarded a copy to the Quai d'Orsay. No reply apparently having been vouchsafed, the Hova minister wrote again on the 12th, requesting the consul in the name of Ranavàlona to suspend further proceedings in regard to the pending disputes until the projected embassy had concluded negotiations at Paris.

M. Baudais disdained to reply to the Foreign Secretary, but wrote to Rainilaiarivony on the 18th that it was not for him to stop the course of events. "As for the mission projected by the Hova Government, it cannot avail towards the solution of the question." The Foreign Minister wrote again to state that the embassy would leave the capital on the 20th of the month, and asked M. Baudais to advise his Government of its advent. Upon this the consul addressed the Prime Minister, telling him that he, the Prime Minister, should himself have addressed him, and informed him of the names of the persons composing the mission, if he wished to fulfil the most elementary usages of diplomacy.

The names of officers appointed to act as ambassadors were duly forwarded, these being (1) Ravoninahitriniarivo, the Foreign Minister, an officer of the 15th Honour, and noted for his successful conduct of a campaign against the rebellious and unruly tribes in the west of the island. He is also, it may be added, nephew of the Prime Minister : (2) Ramaniraka, the son of the well-known Rahaniraka, a distinguished member of the Queen's privy council, and a skilled linguist.

A RESPECTABLE MINISTRY. 91

These two ambassadors were attended by Andrianisa and Rabibisoa as secretaries; the former is the son of the Lieut.-Governor of Tamatave, his mother being a Creole of Mauritius; whilst the latter had received his education in France with the son of the Prime Minister.

M. Baudais not only wanted to know the names of the plenipotentiaries, but their business also. To this request Rainilaiarivony stated that the objects of the mission had already been fully set forth, namely, to do whatever they might judge necessary to restore friendly relations between France and Madagascar. He added that they were furnished with full powers to treat in whatever might be necessary with the European powers.

Finally, the mission arrived at Tamatave on the 8th, and embarked for Mauritius on the 18th August, leaving the latter island on the 7th September by the mail steamer for Marseilles.

On the 29th July the Chamber of Deputies, at Paris, rejected the vote of credit proposed for the protection of the Suez Canal, and the ministry resigned, M. Duclerc coming into office. "M. Duclerc and his colleagues," wrote the *Quarterly Review*, "were respectable men of business, but they owed their position chiefly to the fact that they excited no particular antagonism, because they commanded no particular influence. They could transact the business of the public offices, and that was as much as could be expected of them. They were not credited either with sufficient power in Parliament or with sufficient strength of character to meet any unusual danger, or to control any popular agitation." (December 31st, 1882.)

M. Baudais next made another attempt to get up a grievance, this time a personal one. He wrote a letter marked *private*, calling the attention of the Prime Minister to an article which had appeared in the *Madagascar Times*. He complained that the proprietor of this paper, M. Tacchi (a Mauritian), had insulted him and all the French in Madagascar. This, he said, was not a piece of wit, but an act of madness. The Prime Minister politely disclaimed all connexion with the *Madagascar Times*, and in his turn drew the attention of M. Baudais to a number of a local French journal, called *La Cloche*, published on the 10th September, in which the Malagasy nation were excited to rebellion against their Government. And thus ended this small untimely squabble.

Meanwhile Captain Le Timbre, in accordance with prudential instructions from the Minister of Marine, withdrew the embargo which he had placed upon the *Antananarivo*. The reasons he gave were that during a visit to the north-west coast he had ascertained, with great satisfaction, that the situation in those parts had for some time been noticeably improved, and that perfect tranquillity reigned, whilst the tentative encroachments on the prerogatives of France had ceased and the molestation of the Sàkalàva allies of France was no longer practised. The fact was that by direction of Lord Granville, Lord Lyons was pressing M. Duclerc, who had now succeeded M. de Freycinet in office, for an exposition of the views of the newly constructed French Ministry regarding the recent proceedings of their forces on the coast of Madagascar, and the British Minister was anxious to ascertain on what treaties the French Government rested their claims to a protectorate over the Sàkalàva territory. No satisfactory answer was obtainable as to these treaties, and the Hon. Mr. Plunket again addressed the President of the Council on the 12th October in a note to the following effect :—

"Her Majesty's Government are anxious to receive at as early a date as possible a definite statement on this point from the French Government. Your Excellency is aware that *Her Majesty's Government recognize the Queen of Madagascar as absolute monarch of the whole island*, excepting Mayotta and Nossi-Bé on the north-west coast, which are now occupied by the French. As at present advised, Her Majesty's Government are unaware of any treaty stipulations in virtue of which the French Government claims territorial jurisdiction over any part of the mainland of Madagascar. Your Excellency is also aware that the understanding between Great Britain and France has hitherto been that the two Governments should maintain an identic attitude of policy in Madagascar, and act in concert in the matter; and your Excellency will have no difficulty in understanding the regret with which Her Majesty's Government would view the advancement on the part of France of any territorial claims which might be calculated to disturb that understanding."

The embassy from the Queen of Madagascar arrived at Marseilles on the 2nd October, and on the envoys reaching Paris, the French Government appointed Commissioners to treat with the Malagasy plenipotentiaries, the first conference being held on the 17th October to adjust the preliminaries. MM. Baudais and Campan were summoned to France from Tamatave by M. Duclerc to advise his government in its dealings with the envoys, and thenceforth all chances of a peaceful settlement, if ever any existed, or were intended to exist, were at an end.

The commission nominated by M. Duclerc to confer with the ambassadors were MM. Decrais, Director of Political Affairs, Vice-Admiral Peyron, chief of the staff to the Minister of Marine, and Billot, Director of Commercial Claims. The powers and credentials having been exchanged by the respective plenipotentiaries, the formal proceedings were commenced by the presentation of a note by the Malagasy, in which they requested permission to lay before the representatives of France frankly all the arguments they had to submit, and what they believed to be the rights of their sovereign.

1. From the days of Radama I. all Madagascar had been united under one rule, and although from time to time there had been rebellions, these had been crushed out by military expeditions, organized by the sovereign of the island, and no foreigner had ever interfered or opposed such proceedings.

2. From the days of Radama the inhabitants of the territory now claimed by France had presented the usual tribute or *hasina* to the sovereign of Madagascar, and also the yearly poll-tax to the Madagascar Government.

3. By the treaty of 1862 the French Government had acknowledged Radama II. as sovereign of Madagascar.

4. By the Lambert charter a concession of lands was granted to a French company under the auspices of Napoleon III., which land was within the territory now said to be under a French protectorate.

5. On the withdrawal of this charter, the Queen of Madagascar, Rasoherina, paid an indemnity to the French Government for the breach of contract.

6. By the treaty of 1868 France solemnly acknowledged Ranavàlona II. as Queen of Madagascar.

7. The late French Consul, M. Laborde, had claimed as late as 1874 a rebate of duty overcharged at Ampassambitiky in Passandava Bay, thereby acknowledging the right

of the Malagasy Government to levy dues in that district, now claimed by France.

8. Up to the present time all European and American ships trading at the ports on the north-west coast paid custom-house duties, and that the majority of these vessels were French.

9. The French flag had never been hoisted on the mainland of Madagascar.

10. The Sàkalàva had always looked to Antananarivo for redress of their wrongs.

11. French officials had blamed the Government of Madagascar for not asserting its authority more fully on the west coast.

12. The French Consul, M. Baudais, himself had recently imposed a heavy indemnity for an *outrage* alleged to have been perpetrated on the *Toale* at Marambitsy.

13. British men-of-war and British consuls had dealt directly with the Hova authorities on that coast, without any French interference.

The French Commissioners insisted on limiting the discussion to the questions raised (1) by the violation of the treaty of 1868; and (2) by the pretensions of the Hova Government over certain territories placed under the protectorate of France by special treaties. They therefore concluded in a note handed to the ambassadors in November that " Queen Ranavàlona must voluntarily remove from the north-west coast her flags, garrisons, and customs-stations, and not reduce us to the painful necessity of intervening ourselves to protect our disputed rights and threatened interests."

In a third note (*French version* [1]) the Hova ambassadors expressed a wish above all to come to an agreement on the two points which concerned their political relations. Concerning one of these points—the voluntary removal, by order of Her Majesty Ranavàlonamanjaka, of her flags, garrisons, and customs-stations recently established on the north-west coast—the ambassadors engaged to conform to the desire expressed by the French Government, since the Government of France had notified to them the existence and maintenance of its private treaties with the chiefs of the coast.

In a note dated 25th November, it was stated that the Government of the Republic acknowledged the concession of the Hovas as to the retirement of the Hova garrisons, and in return, *under reserve of its rights*, consented that the Hova military posts thus evacuated should not be replaced, *for the present*, by French troops. The Government of the Republic also made no difficulty in declaring that it *had no intention to possess itself of Madagascar.* It

---

[1] The Hova Ambassadors subsequently informed Lord Granville (February 8th, 1883) that they considered the Yellow Book on Madagascar presented a very inaccurate account of the matters at issue between their Government and that of France, and also of the recent negotiations in Paris.

was ready to aid the progress of the Hova Government and people in the way of civilization.

On the 26th November, the Commissioners forwarded a document, in reality M. Duclerc's ultimatum, which they had drawn up for the ambassadors to sign, embodying the agreement which they had come to with the envoys. One clause appears to have made mention of the general rights of France over Madagascar, and this clause the ambassadors took exception to, as they stated that they had no powers to admit any such general rights over the whole island.

The envoys earnestly begged that the French Government would be good enough not to make mention in writing of "the clause relative to the general rights of France." If the reader turns to the Note as printed in the Yellow Book, he will find nothing in it referring to the "general rights of France." The explanation of this (given by Mr. Chesson in the *Times* of the 27th March, 1883) is that the published version of the Ultimatum is not identical with the document handed to the envoys. Both versions give, with only slight variations, the same sketch of the terms of the settlement proposed by France; but in the Yellow Book the following important passage in the original is entirely suppressed :—
" It is, however, well understood that these assurances cannot in any way question the general rights which France from all time has claimed over Madagascar, which rights the Government of the Republic, under the present

GARBLED REPORTS. 99

circumstances, is bound expressly to reserve, while sincerely hoping that the friendly and confiding spirit of the Hova Government towards us will allow us to refrain from calling them up again."

This objectionable clause was suppressed in the printed correspondence, and the French public were thus designedly misinformed as to the nature of the demand made by their government on the Malagasy ambassadors.

Of the five Notes contained in the Yellow Book purporting to constitute the Malagasy portion of the correspondence at Paris, three were actually drawn up by certain French intermediaries, MM. Revoil and Baragnon, who appear to have given a more or less inaccurate account of their unofficial conversations with the envoys; and the latter cannot be held responsible for these reports drawn up without their sanction.

The Malagasy plenipotentiaries gave the following account of their reasons for not signing the agreement sent to their hotel from the Quai d'Orsay :—

"Our subsequent communications were made through our own consuls, MM. Roux and Rabaud, and MM. Revoil and Baragnon (the latter two gentlemen of whose exact relation to the French Government we are ignorant), who advised us to make some concessions to the national pride of the country with which we were dealing, such as the removal *for a few years* of the custom-house officers and flags which had been lately placed on the north-west in the districts under Binao and Monja, in connection with which the present difficulties arose, and we were given to understand that such a concession on our part would result in a withdrawal of the French claims to a protectorate. On the strength of our expressed willingness to concede this point, a document was drawn up by the Commissioners and sent to us to be signed as an *ultimatum*. Our refusal was made for the following reasons : (1) Nothing was said about our removal of the custom-houses and flags being only for a few years; (2) Recognition of the French protectorate was insisted on ; (3) They asserted general rights over the whole of Madagascar, which was the first intimation we had of any such claims. . . . As it was impossible for us to sign this, and thus betray the independence of our country, we were immediately informed that we were no longer considered as the guests of France, and that our flag must be removed from the hotel. Having received this message and witnessed the removal of our flag against our will, we left Paris for London."

"What then took place?" writes M. Saillens (p. 36). "No official document is there to enlighten us ; but we know from a good source that, in the evening which followed this last conference, the Malagasy envoys were seized with affright. Their insistance in asking the withdrawal of '*the general rights of France*' had doubtless tasked the patience of the honourable French diplomatists.

Harsh phrases had been used to them. At so great a distance from their country, in a land of which they did not understand the language, where everything was strange to them, where they had no friends, they took a dark view of things : they were imagining that our proceedings were as expeditious as theirs of Madagascar. They fancied themselves arrested, put in prison, who knows ? Constrained to sign that which they did not wish to sign. Let us not laugh. That same night they departed for London."

Thus a sudden rupture put an end to the Paris conference, and the Hova envoys departed to England, " where," wrote M. Duclerc, "it is to be hoped they will not meet with the encouragement they have been led to expect."

The President of Council at once concerted measures with the Minister of Marine for the active protection of French citizens and rights in Madagascar.

The former informed M. Raffray, who was acting as consul in Madagascar, that the cabinet of Berlin had lately communicated to him its intention of not mixing itself up in any way with the affairs in Madagascar or the incidents to which they might give rise ; and that it had expressed a desire to place under protection of the French agents the persons and interests of German subjects residing in the island. This was the first step made by Prince Bismarck towards the initiation of a *rapprochement* between France and Germany.

CHAPTER IV.

TORMENTUM BELLI.

RAVONINAHITRINIARIVO and his colleague, Ramaniraka, arrived in London on the 27th November, and met with a hearty reception by many old friends in the English metropolis. A number of gentlemen interested in Madagascar had already formed a committee for the purpose of assisting the objects of the embassy, by placing the British Government in possession of the true facts of the case. Mr. A. McArthur, M.P., the chairman, and an influential deputation from this committee, were received by Lord Granville on the 26th November. This deputation was not only important on account of its numbers but also from its representative character, as both parties in the House of Commons were adequately represented by the presence of many members of Parliament, besides those who quite apart from politics took a deep interest in the Madagascar question from other reasons, commercial, religious, and social. The deputation handed to the minister a statement, in which the French claims were fully discussed,[1] and respectfully asked Lord Granville to endeavour to secure a satisfactory settlement of the difficulty that threatened to interrupt the peaceful progress of a people who had shown a marked capacity for civilization.

Earl Granville thought that the deputation would admit that it was not the business of England to intervene in the affairs of other nations unless her honour and interests were seriously concerned. It was not her business to act as police over the whole world; but the deputation thought that there were various and special reasons why Her Majesty's Government should be stimulated to try and bring this dispute between France and Madagascar to a peaceable solution. France and England had generally acted together in a friendly way with regard to Madagascar. " In 1850 Lord, Palmerston recognized the right of the French to the possession of Nossi-Bé. In 1853 and 1854 there were discussions between the two governments which resulted in *the understanding that neither would take action with regard to Madagascar without previous consultation with the other.* Later on, I think, this understanding was recognized. In 1858, 1859, 1862, and in 1863, most conciliatory assurances were given."

[1] Madagascar Tracts, No. 1. "*What are the French claims on Madagascar?*" A statement of the Madagascar Committee. (A. Kingdon & Co., 52, Moorfields.)

Earl Granville proceeded to say that he understood that there were three points in dispute, viz., the claims of individual French subjects, the claim of Frenchmen to purchase freeholds, and the claim of France to a protectorate over a portion of the mainland. It was impossible for him to give any opinion with regard to the individual claims. With regard to the purchase of land, both France and England (although France had stuck to it more pertinaciously) had contended that the treaty rights gave such a claim to both French and English subjects. With regard to the French protectorate, all Lord Granville would say was that *he was not aware of any treaty which gave such a right to France.* The deputation would understand that it was a strict act of duty for him (Lord Granville) to abstain from saying a single word which could be strained into the slightest discourtesy to the French Government. Equally he had no right to say anything which would commit Her Majesty's Government to any particular course.

On the following day Earl Granville wrote to Lord Lyons at Paris that he was anxious to receive some communication from the French Government on the subject of their existing attitude with respect to Madagascar. Great Britain and France had the same interests in Madagascar, and had hitherto acted in concert in all matters affecting their relations with the Hova Government; Her Majesty's

SUBJECTS OF COMPLAINT. 105

Government attached great importance to the continuance of this good understanding, to promote which it was desirable that no cessation should take place in the system of frank intercommunication which had hitherto been adopted by the two Governments.

On the 2nd December Lord Granville formally received the Malagasy ambassadors, who subsequently submitted statements of their position in relation to the French Government. The chief points of the Malagasy case have already been put forward in a previous chapter. (See ante, p. 95.)

The French ambassador, M. Tissot, also furnished Lord Granville with the copy of a despatch from M. Duclerc giving the French view of the question. M. Tissot in further explanation briefly recapitulated the subjects of complaint on the part of France against Madagascar. These were originally :—

1. The refusal of the Malagasy Government to respect the engagements contracted by the treaties of 1862 and 1868 ; and in particular Art. IV. of the latter treaty, granting to French citizens the right of acquiring landed property.

2. The encroachment of the Malagasy Government on the territories of the north-west coast, in regard to which the native chiefs had signed conventions with France dating from 1840 to 1843. The Hova flag had been hoisted, and

military and customs stations established opposite Mayotte and Nossi-Bé.

The French Commissioner at Antananarivo had presented a note on the 29th May on these points. This had been met by a complete refusal, and by hostile demonstrations against the French Commissioner, who had taken refuge at Tamatave.

The French naval force on the station had then removed two flags improperly hoisted on the north-west coast. The Malagasy Government having announced the dispatch of an embassy, operations had been suspended. Thereupon followed the conferences of Paris. The Malagasy envoys had recognized to a certain extent the rights which France had acquired by treaty on the north-west portion of the coast. They had, however, refused to agree to the claims of France with regard to the right of acquiring real property. They would concede no more than the right of making twenty-five years' leases renewable only with the Queen's authorization. Thereupon the conference had been broken off.

It will be observed that, according to M. Duclerc, the conference was broken off on account of the land question, regarding the tenure of freeholds or by long lease. According to the version of the Madagascar envoys, the rupture of the negotiations was caused by their refusal to sign an ultimatum recognizing general rights of France over Madagascar.

On comparing M. Duclerc's despatch with the statement of the ambassadors, Lord Granville informed Lord Lyons that although there had been a complete misunderstanding at the time on the point of the reparation which was to be made to France, still it seemed to him, both from the fact that some sort of compromise had been discussed, and the absence of any decided difference as to the views entertained by the embassy and France, that this was a matter which might, with a little goodwill and moderation, be at once settled ; and Lord Granville requested M. Duclerc to let him know in what way he could contribute to a peaceful solution of the subject.

On the 13th December Lord Lyons addressed to M. Duclerc a *note verbale*, stating that it appeared to Her Majesty's Government that it was in a satisfactory arrangement of the question with regard to land tenure that a settlement was to be looked for. The French Government asserted the right for French citizens to buy and hold land in Madagascar, while the Hova Government affirmed that by the laws of Madagascar no alien could hold land in fee simple. A similar law had existed in England, and had only been repealed a few years previously, whilst there were still many cases in which, under the law of England, it was impossible to effect absolute transfers of land.

M. Duclerc retorted : " The fact that a similar law recently existed in England may be considered interesting from an historical point of view, but not as a conclusive argument; for it is evident that the English Government under the dominion of such a law would never have consented to conclude diplomatic arrangement."

Victor Hugo has pointed out similar legislation in his description of the peculiarities of the Channel Islands :— "Jersey s'inquiète d'un français propriétaire. S'il allait acheter toute l'île ! À Jersey, défense aux étrangers d'acheter de la terre ; à Guernesey permission."

"Her Majesty's Government," wrote Lord Granville on the 19th December, "have no desire to put themselves forward as mediators, or to press their good offices upon the French Government, but they are at this moment in communication with the Madagascar ambassadors, and would be very willing to use their position in order to pave the way for a more friendly resumption of negotiations at Paris between the two powers."

M. Duclerc haughtily replied : "It is necessary that the whole world should be thoroughly convinced that the conditions expressed by us in the course of the conferences held at Paris mark the limit of possible concessions. On its side, the English Government exactly appreciates the state of affairs when it rejects the idea of offering a mediation which the difference does not admit of. This declaration dispenses us from laying stress upon another expression in the English note. I do not know what the English

Government means by '*to press their good offices upon the French Government*,'[1] but to us this expression is untranslatable in French, for the word, which would be the literal translation, would be absolutely inadmissible."

Lord Granville in a very quiet way pointed out the complete misapprehension of the phrase he had used :—

"That phrase," he wrote, "was only intended to convey that Her Majesty's Government, while they were ready to give their assistance in bringing about an understanding, had no desire to put forward an offer of such assistance if it were not acceptable to France." Our Foreign Minister, therefore, again asked Lord Lyons to ascertain whether the French Government objected to his (Lord Granville's) making any communication of their views to the Madagascar embassy, and, if not, what they would wish the character of the communication to be.

By this time, however, it was evident that mediation was the last object desired by the French Cabinet : and the misapprehension of the phrase "*to press*" was merely a pretext for refusing the English friendly interference.

M. Duclerc observed that the Madagascar envoys were "fully acquainted with the claims of the French Government," and could "have no illusions as to the consequences of the attitude they had chosen to take up." That being the case, the French Government did not think it would be

[1] *Prêter* ses bons offices à la France dans ses differends avec les Hovas.

of any use for a fresh communication of its views to be made to them by Her Majesty's Government. Without further delay preparations for an expedition were made at Toulon.

On the first day of the new year, 1883, France was startled by the sudden death of M. Gambetta ; shortly after which event a ministerial crisis occurred in Paris on the 24th January, on the subject of the expulsion of members of former reigning families, and a majority of the ministers tendered their resignation. The crisis continued on the 25th ; and on the 26th the committee on the Pretenders' Bill decided to report in favour of the most stringent measures. M. Duclerc was taken ill on the 27th, and on Monday 29th he refused to accept the report of the committee, resigning office the following day, when M. Fallières became President of Council in his place. M. Fallières' cabinet adopted the views of the former ministry towards Madagascar, and were resolved to press vigorous and energetic measures against that island without delay.

The news of the rupture of the conferences in Paris at the end of November reached Antananarivo a month subsequently, and in consequence the new year, 1883, saw considerable excitement agitating the population of the capital and its neighbourhood. Exaggerated rumours of sinister designs projected against all strangers somewhat alarmed the foreign residents, and in order to calm their apprehensions, Rainilaiarivony invited the Europeans to a meeting on the 3rd January, when he explained to them that in spite of the prevalent belief that France was preparing for war with Madagascar, Her Majesty Ranavàlona's Government would take every precaution to protect the lives and property of all nationalities. Nevertheless he candidly warned them that it would be better for them to remain at the capital, where his protection could more readily be exercised than in remote parts of the provinces.

At this time M. de Mahy was Minister *ad interim* for the Marine and Colonies, and by his orders Admiral Pierre quitted Toulon in the frigate *La Flore* bound for Malagasy waters on the 15th February, *viâ* the Suez Canal and Aden, touching at Zanzibar in order to receive the latest telegraphic instructions from Paris.

Admiral Pierre was joined by M. Baudais at Zanzibar, and received categorical instructions from M. de Mahy's successor, M. Charles Brun, by that time Minister of Marine. The makeshift ministry of M. Fallières had lasted only three weeks. For it happened that on the 19th February, four days after the *Flore* left Toulon, the new Expulsion Bill sent up by the Chamber to the Senate was rejected by a small majority; and President Grévy accepted the resignation of the ministers; M. Jules Ferry being entrusted with the formation of a cabinet. M. Jules Ferry announced to the Chamber his formation of a new ministry, and on the 23rd February read a declaration of his policy.

The direction of the foreign affairs of the Republic had thus passed within a short period from M. de Freycinet to M. Duclerc, from M. Duclerc to M. Challemel-Lacour. By the death of M. Gambetta the dominant faction in the Republic was literally without a leader, unless M. Jules Ferry can claim the title. His colleagues were obscure, and even the army was without a chief, for General Chanzy died within a few days of Gambetta, and General Thibaudin was the only officer who would condescend to be the Minister of War to this anonymous government. Well might M. Jules Simon exclaim: " At home there is no government, abroad there is no France!" (See *Edinb. Review*, April, 1883. Art. " Dieu, Patrie, Liberté," par Jules Simon.)

As far as Madagascar was concerned the new cabinet adopted the same would-be heroic but aggressive attitude that the previous ministries in the Quai d'Orsay had assumed in Tonkin, Tunis, and the Congo.

The final instructions issued by M. Charles Brun to Admiral Pierre on the 17th March were to the following effect :—

"You will destroy the posts established by the Hovas on those parts of the coast under our protectorate or sovereignty, comprehending not only that part of the north-west coast to the north of Iboina, but also the north-east region as far as Antongil Bay." (Note how the claims grew in extent.) "You will cause the evacuation of any posts existing in this region, notably that of Antsingy (Bay of Diego Suarez). You will then make a demonstration along the north-west coast and in Antongil Bay, to confirm the intention of the Republic to maintain its rights over the whole extent of this territory. (2) You will possess yourself of the custom-house of Mojangà, and leave there a sufficient garrison from Nossi-Bé as well as a ship. You will promptly proceed with your squadron to Tamatave to act in concert with the commissioner. An *ultimatum* is to be sent to the Prime Minister, exacting: 1. The effective recognition of the rights of sovereignty or protectorate which we possess on the north coast. 2. The immediate guarantees necessary to secure the observation of the Treaty of 1868. 3. The payment of indemnities due to our fellow-subjects. A term will be assigned to the Hova Government, which will be warned that if its answer does not arrive within the date fixed upon, the Admiral will occupy the fort of Tamatave, seize the custom-house, and collect the duties until further orders. You will carry out, if occasion requires, the rigorous measures laid down in the summons."

Similar instructions were despatched by M. Challemel-Lacour to M. Baudais, and the *Beautemps-Beaupré* cruiser was despatched to reinforce the French squadron under Admiral Pierre.[1]

The Admiral carried out his instructions with promptitude, his squadron of seven vessels was collected at Nossi-Bé by the 19th April, and the expedition at once departed to carry out the operations decided on. At this time the only British man-of-war on the station was H.M.S. *Dryad*, commanded by Commander (now Captain) C. Johnstone, R.N., which was lying at Tamatave, watched by *Le Vaudreuil*, also in that roadstead.

M. Pierre's first achievement was summoning the Governor of Mourounsanga to evacuate his post, giving him four hours' notice to quit with his men, and half an hour's notice after receipt of the summons to haul down his flag in token of submission.

The Malagasy commander replied verbally :—

"Tell your Admiral that this country belongs to Ranavàlonamanjaka, Queen of Madagascar, and her flag flies on all these coasts. As to your threat to commence hostilities, that is your affair; for we have not received any orders from our Government to make war upon the French. The

---

[1] On the 8th April, 1883, twenty-two days after the despatch of these instructions to commence hostilities, Lord Lyons, on the part of the British Government, asked M. Challemel-Lacour whether the situation in Madagascar was sufficiently grave to justify them in instructing H.M.'s Consul to warn British subjects of impending danger. M. Challemel-Lacour *stated quite positively* to Lord Lyons that *meanwhile no orders for any military operations had been given by the French Government*.

Madagascar Government has placed us here, and we cannot abandon our post. Foreigners possess considerable property here, and we hold you responsible for the damages which may result from your operations."

The Admiral fulfilled his threat, and on the following day, 8th May, the Hova post at Mourounsanga (which is situated on the peninsula of Bavatoubè), was shelled by the guns of the *Flore*, the *Beautemps-Beaupré*, the *Vaudreuil*, and the *Pique*. But a slight formal resistance was encountered, and a landing party of sailors dislodged the small garrison and cut down the flag.

A similar proceeding was carried out on the same afternoon at Bémanéviky, on the banks of the river Congony in Passandava Bay.

The following week another summons was despatched to the Governor of Mojangà,[1] in which the Admiral blandly

---

[1] *Mojangà* is the principal port on the north-west coast of Madagascar, and stands on a long peninsula forming the northern side of a large and deep inlet called Bembatoka Bay, which is eight miles in width, and extends inland about eighteen miles, where the River Betsiboka enters it. The great volume of water from this river has scoured a deep channel many fathoms deep through the bay to the entrance from the sea, where the passage is contracted to three and a half miles across. Mojangà consists of two towns, the upper one on the ridge is the stockaded residence of the Hova garrison. Below is the trading town on the north side of the bay. The upper town was built with considerable regularity, and included the governor's house, with numerous other large houses for the garrison. The stockade is surrounded by a ditch and defended by a number of old English naval guns. The Hova town is surrounded by groves of tamarind, mango, fan palms, and cocoa-nut, with fine old baobabs. The lower town extends half a mile along the shore; in the central parts the rows of houses are five deep. The houses are of slight construction of upright

stated that the resistance offered by the Hova chiefs to the evacuation of territory under French protectorate had involved them in hostilities. He would not enter into discussion, as his duty was confined to devoting all his efforts towards the re-establishment of a durable peace. For this purpose he was determined to possess himself of Mojangà, and he therefore invited the Governor to surrender the place without obliging him to have recourse to arms.

"I grant you," he wrote, "one hour to consider my proposal and come to a decision. After that interval, unless I have received a favourable answer, or if your flag is not lowered, I shall be obliged to open fire upon you!"

A verbal answer almost identical with that given at Mourounsanga was returned, and within an hour, as promised, the ships bombarded Mojangà for six hours, on the 16th May.

Having thoroughly crushed the resistance of the Hova troops, a landing, almost unopposed, was effected by the French marines and sailors. The town was occupied and Commandant Gaillard left in charge of the French garrison

---

timbers, with the interstices filled in with palm leaf and thatched. An important element in the lower town is the stores of the Arab and Bombay merchants, which are of stone or brick cemented with lime, of two or three stories, with flat roofs and terraces; there were some forty of these houses in the town. There are two mosques, and altogether the number of houses in 1875 amounted to 1327, when the population was estimated at 10,000. Before the stoppage of the slave trade Mojangà was an important mart. (See *Twelve Months in Madagascar*, by Dr. Mullens.)

which was placed to hold the position. The Hovas, it is said, suffered great loss; that of the French was *nil*.

All Paris was excited at the publication of M. Pierre's official telegram, 23rd May: "I have the honour to announce that I have destroyed the Hova posts on the north-west coast. Mojangà was taken by assault on the 16th. We have destroyed thirty guns, put to flight two thousand soldiers; seized the custom-house. The occupation is firmly established. I can answer for the security of the position. We have no casualties."

M. Baudais was awaiting the arrival of Admiral Pierre's squadron with impatience to carry out the programme, and received on the 18th a letter from the Admiral announcing his successes in Passandava Bay. Three days afterwards, replying to Consul Pakenham's inquiries, he wrote to the English consul: "Complications between the government of the French Republic and that of Queen Ranavàlona are possible, but *they are not imminent*, as you appear to believe."

Comment on this is superfluous.

The news of the hostilities carried on without any declaration of war against the troops of the Malagasy Government on the north-west coast, reached the capital on the 24th May. Great irritation was felt, and the Prime Minister and advisers of the Queen decided to expel the French residents from Antananarivo and from the interior, as much for the sake of preserving their lives as for retaliation. Accordingly it was notified by Andriamifidy to M. Superbie and others representing the French residents, that they were granted a term of five days to depart from the capital and embark beyond the seas. Bearers and an armed escort were provided by the Malagasy Government, but without waiting for these the Jesuit priests and sisters left the capital on foot, with the evident purpose of exciting commiseration and making a scene.

Admiral Pierre arrived at Tamatave in the *Flore* on the 31st May and found his squadron ready at the rendezvous, and the terms of the *ultimatum* were agreed upon. (See *Appendix*.)

This document was placed on the evening of the 1st of June in the hands of the Governor of Tamatave, who engaged to send it off at once to the Prime Minister, written in French with a Malagasy translation. The term accorded to Rainilaiarivony in which to accept or refuse the conditions was to expire at midnight on the 9th June. After which time, unless a satisfactory answer had been received, fire would be opened on the fort and town. These conditions were also communicated to Mr. Pakenham and the other foreign consuls, and the Admiral intimated that he would give refuge on board his ships to all foreigners who might wish to avail themselves of it. The Governor of Tamatave courteously took means of forwarding to the

French residents on the coast, north and south, the warning circular of the French consul, which otherwise could not have reached them.

Most alarming reports continued to circulate in the town of Tamatave, and the people, who had to some extent returned to the place after the first alarm had subsided, again left. Very few now remained and the native part of the town was almost deserted.

The consul and Captain Johnstone of the *Dryad* met a deputation of British residents, and in reply to the representations made to them expressed their intention of doing all they could for the due protection of the English subjects, who were advised to come into the town and remain as near the consulate as possible. It was impressed upon them that although England was very solicitous for the lives and property of her subjects, yet they must remember that the petty interests in Tamatave were but of little consequence compared with a war with France, and hence it behoved all British subjects to be very circumspect during the troublous times on which they were about to enter; that in the event of hostilities the *Dryad* was prepared to take them all on board.

A standing committee was formed, with Mr. Shaw as president, and steps were taken to provide shelter and provision for indigent British ... coming in from the country. Houses were rented for this purpose, a...

Pakenham consented, on behalf of the Mauritius Government, to supply funds for the purchase of necessaries. Permission was obtained to compel the burial of all petroleum and rum, and no difficulty was experienced in carrying out this measure. All were advised to make preparations, so that on a very short notice they would be able to embark on board the *Dryad*.[1]

On the 8th June Captain Johnstone landed an armed party for the protection of the consulate under Lieutenant Knowles, R.N. The latter officer acted as assistant to Mr. Pakenham, who was at this time so completely broken down that although active in intellect he was evidently incapable of carrying out his duties.

During the whole of the 9th there was a general flight of all the inhabitants to the ships in the roadstead, and by the afternoon there only remained a few Englishmen, together with the *Dryad* party guarding the consulate, and the French consul, with a few of his countrymen, awaiting the reply to the ultimatum.

The answer, as expected, was an absolute rejection of the French conditions, and was brought to M. Baudais at half-past seven on the evening of the 9th; when he at once proceeded with his staff on board the *Forfait*, and communicated the formal refusal of the Hova Government to the Admiral.

See Digest of Information concerning affairs in Madagascar. *Chronicle L. M. S.*, Aug. 1, 1883.

On the 10th June, Sunday morning, at sunrise, the French opened fire with shell on the fort and town of Tamatave from the six ships, the *Flore, Forfait, Beautemps-Beaupré, Boursaint, Creuse,* and *Nièvre*. The retreat of the garrison took place simultaneously, and the fort was abandoned without attempting to reply. Some of the Malagasy troops retired to Manjakandrianombana, at some six miles distance inland, where an entrenched camp had been prepared; and others proceeded towards Hivondro, to the south. A slackened fire was kept up until a quarter past eight, when all firing ceased. Before landing to occupy the fort, Admiral Pierre awaited the report of scouts, who searched for ambuscades and mines; but nothing was discovered, and the disembarkation of the troops was effected in order on the following day under cover of the fire of the ships, which was directed on the entrenched camp where the Hovas were concentrated. The Hova flag was never hoisted at the fort, which was silent and deserted throughout the day.

Considering Hivondro, the first stage of the route to Antananarivo, as a possible rallying point for the Malagasy, M. Pierre sent on the morning of the 12th the *Forfait* and *Nièvre* to shell that village. On the same day, the *Beautemps-Beaupré* and the *Boursaint* attacked Fénoarivo, and destroyed the houses, fort, and customhouse there; whilst later in the afternoon Mahambo experienced the same fate. Again, on the following day, the two last-named ships, reinforced by the *Nièvre*, destroyed Foul-pointe in like manner.

Previous to the bombardment of Tamatave, some active correspondence took place between the French Admiral and the Commander of the *Dryad*. The latter officer incurred the displeasure of the Admiral, and was placed in a most unpleasant and invidious position, but owing to his great tact and judicious demeanour, a grave complication, which might have led to the most serious consequences, was happily averted.

M. Baudais reported that at the first shot, as the Hovas had threatened to do, fire was set very cleverly to the four quarters of the town; but Mr. Shaw, who was on shore, positively states that he saw the first shell fired burst in the market-place, and shortly afterwards fire and smoke were seen rising from the market; hence he believed that the fires were not the work of incendiaries, but caused by the French bombardment; on the other hand, the officers of the *Dryad* appear to have no doubt that the fire was designedly effected by the Hovas.

The Admiral in his official account of the operations to the Minister of Marine wrote that it required two notices of a friendly nature, and at last a third formal summons, to make H.M.S. *Dryad* move out of the French line of attack. "She obeyed, but manœuvred so as to make it appear in the eyes of the Hovas, to whom she had promised her interposition, that she retreated *en échelon*."

It was not until the 14th June that Admiral Pierre formally hoisted the French flag on the fort and took possession and civil charge of the town. On this date he proclaimed a state of siege, nominated M. Raffray mayor of Tamatave, and intimated to the foreign consuls that their flags must be hauled down and their consular functions cease.

The Shaw Incident.

On Saturday, 16th June, Mr. Shaw, of the London Missionary Society, was requested by M. Raffray, the newly appointed French mayor, to go to the fort. Here, after some examination by the commandant, he was made a prisoner and marched down under an armed escort to the landing-place and taken on board the *Nièvre*, where he was confined in close arrest without being informed of any charge being brought against him. Ten days subsequently one of the Donald Currie line of steamers, the *Taymouth Castle*,[1] arrived with mails and passengers from England.

---

[1] Sir Donald Currie, M.P., speaking in the House of Commons during the late autumn session of 1884 on the state of the Navy, said :—

" In Madagascar we were very near an outbreak of war with the French. Captain Johnstone, of Her Majesty's ship *Dryad*, was acting consul, owing to the death of Consul Pakenham. Admiral Pierre took the British mails from the *Taymouth Castle*, instead of allowing them to be delivered on board the *Dryad*, and he placed armed sentries on the deck of the mail packet. He forbade the embarkation of mails except through the French flag-ship, and absolutely refused to allow the captain of the packet to receive Captain Johnstone's despatches for the Admiralty, unless they were first of all sent to the French flag-ship (*La Flore*). Acting under the instructions of Captain Johnstone, the British packet steamed past the French fleet, went alongside

Mrs. Shaw, who was on board, made every effort to obtain permission to communicate with her husband, but she was not allowed to see him, and he was not apprised of her presence. Several of his letters never reached her, whilst her letters to him were not delivered to him until after the departure of the steamer, and then opened. It was not until the 1st July, after fifteen days of close confinement, that Mr. Shaw was examined by a French officer, who now for the first time informed him that he was accused of having tried to poison French soldiers ; and four days afterwards the English missionary was transferred on board the *Flore*, where he was placed in a small cabin on the lower deck, and only permitted to take exercise on the upper deck for one hour daily. On the 22nd Mr. Shaw was again examined, and told that the charge of poisoning was withdrawn, and another charge of being *imprudent* substituted. It appears that Mr. Shaw's dispensary had been broken open and rifled subsequent to the bombardment, and all the bottles which had not been stolen or broken had been thrown into the garden. Some of them contained medicines and poisons. At last, on the 7th August, nearly two months after the date of his first arrest,

the *Dryad*, took the Admiralty despatches on board and steamed out to sea. A conflict might at that moment have taken place notwithstanding that the *Dryad* was only a sloop of war, face to face with four powerful French ships, one of them an ironclad. The *Dryad* had nine guns, but orders had been sent to that vessel not to fire eight of them, as they might burst."—*Times* Report, December 3rd, 1884.

Mr. Shaw was set at liberty, and shortly afterwards proceeded to join his wife at Mauritius, and Mr. and Mrs. Shaw arrived together at Plymouth on the 24th September.

The Hova ambassadors, meantime, before leaving Europe, had another interview at Paris with M. Jules Ferry, who gave them a safe conduct through the French lines at Tamatave to return to Antananarivo. At this interview, which took place on the 18th June, the following bases for a renewal of friendly relations were communicated to them by the President of the Council :[1] viz., " 1. The Hova Government must engage not to occupy any territory, nor exercise any authority within the region which was indicated in the arrangements concluded by France in 1841 and 1842 with the Sàkalàva, and which included Mojangà.

" 2. Formal guarantees which will secure to our fellow-subjects in every respect the right to possess real property, which advantages were recognized by the Treaty of 1868.

" 3. A sum, which cannot be less than a million francs,

[1] M. Jules Ferry wrote to M. Baudais (No. 16, *Diplomatic Documents*), under date, Paris, 19th June, 1883 :—" In order to reserve our historic rights over Madagascar, it will be expedient, in the forthcoming treaty between ourselves and the Hovas, to formulate the clause relating to the N.W. coast as follows :—

" 'The Hova Government engages not to occupy any territory, nor exercise any authority within the region which was indicated in the arrangements made by France with the Sàkalàva in 1841 and 1842.'

" You will take care that the Port of Mojangà and its neighbourhood are expressly mentioned ; our sovereignty is not the less certain, but you know that it has been disputed." JULES FERRY.

shall be paid to the French Government, which will reserve it for payment of the indemnities due to French subjects.

"It may be added that the Commissioner of the French Republic in Madagascar has received extended powers, and that in presence of the situation created by the resistance of the Hova Government, it is impossible here to detail the modifications which the development of events may bring about to modify the programme traced out in general terms since his departure. (*Documents Diplomatiques*, Nos. 16, 17, 18.)

On the 18th June, in consequence of the serious illness of Consul Pakenham, Captain C. Johnstone, of H.M.S. *Dryad*, obtained from him a commission as vice-consul for Madagascar, and also a commission as acting-consul in case of his being incapable of performing his duty, and on the 22nd Mr. Pakenham died (No. 53, Blue-book). Mr. Pakenham had been apparently in failing health for some time, and his increased duties and anxieties of late, combined with the actual noise and disturbance attendant on the capture of the place, completely broke him down. Later, the native secretary at the British consulate, on account of his Hova name, Andrianisa, was arrested by the French authorities—a most unfriendly proceeding on the part of the Admiral. It may be remarked that Mr. Andrianisa was born in Mauritius; his father was a Hova refugee, and his mother a Creole and a British subject. He was educated and married in Mauritius, had children there, and had remained in that colony as a British-born subject, until he became secretary to the British consulate at Tamatave. This high-handed proceeding on the part of the French commander-in-chief was followed up by a peremptory order for the consul himself and his staff to quit Tamatave within twenty-four hours' notice. Now this order was not really directed against Mr. Pakenham personally, but only ostensibly so ; in truth it was directed against the British commander, who at this time was practically consul, and who had already removed the consular archives on board the *Dryad*. The Admiral's excuse, or rather the one made for him, was that it was found necessary for the security of the place that the officer in command should forbid all communication with the exterior. This reason led that officer to consider it expedient to forbid the presence of the British consul (*and British officers acting for him*), whose correspondence with the Hovas had become so frequent and so important as to make it necessary to attach to him an officer in active service. Mr. Pakenham's death occurred, however, before any measures had been taken to put the order into execution, and although coincident with, was not accelerated by the order given for his expulsion. Mr. Pakenham was buried on the following day, and all due honours rendered to the deceased by the French troops.

"The attacks of the Hovas and the necessities of the defence," wrote M. Challemel-Lacour, "compelled the French superior authorities to take notice of the presence of foreign officers, who interfered in matters which it belonged to them alone to deal with. It was decided that they should be forbidden to stay in the place." All communication, therefore, between the English ships of war and the shore was forbidden, and Admiral Pierre refused to hold any written communication with the commander of the *Dryad*. "It was only after the pretension advanced by the commander of the *Dryad* to exercise a control over the military orders (*consignes*) that the interdiction was positively carried into execution."

The voluminous correspondence exchanged between Admiral Pierre and Captain Johnstone has not been published by either government, but from the specimens which leaked out in the pages of a French newspaper, and which have been republished apparently with pride by at least one French author, it would appear that the tone of the superior officer was somewhat unusual; although the French Minister tried to point out the conciliatory disposition of the Admiral at the beginning of the communications, "a disposition which it was in Captain Johnstone's power to have confirmed. Unfortunately, by a daily interference, often without foundation, and by insisting on putting questions to the French authorities with which they had not authority to deal, by raising discussions which hampered their action, and by the tone of some of his communications, Commander Johnstone seemed to have himself endeavoured to induce the French Admiral to refuse to continue a correspondence which threatened to lead to regrettable complications." However, in a despatch dated October 15th, the French Government expressed as well as they could their regret, qualified, it is true, but which Lord Granville was able to accept.

M. Challemel-Lacour wrote: "We have, nevertheless, only the more reason to regret that owing to a series of circumstances which it did not depend upon him to avoid, but of which the simple recital is enough to show the effect, the tone of the communications from the French Admiral to the commander of the *Dryad* ceased at one time to correspond as much as we could have wished with the friendly character of the relations existing between the two nations, and with which our instructions were inspired."

Lord Granville said that Her Majesty's Government did not doubt that the Government of the Republic, on learning the facts, would be anxious to express regret that a departure should have taken place from the traditional courtesy of the French nation, &c. They were satisfied that there was no failure on the part of Commander Johnstone to fulfil his weighty international duties. Commander Johnstone did the best he could to comply with the wishes of the Admiral, consistently with the dictates of humanity and with his duty toward his countrymen on shore. The five distinct charges formulated against Commander Johnstone by Admiral Pierre in his letter of the 2nd June are shown to have been unfounded. The expression of regret which appeared in M. Challemel-Lacour's despatch showed that the French Government were acting consistently with the friendly feeling and the good disposition existing between the two governments, who both felt the same desire to smooth the differences which had arisen.

Moved by these sentiments Her Majesty's Government accepted the acknowledgment offered by the French Government with a view of preventing a controversy inconsistent with the interests and dignity of the two countries, &c. The approbation of the British Government was conveyed to Commander Johnstone, who was also deservedly promoted to the rank of captain.[1]

[1] It may here be noted that Capt. Charles Johnstone, R.N., found distraction from the monotonous and distasteful duty at Tamatave, whilst lying at anchor unable to communicate with the shore, in writing the *Naval Prize Essay* (1883-84), which gained the gold medal presented by the Royal United Service Institution. His motto, attached to the essay, indicates sufficiently the prudence and circumspection exercised by this able officer during an anxious season of responsibility and provocation. It is this :—" Let reason go before every enterprise, and counsel before every action."

CHAPTER V.

NEUTRAL SENTIMENTS.

THE French subjects expelled from Antananarivo by order of the Malagasy Government, and who left the capital on the 29th May, arrived at length at Tamatave on the 23rd June. The bearers who accompanied them from the time of their departure had received orders not to go beyond the village of Maromby, on the Iharoka near the coast, about sixty miles from Tamatave, as they could not trust themselves within reach of the French.

It is highly creditable to the Malagasy that this large party of French people should have been able to traverse the country held by the Malagasy troops driven out of Tamatave safely and without injury and insult within a fortnight of the bombardment of the fort and other villages along the coast, at a period when the exasperation against the French was most profound. This example shows what a firm hold the Prime Minister retained over the people, the slightest relaxation of which would have resulted in terrible retaliation.

Père Felix, one of the refugees, relates that when at Beforona on the 8th June, the news arrived that the French were just going to bombard Tamatave. During the night he overheard some of their escort, half drunk, talking to one another. "What shall we do with these French?" said one. "Kill them!" "And the sisters?" "Sell them!" "Unfortunately," added one of them, "we are not sufficiently numerous to kill all these Europeans." No wonder the priests and sisters each ejaculated: "*In manus tuas, Domine, commendo spiritum meum.*"

Another party of French missionaries expelled from Fianarantsoa was escorted to Mananzary, where they embarked, and others from the Betsileo country to Masindrano, whilst the last to arrive were the Jesuit fathers from Ambositra, who did not reach Mananzary until the end of July. Two of these unfortunate Jesuits died of fever on their arrival at the coast, Frère Brutail and Père le Batz; but their deaths were attributable solely to climatic influences, and the Hovas were in no way responsible for the lamentable event. Full details of the expulsion and journeys to the coast of the members of the Catholic Mission in Madagascar are given in the second volume of the History by Père de la Vaissière published in Paris last year.

The first arrivals of the expelled missionaries reached Tamatave in time to witness the funeral of Mr. Pakenham, and two nights afterwards they were aroused by the sound of the firing during the repulse of a night attack by the

Hovas on the French outposts. Since the occupation the fort of Tamatave had been cleared of the somewhat dense groves which surrounded the works, and formerly nearly hid it from the view of the ships. All this cover was now removed, and the fort was therefore perfectly visible and within easy range of the guns of the squadron.

The Hovas from time to time made night attacks on the French pickets, more with the purpose of harassing them than with any serious intentions of retaking the fort, which they well knew was at the mercy of the men-of-war. The entrenched camp, however, at Manjakandrianombana was strengthened and reinforced, and being judiciously placed and flanked by morasses, it thoroughly cut off the French from communication with the interior. The French were and have been only masters of the situation within range of their heavy guns. The road to Antananarivo was of course closed, and no intelligence could pass between the port and the capital.

Night attacks were repulsed with vigour on the 19th and 25th June and on the 5th and 17th July, when demonstrations were made by the Hovas, who penetrated the village and fired some shots, killing one and wounding two of the French.

The first news of the capture of Tamatave reached Paris on the 19th June in a telegram from Admiral Pierre, dated June 13th :—

"The ultimatum which I addressed to the Hova Government having been rejected, I have taken the town of Tamatave and the custom-house. The towns of Foulepoint, Mohambo, and Fénoarivo are destroyed. No wounded on our side. The position which we occupy is strong. The Hovas have taken to flight, which puts an end to our principal action. I have proclaimed a state of siege because of the mixed state of the population."

This news was received with great satisfaction in France and regret in England, where great anxiety was manifested; but a profound sensation was made later when the English Government received a telegram from Colonel Miles at Zanzibar reporting the death of Consul Pakenham, that the French Admiral had ordered him to quit Tamatave in twenty-four hours, though dangerously ill; that he had died seven hours before the time had expired; the commander of the *Dryad* had embarked the consular archives; the admiral had stopped communication between the British men-of-war and shore, and had refused to hold written communication with the commander of the *Dryad;* that Tamatave was practically a French town and all the foreign consuls' flags had been hauled down.

This was announced in the House of Commons by Mr. Gladstone on Wednesday, 11th July, and the gravity of the intelligence startled Europe, for it was evident that the Madagascar question was about to assume a serious aspect.

Sir Stafford Northcote questioned the Government regarding a serious occurrence which had been reported as having taken place in Madagascar, when the Prime Minister made the following unexpected and alarming statement :—

"The House is aware, from the statements of the Under-Secretary for Foreign Affairs, that on June 14th a state of siege was proclaimed at Tamatave. The British consul was unhappily at the time very ill, and the information received is to the effect that his illness was seriously aggravated by the political crisis. His secretary was arrested in his presence. In these circumstances he received an order from the French Admiral to quit the place within twenty-four hours, and seven hours before the expiration of that time he died. The French Admiral invited the British to attend the funeral, and the British officers and men of the *Dryad* attended in some numbers. The French Admiral stopped communication between the British men-of-war and the shore. The captain was allowed only verbally to protest against the proceedings, and the flags of all other foreign consuls have been pulled down. There is a portion of the telegram affecting another person in addition to the secretary of the consul. One British subject, a missionary of the London Missionary Society, was arrested on the 16th, and remains in prison. The charge against him is not made public, but it is surmised to be for correspondence with the enemy, as the French phrase would be in the circumstances. The answer that has been received is that the law must take its course. In announcing these grave and painful occurrences, I have only to say that we wait for further information as to the facts, and for those communications from the Government of France required in such a case which we have intimated we expect, and which it would be our duty to make under similar circumstances."

Telegraphic instructions were at once forwarded to Lord Lyons at Paris by Lord Granville to inquire whether the French Government were in possession of the facts of the case, and whether M. Challemel-Lacour was able to give any information explanatory of the action of Admiral Pierre; and Lord Lyons pointed out to the French minister the unfortunate effect which could not fail to be produced should this painful intelligence remain for any time without explanation.

The feeling of irritation and annoyance in England was manifest, but the French Government could or would only state that they were without information, but had telegraphed without delay to Zanzibar to hasten the despatch of explanations of the alleged action of the French Admiral. M. Challemel-Lacour stated to Lord Lyons that he was quite unable to account for what had occurred, and was at a loss to conceive circumstances under which Admiral Pierre could have thus acted.

M. d'Aunay, the French chargé d'affaires in London, also called on Lord Granville to say that, although he had no instructions, he had no doubt that the French Government would be willing to give all proper satisfaction to England if the facts turned out as represented, but he requested that no publicity should then be given to what was only his impression.

A lively debate ensued in the Chamber of Deputies on the 16th July, when the Minister of Foreign Affairs, in reply to a question put by M. Francis Charmes, made a long statement, in the course of which he stated that the French Government had received a telegram from Admiral Pierre, dated from Tamatave on the 6th July, giving various details of the situation, but not a word, not the least allusion, to the facts brought to their notice by the English Government. M. Challemel-Lacour proceeded to state :—" I cannot conceal from you, gentlemen, that we have experienced considerable surprise at the news which has been announced by the English despatches, of which the Admiral makes no mention. We have the honour of knowing that officer, a gentleman of distinguished abilities, and whose prudence equals his resolution." The minister concluded :—" You have seen that the explanations demanded of Mr. Gladstone in the House of Commons and of Lord Granville in the House of Lords have been given with becoming moderation, and in language bearing the impress of that courteous confidence on which we congratulate ourselves. And although we may still at this moment be thoroughly convinced that the general officer in command of the squadron before Madagascar cannot have misunderstood the respect due, one to the other, by two great civilized nations, or have forgotten the rules which govern and should govern international relations, I do not, however, hesitate to declare that if, as is possible in certain circumstances, any error or misunderstanding in which passion has been displayed has, in fact, taken place, we shall not fail in the duty imposed on us, nor shall we hesitate to act in accordance with the dictates of the spirit of justice and with the interest of the country."

The effect of the attitude of the British Government was soon apparent, for by the following mail M. Challemel-Lacour modified his instructions to M. Baudais. After referring to the north-west coast, in regard to which he confirmed his former instructions, he added :—" At Tamatave and on the east coast, to the south of Antongil Bay, the situation is not the same. There we do not intend to claim *for the present* the exercise of an effective sovereignty ; and, without renouncing our historic rights, which we can claim over this coast, our occupation must remain temporary. The possession of Tamatave is, in our hands, but a means of bringing the Hovas to a settlement. We should confine ourselves to measures strictly necessary for the realization of the result foreseen in your general instructions, to hasten the determination of the Court of Antananarivo, *whilst counteracting as little as possible the commerce and the relations of neutrals.* From this point of view, the instituting a French mayoralty and the summons calling upon the consular agents to suspend their duties, were not sufficiently justified by the character of our establishment, and exceeded the limits assigned by the Government of the Republic. I shall be pleased to learn that you have arranged with the commander-in-chief, on his receiving like instructions, to permit the foreign consuls to resume their functions, and to instruct M. Raffray to confine himself within the limits of his consular duties."

Admiral Pierre's bad state of health forced him—now, as he himself reported, *utterly broken*—to quit Tamatave, and proceed to Réunion, leaving his flag-captain, M. Rallier, in charge of the naval division off Tamatave. The latter, in answer to inquiries from the Minister of Marine, telegraphed on the 28th July from Tamatave that the Admiral was sick at Réunion, and that the correspondence with Captain Johnstone would be received in Paris on the 10th August. He next stated:—"The English consul, Pakenham, is dead : we have accorded him full honours. The secretary of the English consul being a Hova, son of the late Governor of Tamatave, had been arrested as dangerous, but he has been released on parole. The missionary Shaw is accused of an attempt to poison our soldiers. The appearances are very serious. The examination is being carried on."

This telegram was despatched from Zanzibar on the 5th August, and must have reached Paris on the 6th August. The English Government received the bulky despatches containing the Pierre-Johnstone correspondence on the 7th or 8th August, and on the evening of the 8th August, Mr. Gladstone, after a dinner at the Mansion House, made an allusion to the death of Mr. Pakenham, which he was able to state had not been accelerated by the order for his expulsion, and also said that the facts being now clear, made it easy for the French Government to meet Her Majesty's Government.

"But a short time ago," said Mr. Gladstone, "turning to another quarter of the globe, pain and apprehension were excited in this country by intelligence which reached us in telegraphic form from Madagascar, and we had experience on that occasion which ,suggests the general rule of prudence, the rule, namely, that while we acknowledge the enormous benefits which the telegraph has conferred, we should be on our guard against the special risks of misapprehension with which that succinct method of communication is specially attended ; for the knowledge of important, perhaps of painful, at any rate, of critical events, is conveyed in a fewness of words which would not be observed in the more ordinary methods of communication. When the telegraphic news came from Madagascar we felt satisfied that it contained nothing that need present to us any difficulties except such as would be solved by frank communication between the governments concerned, and by those generous and honourable dispositions which, I trust, will always prevail among friendly nations, and especially, if I may say so, between ourselves and our great neighbours across the Channel. I will only now say that that fuller knowledge which we claim at this moment to possess, which has hardly come to our eyes, though it has partially reached them (I myself have not yet become minutely acquainted with all the particulars), justifies me in saying that those cheerful hopes we entertained are confirmed by the better and larger means of judgment which we now possess, and I feel confident—reasonably, and even sanguinely confident—that nothing will arise out of those transactions that can disturb the long accord between England and France which has now survived an anxious and unlucky struggle."

Mr. Gladstone's speech created a favourable impression in France, and M. Waddington said that his Government believed that that of Her Majesty would be confirmed in their impression that the commander of the French forces had shown all the consideration which circumstances allowed. Lord Granville speedily disabused the mind of the French ambassador of this misapprehension, as his Government, he said, had no opinion of the kind.

The semi-official journal *Le Temps* announced on the 9th August that Admiral Pierre was about to resign the command of the squadron off Madagascar on account of ophthalmia, and M. Ledoulx informed Sir John Kirk, at Zanzibar, on the 15th August, that Admiral Pierre having gone to Réunion on the ground of ill-health, it might be thought imprudent for him on this account to resume his command. In fact, it appears to have been known, at all events expected, at Réunion, that Admiral Pierre would be recalled, and indeed, on the 16th of the month, that officer embarked for Europe in the mail steamer, reaching Europe only to die at Marseilles on the 11th September. The death of the unfortunate Admiral enabled the French Government to evade further explanations beyond regret, &c., with regard to the Pierre-Johnstone correspondence, and that matter was allowed to drop.[1] So concluded an

---

[1] "As regards the part taken by Admiral Pierre," wrote Lord Granville, "in the proceedings which have given rise to the complaints of Her Majesty's Government, and the remarks thereon which are contained in M. Challemel-Lacour's despatch, I have only to observe that Her Majesty's Government can readily understand the disposition with which the French Government would not fail to approach the subject, and their leaning to a favourable view of the conduct of a distinguished and gallant officer, who has long served his country with honour, and who at last, while suffering from an attack of illness which ended fatally, wrote and acted in a manner which, under the circumstances, would (as Her Majesty's Government cannot doubt) have been repugnant to his feelings and inconsistent with the friendly relations which, during a residence of some months, he had established in England."

A RECITAL OF WRONGS. 143

incident which might have engendered war between France and her neighbour across the Channel.

With regard to the Shaw affair also, a not unhappy conclusion was arrived at shortly afterwards. As before mentioned, Mr. and Mrs. Shaw arrived at Plymouth on the 24th of September; and on the evening of September 27th a public meeting at Exeter Hall was held, under the auspices of the London Missionary Society, to give them a welcome, and hear the statement of Mr. Shaw's recent experiences whilst in the hands of the French. The hall was crowded, the greatest enthusiasm prevailed, and Mr. Shaw's unvarnished recital of his wrongs produced a great impression throughout Great Britain.

Mr. Shaw, who might have posed as a martyr, and pressed on the Government to exact heavy reparation for his unjustifiable imprisonment, refused to agitate in any way the public mind. He confidently left his case in the hands of his own Government and that of France to settle between themselves.

"I can leave this matter," he said, "to the sense of justice which, although ignored by some of her officials in some parts of the world, must animate the conduct of a great and honourable nation like France."

On the 17th October, within three weeks of the meeting at Exeter Hall, the French ambassador, M. Waddington, visited Lord Granville at Walmer Castle, in order to communicate to him a satisfactory solution of the "Shaw" incident. He observed that it was entirely contrary to French practice to give any indemnity to persons who had been arrested and examined because the prosecution failed; that no Frenchman (although complaints of some hard cases had arisen) had ever received such an indemnity. But the French Government had resolved to make an exception, and to make the spontaneous offer of £1,000 to Mr. Shaw, although it was a much larger sum than they thought was his due. Lord Granville accepted this offer, and M. Challemel-Lacour wrote to M. Waddington the next day, concluding thus :—"However this may be, it is certain that an innocent man, the subject of a friendly power, was for fifty-four days deprived of his liberty, to the prejudice of his interests, and kept in painful circumstances under the weight of an accusation which was not found to be justified. The Government have decided that you should be authorized to offer a sum of 25,000 francs as evidence of our wish to lighten the consequences of the hardships endured by Mr. Shaw. Her Britannic Majesty's Government will, I am convinced, see in this decision a proof of the sentiments by which we are animated, and a fresh motive for continuing on both sides, and in the same friendly spirit, the settlement of the difficulties which may arise between the two countries."

In July the Malagasy envoys took leave of Earl Granville

and the many and influential friends who had interested themselves sympathetically in the Malagasy cause. A safe-conduct was offered to them by M. Jules Ferry, but they returned to their own country in safety by way of Natal and Mananzary, without the necessity of passing through the French lines. We may here briefly recapitulate the work which they had accomplished since leaving their native capital a year before.

It will be remembered that an account has already been given of the proceedings of the Hova ambassadors up to the time of their arrival in England and their reception by Lord Granville.

Soon after their arrival in this country Ravoninahitriniarivo and Ramaniraka were graciously received by Her Majesty, and subsequently by the Prince and Princess of Wales. On the invitation of the local authorities, and with the co-operation of the Madagascar Committee and the London Missionary Society, the envoys were able to visit several of the most important towns in Great Britain, and wherever they went they met with a cordial sympathy on the part of the English people. They had frequent communications with Lord Granville, who interested himself warmly in their cause, and did his utmost to bring about a solution of their dispute with the French Government through the mediation of England; but his efforts, as we have seen, were vain, and the proffered kind offices were rejected.

So far, indeed, in this primary object of staving off hostilities which were hastened on by France, the mission of the Hova plenipotentiaries was unsuccessful. Rebuffed and insulted on the Continent, the ambassadors of Queen Ranavàlona must have felt the contrast when they experienced such hearty kindness in England.

In England, however, the treaty of 1855 was revised, and Mr. Lister, Assistant Under-Secretary at the Foreign Office, was able to make some suggestions regarding freedom of contract in leases between British and Malagasy subjects, which ultimately led to a formal declaration between the Governments of Great Britain and Madagascar amending Article V. of treaty of June 27, 1865. This declaration was signed by Lord Granville and the envoys on the 16th February, 1883. In addition to the alterations of this Article the envoys proposed modifications in the XIth Article on the subject of the sale of intoxicating liquors. This question of restricting the importation of intoxicating liquors into Madagascar excited considerable interest in England, and the ambassadors were warmly supported by the United Kingdom Alliance.

The plenipotentiaries, who resided during their stay in London at the Alexandra Hotel, Hyde Park, received there on the 29th December, 1882, a deputation of the Alliance, headed by Mr. Whitworth, M.P. On this occasion Ravoninahitriniarivo made a speech, which was translated by Mr. Tacchi, and it is so interesting that it can hardly be omitted here :—

"Although we cannot speak of ourselves as citizens of a country which has long enjoyed the blessing of Christian civilization, we can join with you both mind and heart in the object of your United Kingdom Alliance. It was only yesterday that we began to receive enlightenment, but we have very soon seen the evils which are the fruits of the traffic it is your aim to suppress. And we are glad that the thing which was in our minds already has thus secured friends like yourselves, who in this matter thoroughly agree with us. Your words are perfectly correct respecting the surrender of revenue, for although this traffic is a source of wealth, our Government never rejoices in the money which comes therefrom. We would rather have a small exchequer than a degraded people. In witness of this I may remind you that the barrels of rum taken as custom dues used to be publicly poured out on the beach, by way of showing to all importers that the introduction of this article into the kingdom was a thing which our Government hated. But the greedy of money were not ashamed, for they still force in their traffic, and we are grieved to inform you that imports of rum are apparently on the increase. Last year there were over 9,500 barrels brought in and sold at sixpence a pint. And yet, as has just been said, our Government has no pleasure in this ; we wish to prohibit the sale, but it is foreigners who push in the trade, and the treaties, called treaties of friendship, support them in their doings. But we trust that the kingdoms of Europe which have brought Christianity and civilization to our land will see the unrighteousness of an evil traffic conducted by a few to the killing of many, and will combine with us for its suppression."

After considerable trouble the ambassadors had the satisfaction of concluding with the British Government an agreement for regulating the traffic in spirituous liquors. This agreement was signed at London on the 29th May, 1883.

The embassy next paid a visit to America, where by the courteous forethought of the United States Consul for Madagascar, Colonel Robinson, the envoys met with a reception as hearty and sympathetic as that which had everywhere greeted them in England.

Colonel W. Robinson had previously concluded at Antananarivo on May 13th, 1881, a Treaty of Peace, Friendship, and Commerce on the part of the Government of the United States with Madagascar. The ratification of this treaty was advised by the Senate on the 27th February, 1883, and the treaty was ratified by the ambassadors of the Queen of Madagascar at Washington on the 12th March, 1883.

In this important treaty it is formally laid down that

"*The dominions of Her Majesty the Queen of Madagascar shall be understood to mean the whole extent of Madagascar.*"

Returning across the Atlantic on the 17th April, the envoys received a deputation of the Madagascar Committee when the chief ambassador spoke as follows :—

"As friends of Madagascar, you will be happy to hear that the Americans are not less hearty than yourselves in sympathy with our cause. They begged us to understand that there was no lack of cordiality on their part towards France. 'Ever since the days of Lafayette,' they said, 'there had been a sentiment in our hearts which is still alive, but none the less,' they added, ' do we recognize that in her present policy towards Madagascar, she is acting unrighteously and betraying her national honour.' Those are words which we heard in every city we visited, as we were wished 'God speed' and fullest success to our mission. And so certain was the United States Government of the people's desire for our continued independence that, in ratifying its treaty with our Queen, it expressly acknowledged her as sovereign of the whole of Madagascar; and as a further illustration of active American interest in our welfare, we may remind you of the reported intention of the United States Government to promote its representative in our island to the rank of Consul-General, with an appointed residence at the capital."

The enterprising Malagasy plenipotentiaries next made

their way to Berlin, where in June the draft of a short Treaty of Amity and Peace between Germany and Madagascar was signed. This consisted of three articles only, containing a most-favoured nation clause. Previously in 1880 drafts of a formal treaty and of a consular convention between the Empire and Madagascar had been submitted to the Federal Council by Prince Bismarck, but the negotiations had then fallen through, and although the envoys were desirous of renewing these negotiations, the shortness of their stay at Berlin rendered such a course impossible. A similar most-favoured nation treaty was also concluded by the Madagascar mission with Italy for the first time. So, altogether, the peaceful errand on which the ambassadors had been despatched by their Sovereign had by no means met with unmitigated defeat, and the returning embassy had the satisfaction of feeling that they had at least secured the sympathy of all English-speaking nations, and otherwise reaped a fair return for their labours.

CHAPTER VI.

REGINA DE GRATIA.

BEFORE her ambassadors had returned to Ankova, Ranavàlona II., who had been ailing for more than a year, died in her palace at Antananarivo on July 13, 1883, after a reign of fifteen years; and Razafindrahéty, her cousin, was proclaimed Queen of Madagascar, under the title of Ranavàlona III.

Ranavàlona II. was born in the same year as Radama II., her unfortunate cousin, that is, in 1829; and her mother was Rafàrasòa, a younger sister of the famous Queen, the first Ranavàlona. Previous to her coronation the name of Ranavàlona was Ramòma or Ramòrabé (*very gentle*), and she was the youngest of a family of four; the eldest of whom was Rambòasalàma, the rival claimant to the throne of Radama II; the second was Ramàhatra, a judge; and the third Ramònja, whose name was made familiar to English readers by the missionary, William Ellis. Genealogical descent in Madagascar is traced through the female line, but the father of Ramòma is stated to have been named Razàkaratrìmo. Before she came to the throne, notwithstanding her rank, the princess was brought up in comparative seclusion and little state, having but few attendants and slaves to wait upon her. In her youth she was a scholar in one of the earliest schools established by the first missionaries of the London Missionary Society, and consequently her sympathies were enlisted at an early age in favour of the unfortunate Christians who suffered such terrible persecution during the sanguinary reign of her aunt; and, indeed, it is said that she was accused by her brother the judge, Ramàhatra, of being a Christian, and only saved from conviction by the Prime Minister, Rainihàro. Ramòma grew up among the dark and pagan days, when Madagascar was a closed country to all foreign influence, when the *sikidy* (divination) and the will of the idols governed the actions of the sovereign for a period of thirty years. When the princess was in her thirty-second year, her aunt died, and brighter days dawned when her more enlightened and merciful cousin Rakòto-Radama ascended the throne in 1861. Nevertheless her brother, Prince Rambòasalàma, who had plotted to seize the throne by force if necessary, was banished to Ambohimirimo, where he died on the 9th April, 1862. It will be remembered that the treatment of his unsuccessful rival by the King Radama II. was most honourable. He not only preserved his life but refused to allow any of his possessions to be confiscated, so that the entire property of Rambòasalàma descended undiminished to his widow and children.

CONSPIRACY DEFEATED. 153

Both at the coronation of Radama II. and at the crowning of his widow, Rabòdo, under the title of Rasoherina, two years subsequently, the presence of the national idols was considered indispensable at the ceremony ; and the idol-keepers continued to exercise considerable influence throughout the reign of Rasoherina until the death of that Queen. During the last illness of Queen Rasoherina a plot was discovered to take the reins of government out of the hands of Rainilaiarivony, her Prime Minister, and to place on the throne, as successor to Rasoherina, a young noble named Rasata, son of the late Governor of Tamatave, and said to be the direct male descendant of Andrianimpoinimèrina, the founder of the Radama-Ranavàlona dynasty. The plot was formed, it is said, by the coalition of two very different parties : the one comprising several of the older and reactionary chiefs, heathen, and those jealous of the position and influence of Rainilaiarivony and the family of Rainiharo ; and the other consisting of younger men, ambitious of self-advancement and with radical ideas; amongst this party were several of the most intelligent among the native Christians. This conspiracy was discovered on March 27, 1868, and at once quelled by the prompt measures taken by the Prime Minister. The dying Queen, whose throne was thus contested for, died on the following Wednesday night, April 1st ; and early on 2nd April, Ramòma, her first cousin, was proclaimed Queen under the title of Ranavàlona II. Rasata and the conspirators were condemned to death, and at any former period no hesitation would have been felt in carrying out their execution ; but Rainilaiarivony was able, in the strength of his position, to be merciful, and Rasata was banished to Mahabo, on the west coast, where he yet remains. M. Cremazy affirms that if Rasata had succeeded to Rasoherina, there is no doubt that his rule would have been favourable to French influence.

No idols were brought forth when Ranavàlona II. made her first appearance to the people on the balcony of the great wooden palace ; and no idols were permitted to accompany the funeral procession of Rasoherina, the late Queen, whom M. Laborde claimed to have baptized under pretence of administering medicine previous to her death. (*Hist.*, Père de la Vaissière, vol. 1.)

At her coronation, which took place on the 3rd September, 1868, Ranavàlona II. had a Bible placed by her side, with a copy of the laws of Madagascar ; whilst on the canopy above her were emblazoned texts of Scripture. In her speech to the multitude the newly crowned Queen quoted two passages of the Bible, and she directly referred to the *praying*, which in future she declared should neither be compulsory nor forbidden. Various changes soon indicated that a total change of policy was initiated. All Government works were suspended on the Sunday ; the markets, usually held on that day, were ordered to be changed to some other day of the week; and it was proclaimed throughout the country that the Queen desired all the people to abstain from all work on that day. Sunday services were commenced in the palace, and the Queen and Prime Minister were baptized by a native pastor, Andriambelo, in February, 1869. In September of the same year, the *ancestral* idols of the Queen were publicly burnt, together with the basketfuls of rubbish, such as charms, &c., belonging to them; a Government press was set up in the Anaty-Rova or palace yard, and a stone-built church erected close to the south side of the large palace. The reign of idolatry was over, although there remained long after in the provinces, and still remain in the out-of-the-way and unexplored parts of the island, many of the old superstitious rites and ancient pagan practices.

From all accounts the profession of Christianity by the Queen was sincere, and not adopted only from motives of policy; whilst her religion did not consist in the mere external ceremony, for she acted up to her creed by the performance of constant deeds of charity and mercy. She took an active personal share of labour in the distribution of medicine and clothing to the sick and poor during the epidemic which prevailed during her reign. She supported the native churches with queenly donations, and employed two English medical practitioners for the public benefit of her people, defraying all expenses (about £1,000 annually) out of her own money.

The good Queen Ranavàlona [1] first became seriously ill in May, 1882, and during the greater part of her illness she was under the care of Dr. Rajaonà, a skilful Malagasy physician, who had learnt his profession in Scotland, and who for about four years was the resident medical officer of a dispensary near South Shields. In October, a change of air having been advised, the court proceeded to Tsinjoarivo, a pleasant summer resort, until December, when the Queen returned to her capital. Finally, after lingering six months at Antananarivo, the second Ranavàlona died on the 13th July, 1883; her hitherto peaceful reign over a kingdom giving promise of steadily increasing civilization ending in dark prospects of the future for Madagascar, whose independence was threatened by the French invaders.

The reign of no former sovereign was so fraught with good for Madagascar and so full of beneficent changes as that of Ranavàlona II. Under her rule, guided by the sagacity of the veteran Rainilaiarivony, more improvements were made of a political, educational, and social character than in any previous period in the history of the Great African Island. The religious progress inaugurated

---

[1] See Article on Ranavàlona II. by the Rev. R. Baron, F.L.S., in the *Antananarivo Annual* for 1883.

by the burning of the idols has already been alluded to. It may be added that, when Ranavàlona came to the throne in 1868, there were about 120 churches in her kingdom, and when she died there were upwards of 1,200 in active operation, a tenfold increase. The schools which had numbered about 25 at her accession had increased their number to 1,200 by the date of her death. In political matters also the changes were numerous. The government of the country, the burden of which formerly fell almost entirely on the shoulders of the Prime Minister, was divided into eight departments. These departments are presided over now by the following ministers :—

1. Rainitsimbazafy, 15th honour, Home Department.
2. Ravoninahitriniarivo, 15th honour, Foreign Affairs. (He succeeded Rainimaharavo, and was first Ambassador to Europe.)
    Andriamifidy, Assistant Secretary.
3. Rainilambo, 15th honour, War Office.
4. Ralaitsirofo, Minister of Justice.
5. Razanakombana, 15th honour, Minister of Law.
6. Rainimiadana, 14th honour, Department of Commerce and Agriculture.
7. Rainimahazire, 14th honour, Finance.
8. Andriamananizao, Civil Officer, Education.

In 1878 great improvements were made in the administration of justice by the formation of additional courts for the examination of witnesses, upon whose reports judgment was to be declared from the palace. A thorough reorganization of the army was carried out. Hitherto the whole male adult population belonged to two classes; they were either soldiers or civilians. If the former, they were called out for drill and military services; if the latter, they were required to perform other work, or *corvée*, for the government. In 1879 an edict was published that all classes, rich and poor, would have to serve, without excepting any favoured people from the conscription, except the sick and regularly appointed pastors; but instead of for life, the term of service was limited to five years. A rural police was established, and taxes levied on guns, slaves, cattle, &c. Another reform was effected in placing new governors with subordinate officials in charge of the distant provinces of the island.

Finally a new code of laws, comprising 305 statutes, was drawn up and promulgated, and all the Mozambiques in the island were emancipated.

Razafindrahéty (*i.e.*, "the little daughter of Rahéty") is the daughter of a sister of the late Queen, and about twenty-two years of age. Her mother and grandmother are still living, but her late husband, Ratrimo, also a relative of the late Queen, died in April, 1883. This princess was educated in the country district by one of the London Missionary native teachers. She then entered a school in the capital, and was afterwards for some time at the school under Miss Gilpin of the Friends' Missionary Association ; later for some years she attended the girls' school at Andohalo, where she was considered clever and in the first class. She was well behaved and spirited. It was doubtless her behaviour and Protestant education which prompted the Prime Minister to consider her eligibility for the crown. Being a widow and childless was also in her favour, as being formally married to the Prime Minister, the protection of such a powerful consort is a safeguard against usurpation. Thus her elder sister, Rasendranoro, who is twenty-six years of age, might have been considered eligible, but she was educated by the French Sisters of Saint-Joseph as a Catholic, and married and is divorced from Andrianaly, who remains exiled in Betsileo, whilst she has three children.

The late sovereign was buried in state at Ambohimanga in the same tomb as the first Ranavàlona ; but the funeral ceremonies were much curtailed in order to prevent as little as possible any interruption of the war preparations.

The accession of the new sovereign under the title of Ranavàlona III. took place on the 13th July, but the coronation did not take place until the 22nd November, when the *Misehoana* (literally " apparition " or " manifestation "), or public presentation of the sovereign on the *vatomasina*, the traditional sacred stone at Andohalo, and again on the plain of Mahamasina, took place amidst great enthusiasm.

The brave young queen repeated the following speech:—

THE QUEEN'S SPEECH.[1]

"This is my message to you, O people: God has given me the country and the kingdom, and I thank Him exceedingly. The blessings of Andrianimpoinimerina, and Lehidama, and Rabòdo, Rasohèrina and Ranavàlona have come down to me. You, the people, have assembled here on this day of my public appearance, and you have not deceived me, and so I thank you, and may the blessing of God be on you. This also I say to you: As you have not altered the word of the five sovereigns, and seeing that their memory is dear to you and you do not depart from the charge they left you, I rest in confidence. Rest in confidence, for it is I whom God has chosen to reign in this island as successor and heir of the five. It is I who am your protection, the refuge of the poor, the glory of the rich. When I say 'rest in confidence,' you can really be confident. My desire from God is to benefit you and make you prosperous. Is it not so, O people?

"I call to your mind that Andrianimpoinimerina was lord of the land, and Radama put forth strenuous efforts

---

[1] The Coronation of Ranavàlona III., by the Rev. J. Richardson, L.M.S., *Antananarivo Annual*, 1883.

to make his kingdom stretch to the sea ; he left it to his three successors ; they have left it to me. *Should any one dare to claim even a hair's breadth, I will show myself to be a man, and go along with you to protect our fatherland.* Is it not so, O people? We have treaties with our friends from across the sea. Observe them strictly, for should any one break them, I shall account him guilty of crime. I also announce to you that it is Rainilaiarivony who is Prime Minister and Commander-in-chief. I also tell you, the army, that as to the vows you made with Radama, and which you ratified to his three successors and which are now renewed to me, I can accept nothing less, O army! Is it not so, O soldiers? . . . .

" The laws of my kingdom will be printed and issued to all the people. Let each one beware, for the law is no respecter of persons ; it is what a person does that condemns him, for both you and I must submit to the law. Observe the laws, for I have no desire to condemn you, and I wish no one's life to be taken. Whoever forsakes the path of righteousness walks in the way of darkness. Is it not so, O people?"

At the part referring to the fact that she would not yield as much as a hair's breadth of her country to the French, the Queen raised her golden sceptre, and the people answered by shouts, waving their shields, spears, and rifles (for every man and boy in the whole assembly had a weapon), and immense enthusiasm prevailed. The Prime Minister and popular Commander-in-chief, Rainilaiarivony, was requested by the head of the people to reply for all. He is a great orator among a nation of orators, and when with his uplifted sword he stood on the platform in front of the Queen and told her that his own body and the bodies of that vast multitude would be her wall of defence, the people were frantic with excitement. "I never saw such a wild scene," writes the Rev. J. Richardson; "cannon, swords, spears, shields, rifles, hats, handkerchiefs, and hundreds of thousands of throats gave forth the wild assent. If ever Queen had a royal welcome from her people, she had that day."

The same day the teachers from town and country and all the school agents were gathered together, and were informed by the Queen's command that one day a month was to be devoted to spear and shield drill.

It is noteworthy that the well-known Juliette Fische, the daughter of Fisatra, the last of the Betsimisaraka chiefs, who had been educated in Réunion, and had always been noted for her French sympathies and proclivities, came up from the coast to pay homage and to declare that not an inch of Madagascar soil should be yielded to the French invaders.

It may not be out of place here to recall to mind the

past career of Rainilaiarivony, the actual prop and mainstay of the royal throne of Madagascar. He has held the reins of government individually for twenty years, since the 14th July, 1864, on which date his elder brother was deposed from his proud position as chief Minister of State.

Rainivoninahitraniony and his brother Rainilaiarivony were the sons of the great Rainiharo, who was the Prime Minister of the great and terrible Queen Ranavàlona I. The elder brother it was who placed the second Radama on the throne in 1861, and who, two years afterwards, deposed and caused to be slain that unhappy monarch, placing his widow Rasoherina on the throne. Intemperance, brought on perhaps by remorse and an ever-present sense of insecurity from revenge, seems to have weakened his intellect and broken down this once all-powerful noble, and at length his intemperate deeds, his numerous executions, and threats against his brother, and finally treasonable intentions expressed against the Queen herself, brought about his undoing. For two successive days his destiny was the subject of grave deliberation between the Queen, the nobles, judges, and high officers, and the heads of the people. Finally Rainivoninahitraniony was banished to Mananzary, stripped of all his honours and dignities, disgraced and ruined.

Rainilaiarivony succeeded to his brother's position, and retained also his former control of the army as commander-in-chief. On his accession to office he at once assured the foreigners that there would be no alteration in the views of the Government in respect to the liberty and security of the Christians, nor any wish to interfere with the missionary labours of teaching and preaching. He commenced his new career with mercy, as he attributed the cause of his brother the late minister's removal to the needless sacrifice of life, and to the fear of the people that when under the influence of drink he might put many people to death and do great mischief.

Rainilaiarivony had a very difficult part to play during the first few years of his ministry; the reactionary party of old Hova nobles, their jealousy of his family and its position, the hatred of the idol-keepers in those days, rendered his position precarious; and it was only owing to the firm hold he possessed over the army, who were greatly attached to him, that he was able to preserve and direct the government of the country. At the outset he informed Mr. Ellis that his great desire was to promote the prosperity of his country and to be remembered as its benefactor. The people appeared to think that the change would be better for the country. He had more industry and power of application than his brother, and also possessed the peculiarly valuable recommendation of being a temperate man.

The history of the political, educational, and social improvements during the past fifteen years which has been glanced at is the history of reforms instituted by Rainilaiarivony, the septuagenarian veteran whose name will always be held in respect by all races of the Malagasy through future ages. Prudent and cautious, Rainilaiarivony has introduced by degrees measures and institutions which, had they been thrust suddenly and inopportunely on the people, might have given rise to revolution, or at all events dissatisfaction. Although often pressed by ardent and zealous European advisers to hurry on this or that change, he was always slow to move until he was thoroughly convinced that the temperament of the masses and public opinion in Imerina were prepared to admit the innovation; and thoroughly understanding the disposition of the people, he was always well informed of what occupied the minds of the upper and lower classes, and could prepare his plans accordingly. Sagacious and firm, Rainilaiarivony possesses, as we have seen, a strong hand, and keeps a tenacious hold on the people; whilst with an intelligent surrounding of well-educated young men, and backed by the devoted adherence of the regular army, he can retain his impregnable position as long as his physical and mental capacities last out. For the sake of Madagascar and her brave young sovereign we sincerely trust that health and vigour may long be enjoyed by the present hale Prime Minister of Madagascar. How much the fate of Madagascar depends upon the life, temper, and conduct of this man!

The return of the ambassadors from Europe after their fairly successful mission enabled the Prime Minister and the advisers of Ranavàlona III. to understand that although the independence of Madagascar was recognized by all the leading European states except France, nevertheless merely sentimental sympathy would not much avail against the active operations of the French.

Like former Malagasy potentates, the sovereign of Madagascar and her minister found that the greatest protection to Antananarivo and Imerina were the famous two generals of nature, Generals Hazo and Tazo, that is to say, forest and fever, which fought on their side as Generals *Janvier et Février* fought for Nicholas of Russia, and as similar genii—malaria and trackless jungles—have prevailed to save many native races from highly civilized invaders,

> "Thou hast great allies,
> Powers that will work for thee, air, earth, and skies."
> (Sonnet to *Toussaint l'Ouverture*, by Wordsworth.)

After the arrival of the embassy, the chief ambassador, Ravoninahitriniarivo, made a public address at one of the periodical Isan-Enim-Bolana meetings, when the delegates from the churches assemble at the capital to discuss the affairs of the united church.[1]

It had been a matter of some speculation as to how far

---

[1] *Chronicle of the London Missionary Society.* New Series, No. 28. "Native Church and Evangelistic Work," by Re . James Wills.

the embassy would dare to state publicly what they had seen and the impressions produced on their minds. But from the first it was clear that Ravoninahitriniarivo felt under no restraint whatever. He evidently endeavoured to present as faithful a picture as he could of England and other countries, and spoke most emphatically of the advantages which would follow the adoption by Madagascar of many of the ideas and practices prevalent there. His address, says Mr. Wills, took a wide sweep, and embraced material subjects, such as roads, railroads, manufactories, steamships, &c.; social subjects, such as courtship, marriage, and household arrangements ; commercial matters, as companies, mining, chambers of commerce. And here he mentioned two points which lie at the very root of the obstacles to any great advance on the part of the Malagasy—one, that every one had wages for his work, whatever that work might be, and was thereby stimulated to do his best ; and he expressed a hope that it might ere long be like that in Madagascar. The other, that no one thought it a disgrace to work. His wish, on the first point, if realized, would destroy the system of *fanom-pana*, or *corvée*, which labour, rendered as service without pay, is in reality the great hindrance to progress in the island. There is no doubt that the Prime Minister will, as soon as he sees his way to do so, gradually substitute paid for unpaid labour.

The political allusions made by the ambassador were

apposite, and he reiterated again and again that England loved Madagascar and desired her independence.

The ambassadors did not fail to show the Government the advantage of printing the correspondence between themselves and the French Government, especially because the notes published by the French Government as emanating from the Hova envoys were disclaimed by the latter. The consequence was the production of the first Red book containing the correspondence between the French Commissioners and the Madagascar Government from 1879 down to 1882. This was a most creditable production from the Royal Palace press, and the effect of its appearance in Europe was considerable. It shed a new light on the aspect of the tiresome Madagascar Question which has been for so long an unintelligible bugbear to European diplomatists.

CHAPTER VII.

OPERATIONS CIVIL AND MILITARY.

AFTER this interlude, we now revert to the position of the French forces in Madagascar subsequent to the death of Admiral Pierre, and the effect of the reprisals exacted by the French men-of-war on the neutral commerce. During July Commander Johnstone took H.M.S. *Dryad* to the following Hova stations, viz., Foule Point, Fénoarivo, Mananhar, Maroantsetra, and Amboditsania, a small village in Diego Suarez Bay. At Fénoarivo all facilities were afforded for obtaining provisions for the English sloop; but at all the other places considerable suspicion was displayed, for the British man-of-war flag appeared to be unknown, and although oxen and supplies were plentiful, the sale of them was not permitted. At Amboditsania the Hovas were so alarmed that they left their village and could not be induced to approach the officer and the interpreter sent by Commander Johnstone in a small boat with five men. It was thought by the authorities in these parts that the *Dryad* was a French ship in disguise.

As soon as the French commenced hostilities, the Malagasy Government issued orders to their governors at all the ports, forbidding all kinds of food supplies from being exported, because, "in the first place," said the Prime Minister, "we have to look out that no famine may ensue from the effect of the war now waged on us by France; and, in the second, we do not wish that our enemy should get supplies of food from our country." On complaint being made by the British commander, the Governor of Mahanoro was instructed to furnish the English men-of-war with all supplies required, because at that place there was a British vice-consulate.

Commander Johnstone protested against the prohibition to export articles of commerce such as hides and rubber, &c. Upon which Rainilaiarivony stated that British subjects, having provisions in their stores, and wishing to sell them, could dispose of them in any part of the country where the enemy was not present; and no restriction whatever would be placed on the export of other articles. He added—

"I have to bring to your cognizance that even though the Government desires to see commerce increasing, I regret to state that as soon as that part of Admiral Pierre's ultimatum became known among the public in general, which part intimates that our ports on the eastern coast are to be destroyed if it (the ultimatum) be refused, commerce in consequence is at a standstill, as the traders in the interior, on the one hand, do not care to send goods down to the coast; while those on the coast, on the other, remove theirs inland, for fear of losing them somehow or other."

The *Dryad* again visited the eastern ports, including Ngoncy and Antalatsa, in September, and at only two of the ports was it permitted to the ship to obtain freely the supplies required; whilst the officers sent on shore to convey courtesies to the local authorities were received with great coolness and suspicion. Such were a few of the effects produced by the harassing state of affairs consequent on the French occupation.

Admiral Pierre was succeeded by Admiral Galiber, who was, together with M. Baudais, the civil commissioner, armed with plenipotentiary powers to treat with the Malagasy Government.

In the middle of October Rainilaiarivony informed the commmander-in-chief that he was ready to reopen negotiations, and Admiral Galiber replied on the 22nd October that he would agree to the proposal on condition that the operations of war should not, in the meantime, be suspended; and as an earnest intimation of his active intentions, he proceeded to bombard afresh the various small ports on the eastern coast, commencing with Vohémar.

On the 31st October the aviso *Boursaint*, commanded

by M. Boutet, anchored off Vohémar.[1] Scarcely was the anchor down when a boat was lowered and an officer came in it towards the beach, and when within speaking distance of the shore, inquired for a Malagasy subject named Beguinne, who was employed by a French firm at that place. The reply was that this man had been taken as a soldier and was with the Hova authorities. Upon this the boat returned to the ship and was scarcely alongside when the *Boursaint* opened fire, and M. Boutet shelled the village leisurely for about an hour. At the first shot the few British subjects took refuge with M. de Charmoy, the British consular agent, who had hoisted the British flag on the roof of his house. Four of the natives were killed at once, and a fifth died of his wounds. The fire from the *aviso* was principally directed towards the customhouse in the centre of the village,

The French then landed in two launches and set fire to all the houses left in the village which had not been burnt

[1] On the 11th June, 1884, M. le Commandant Boutet stated before the Madagascar Committee in Paris :—" L'amiral Galiber me donna l'ordre de parcourir la côte jusqu'à la baie de Diego-Suarez et d'y faire tout le mal possible. Je brûlai tout ce que je pus brûler, et je suis arrivé à Vohémar. . . . Enfin, d'après mes instructions, je devais aller à Vohémar et brûler tout sur ma route. . . . En arrivant, ayant vu sur la côte des Hovas armés de vieux fusils, j'en ai blessé beaucoup. Au bout de deux ou trois décharges, ils sont partis à leur camp, à 2 ou 3 kilomètres à l'intérieur. J'ai fait parcourir la côte par des embarcations armées en guerre, qui ont également tiré de façon à faire partir les Hovas sans laisser tuer mes hommes. Aussitôt après je débarquai, et on a tout brûlé. Les instructions que j'avais données à mes officiers étaient de brûler toutes les cases des Hovas, en prenant les précautions nécessaires pour que celles des Anglais fussent respectées."

by the shells, amongst others the houses of two Mauritians, British subjects, and all the houses of the Indians from Bombay. It was impossible to mistake the better sort of houses belonging to the Europeans, such as that of Mr. Lionnet, for those of the natives. In striking contrast to the burnt houses remained the establishment of MM. Roux, Fraissinet et Cie, a French firm, the buildings of which stood intact.

Captain Boutet, after this bombardment, offered a passage to the Europeans and Indians, who, having lost everything, were without means of support, and took them to Tamatave, where they were relieved by Mr. Bardel, the British agent, as distressed British subjects, until the arrival of the *Dryad*. Thus it appears that a considerable amount of British property was sacrificed by this bombardment, which was begun at Vohémar without notice, and which caused the destruction of a thriving little settlement of British subjects, who were obliged to leave what remained of their goods to be plundered by the natives. The attention of M. Ferry was shortly afterwards drawn to the occurrence, and Lord Lyons was instructed to press the Government of the Republic for an inquiry into the matter. All the other ports to the south of Tamatave were treated in a similar manner by the *Vaudreuil* or other French men-of-war.

Thus Mahanoro was shelled on the 12th November, and

Mahela and Mananzary both suffered a similar fate on the 14th of the same month. Fort Dauphin was bombarded on the 16th and again on the 19th November; whilst Mahanoro was again attacked on the 20th. Later, Fénoarivo received a second baptism of fire on the 23rd, and Mahambo for the *fifth* time was burnt by the shell fire from the French naval force.

These operations could have no other effect than that of exasperating the coast tribes against the French, and the object seems to have been to raise up a spirit of irritation against all the neutral foreigners, and break up the neutral establishments at these small trading ports.

France, by the unjustifiable behaviour of her irresponsible agents in the great African island, was laying up for herself a legacy of reciprocal hate which will last for several generations.[1] These *acts of vigour* were, however, considered necessary by the Commissioners to bring the Hovas to a proper sense of French power and to emphasize the determination of France to enforce her ancient and historical rights.

Rainidriamanpandry, the Governor of Tamatave, and at

[1] "On ne peut s'étonner que Madagascar refuse aujourd'hui de se laisser civiliser par les descendants de ceux qui, les premiers et les seuls parmi les Européens, lui firent subir de pareils maux. Les peuples encore enfants ont une longue mémoire et le récit de ces attentats, passant de hutte en hutte, et de génération en génération, ainsi grossi de bouche en bouche et devenu une feuille légende, n'a pas été propre, certes, à donner aux Malgaches l'amour du nom français."—M. Saillens, p. 3.

this time commanding the Hova forces in their entrenched position at Manjakandrianombana, was appointed by the Madagascar Government as their principal plenipotentiary, and with him were associated Andriantasy, Rainizanamanga, and Ramarosana as his colleagues, with full powers to treat with the French representatives. These envoys were appointed as early as the 9th November, but the various *pourparlers* and correspondence which ensued delayed the preliminaries being settled before the 19th November, on which date the first conference took place at Ambodimanga near Tamatave. After some fruitless discussion the negotiations were adjourned until the 24th November, when the plenipotentiaries again met, and the Malagasy envoys requested two days in order to submit on paper the concessions which their Government was willing to make towards meeting the conditions imposed by the French ultimatum. This document was presented on the 26th November; and after a short preliminary three articles were drawn up to the following effect :—

1. As to the renting of land. This shall be free, in conformity with the mutual arrangement between the lessor and lessee for any number of months or years agreed upon. The lands then let will be registered by duly appointed officials by the French and Malagasy Governments; and no freehold ground will be sold to any foreigner whatsoever.

2. The sum of 200,000 dollars (£40,000), demanded by the Government of the French Republic, as indemnity for the French claims for the last twenty years, this sum we consent to pay.

3. With regard to the "sovereignty or protectorate over the territories indicated by the French Government," Madagascar has her independence to preserve and cannot give it up to any one whosoever; but the Government of the Queen consents to pay a certain sum to arrive at an understanding which will put an end to all the dissensions and misunderstandings between the two Governments in the matter.

To this a verbal answer was returned refusing to treat on the above terms, and the situation remained unmodified.

Meanwhile the Hovas were strengthening their camp at Manjakandrianombana, whilst a good deal of sickness prevailed among the French garrisons on the coast.

A few days after the close of the conference on the 3rd December, 1883, Mr. Hicks Graves, the newly appointed British consul for Madagascar, arrived at Zanzibar and took over the archives of the Madagascar consulate from Commander Johnstone, R.N., of the *Dryad*, who, as already stated, was promoted for his valuable services rendered under exceptionally trying circumstances. The *Dryad* was at this time relieved by H.M.S. *Tourmaline*, commanded by Captain R. Boyle, who embarked Mr. Graves and Mr. Pickersgill, the recently appointed vice-consul for Antananarivo, and landed the latter at Fénoarivo, where the Hova authorities had made dispositions to enable him to proceed thence direct to the capital. Mr. Graves proceeded in the *Tourmaline* to Tamatave, reaching that port by the 15th December, where the French squadron of four ships was lying, while the United States corvette, *Brooklyn*, bearing the broad pendant of Commodore Phelps, was leaving the port for Zanzibar.

Captain Boyle opened communications with Admiral Galiber, and, having received satisfactory assurances with reference to the proposed landing of the British consul at Tamatave, he requested the Admiral to have a private and unofficial interview with Mr. Graves, a proposition which he accepted most cordially, and which was followed by a reiteration of friendly sentiments. On the 19th the British consul landed, with the usual complimentary salute of guns, and once more the Union Jack was hoisted at the consulate. The spontaneous offer of the French Admiral that the boats of the *Tourmaline* should communicate between that vessel and the shore, showed the amicable and conciliatory disposition of M. Galiber, and the relations of the new consul with the French naval authorities were thus fully established without the surrender of the neutral attitude on the part of the British.

Thus the year 1883 closed, leaving the French no further advanced towards a solution of this complication with the Madagascar Government than they were at the capture of Tamatave six months before; and the new year opened by a demonstration from the guns of the *Boursaint*, which vessel bombarded a village beyond Tanio Point, by firing fifty rounds of shell into it.

On January 14, 1884, the French made a reconnaissance in the direction of the Hova camp. About 400 men, including some of the volunteers lately brought from Réunion, with five small field-guns drawn by mules, started at an early hour in the morning, and penetrated as far as a marshy valley immediately in front of the hill on which the Hova camp was established. Soon after daylight the ships in the harbour began firing, at the range of 8,000 mètres, to cover the advance. The reconnoitring force returned to the fort about 9 A.M. with four prisoners, without having lost any men or inflicted any loss on the Hovas. A river prevented the approach of the French nearer than 1,800 mètres to the Hova position, and it was stated that they were replied to by rifled guns from the entrenchments.

During the month of January Captain Boyle visited in the *Tourmaline* all the various points along the coast where British subjects were known to live, and which had been, almost without exception, bombarded by one or other of the vessels composing the French squadron. The complaints of the sufferers from various causes arising from the state of war on the coast were forwarded to Mr. Graves to be dealt with; whilst Captain Boyle confined his own action to displaying the white ensign at the various ports, and communicating officially with the Hova governors along the coast. These constant visits were most useful in furtherance of the general purposes of British commerce.

"An occasional visit during these times," writes Captain Boyle, "when law is apt to be in abeyance, brings home to the governing and governed alike that the distinction between enemy and neutral must be observed, and that a general disregard of treaty rights is no part of a state of war."

Lieutenant Hayes, R.N., under the direction of Captain Boyle, was detached in the pinnace to coast southwards, for a distance of 150 miles from Port Choiseul, Antongil Bay, to Tamatave, in the course of ten days, calling on the Hova governors of Mananhar, Tang-tang, Fénoarivo, and Foule Point. He touched at these and several other points of the coast, and his observations contributed several additions to the yet scanty knowledge of this coast. At several places this intelligent young officer found that ignorance of the British flag had induced the flight of the natives, who had the fear of the French greatly before them. When the *Tourmaline* visited Mahanoro further to the south, Lieutenant Hayes again visited the neighbouring ports, taking with him Mr. Consul Graves to Vatoumandry.

On the 18th February the Malagasy plenipotentiaries, in consequence of a visit made to them by M. Campan, again proposed the reopening of negotiations with the Commissioners and Admiral Galiber, and, after the usual *pourparlers*, an interview was arranged and took place at Ambodimanga on the 21st February.

In a note, dated February 23rd, which the French plenipotentiaries addressed to the Prime Minister, a proposal was made by them to the Madagascar Government that the latter should agree not to occupy any territory or exercise any authority in the region named in the arrangement concluded with the Sàkalàva chiefs in 1841-42.

To this the Prime Minister replied on the 5th March that the Government of Ranavàlona could not consent to cede to France any portion whatever of the territory in question ; it was willing to grant the same privileges to the French subjects as were accorded to the most favoured nation. So the negotiations dragged on, at one time broken off, at another time renewed, whilst constant delays intervened in consequence of the frequent references to Antananarivo, the route to the capital at this time of year being difficult to traverse.

On the 4th April the Malagasy envoys made renewed

appeals to the generosity of France to put an end to the existing difficulties by the payment of an indemnity, and on the following day the fifth conference took place between MM. Galiber and Baudais and the Hova plenipotentiaries.

The Admiral and M. Baudais pressed the envoys to consent to the withdrawal of the Hova garrisons from the north-west Sàkalàva territory, which in turn they promised would not be occupied by French troops. "This," said they, "is no cession of territory," but naturally Rainidriamanpandry argued that by the evacuation of that region the independence of Madagascar would be compromised, and that if the Sàkalàva tribes were left to themselves, without any authority over them, a state of anarchy would arise which would be prejudicial to their interests.

There was another meeting on the 8th April, when the Hova Ambassador read a statement which he had drawn up, to the effect that the Madagascar Government would consent to giving up the islands of Nossi-Mitsiou and Nossi-Faly to France. It would besides agree to pay the sum of 200,000 dollars (£40,000), which France claimed as indemnity for losses to her subjects during the past twenty years; but it could not consent to yield up any portion of the mainland, although it proposed as before to arrive at an understanding by means of a money payment. This by no means satisfied the French negotiators, and, as previously, the meeting broke up without any approach to an understanding being arrived at. This was the last conference at which Admiral Galiber was present, as at this date he was expecting to be relieved by his successor, who was on his way from France.

Meantime at Paris a debate, on an interpellation by M. Lanessan, relative to the affairs of Madagascar, was begun in the Chamber of Deputies on the 24th March, and in the course of it a very remarkable speech was made by the Comte Albert de Mun, the well-known champion of the Legitimist party, who said :—"The historical right of France to the sovereignty over the entire island is established by two centuries and a half of successive establishments and constant claims. It was recognized in 1816 by a solemn diplomatic negotiation, and the authentic cession of part of the west coast by its inhabitants again served to ratify and justify it. These repeated titles, the condition of the Hova people, the attempts it repeatedly endeavours to make to extend beyond its frontiers, all justify the firm assertion of our rights. Where, therefore, is the objection which stops us? It is necessary to say a word of the question which is at the bottom of this debate. I know how delicate a one it is, and I shall only indicate it with all the reserve it requires, with all the regard which public speaking imposes, when it deals with a neighbouring and friendly nation. England, gentlemen, is at Mauritius, as

RIVALRY. 183

we are at Réunion, opposite Madagascar. She meets us on its coasts, she penetrates into the great island by her subjects, by her missionaries, by a thousand means which her genius, always active and practical, can dispose of. Thence arise, no doubt, on that land open to the efforts of civilization, rivalries and struggles for influence which have been mentioned and which are inevitable. I need not enter into the details of these contests; it is a difficult subject, often a sad one for us; but the Methodist Independents who rule at Antananarivo are not England; it is with them that there are disputes, not with her. What has it to do with England? She has no rights over Madagascar . . . (*cheers*). She has neither rights ancient nor rights modern; she has only treaties of commerce and residence with the Hova Government. She recognized our rights in 1816; she has never disputed them since; she does not dispute them. Wherefore should there be on this side an obstacle to our legitimate intervention? . . .

"Well, gentlemen, we have heard in the Mediterranean the English cannon which destroyed Alexandria whilst the French fleet sailed away (*sensation*). We have seen our colony of Egypt destroyed and our fellow-countrymen dispersed; we have seen England the mistress of Gibraltar and Malta, England, who holds the island of Cyprus, and who extends her arms over Asia Minor, occupy under our eyes the mouths and banks of the Nile, where France has marked, from the days of St. Louis to those of Bonaparte, the traces of her glory . . . (*sensation*). I do not recall these recollections in a spirit of recrimination or of jealousy towards a neighbouring nation, but I beg you not to forget what you are ; I beg you not to forget that France seated between three seas is also a maritime nation, and that there is no maritime nation without colonial possessions (*cheers*)."

The Count de Mun concluded : " Gentlemen, do not act like the Chamber of 1846 ; do not confine yourselves to platonic manifestations ; give to your government the necessary force to act vigorously (*interruptions*) in order that it may renounce fruitless negotiations, as if it wished for peace at any price, to enable it to advance and cause to be respected on the mainland, on *La France Orientale*,[1] the right of sovereignty of which it has the care, and which it has found in the legacy of centuries. This is the only policy I can comprehend. Otherwise, if we mark time for six months, the evil can only be aggravated, and every day the solution will become more difficult and more costly" (*loud applause*). The Count, on returning from the tribune, was congratulated by a large number of the deputies. M. Pierre Alype, who followed, deprecated an

---

[1] " La France Orientale " was the name given to Madagascar by the French Government in 1665. " Cette île, avec Bourbon et l'île de France, formait la ' Gallia orientalis,' la France Orientale."—M. Saillens, p. 4.

A COLONIAL DEPUTY. 185

advance on Antananarivo as risky, and advocated the occupation of certain points on the coast. And then the debate was adjourned to the 27th March.

On this day the discussion on the interpellation of M. de Lanessan was resumed by M. Durcau de Vaulcomte, deputy for the island of Réunion, who stated that although Réunion could not contribute money to the cost of the expedition, yet that colony had contributed volunteers, that when the recruiting lists were opened and 300 men asked for, that at least 600 had responded, so that they had to draw lots who should go. Finally he claimed protection for the French in Madagascar.

The tone of the whole debate was in favour of strong and immediate action in Madagascar; and, indeed, the advisability not only of asserting the sovereignty of France over the whole island, but of establishing it at once, practically by the use of force, did not lack advocates.

M. Jules Ferry, the President of Council, speaking next for the Government, found it advisable rather to restrain than to urge on the Chamber. He began by remarking that the Government now found no opponents to their colonial policy, a situation of happy novelty to the Government, that it was no longer their spirit of adventure, that it was now their too great moderation which was found fault with. He observed that there were no rights more certain, more entitled to respect, than the ancient historical rights of France over Madagascar ; that these rights were very strong, and could be maintained in face of all the European powers, in virtue of the international law of old Europe. He went on to say that the question of sovereignty was reserved, but that it would always be in the power of France to assert it when she might think it expedient to do so ; and he stated the obstacles to an immediate and uncompromising assertion of it in the following terms :—

"If you desire to raise the sovereignty in Madagascar, then it is a case of war to the death between you and the Hovas ; it is necessary that the Hovas disappear from Madagascar ; if you are desirous of proclaiming the sovereignty of France, then the object of our policy is no longer only the protection of the Sàkalàva, of our countrymen, and the vindication of our secular rights ; it is no longer that policy, it is the policy of entire occupation, of conquest pure and simple ; it is the project of creating at this immense distance from the mother-country another Algeria, assuredly less costly to conquer—the military difficulties cannot be compared—but I am afraid infinitely more difficult to populate, to render healthy, to render fertile ; for the island is entirely covered by forests ; there are neither roads nor tracks, not even mule paths—what am I saying? there are no mules."

He then proceeded to inform the Chamber that negotiations had been resumed in February; that it would be too soon to say that they would fail; that, for his part, he had the strongest desire that they should succeed; that he desired very sincerely to make a treaty with the Hovas, and that he did not desire that the Hovas should give France occasion to break definitely with them. On the question, however, as to what the Government would do if the negotiations now pending should fail, he made the following declaration: "Gentlemen, I reply that if these negotiations come to nothing, it is our duty, in order to terminate this affair, in order to bring the Hova people to reason, not to omit the employment of any means; and to see that from what is spoken in this Tribune, this obstinate people, of an obstinacy entirely peculiar to them, cannot conclude that from the heights of their eagles' nest of Antananarivo, they can indefinitely brave the will and the arms of France. But, however, gentlemen, without the extreme measure, which I do not yet wish to examine, there are others; there are intermediate measures, if I may say so; some of them have been pointed out; I might indicate others. There is only one solution which we discard; it is the policy of the past—the policy of weakness and of abandonment. We will solve, with your assistance, the question of Madagascar; we will never abandon our rights. We are determined that this should be known, and it is necessary that it should be spoken sufficiently loudly for the Hovas, or *those who advise them*, to take good note of it" (*applause*). "We shall not leave, we shall not evacuate, as the other Governments who preceded us have had the pain of doing, the places which we occupy; we repel the solution to be found in withdrawal, and we entreat the Chamber to give us an order of the day, which will exclude in an absolute manner the policy of abandonment."

M. Georges Perin finally proposed the following order of the day, which was carried by 437 votes to 26, the Government voting for it: "The Chamber, resolved to maintain all the rights of France over Madagascar, remits to a special Commission, which will be nominated in the Bureaux, the examination of the credits applied for, and passes to the order of the day."

The credits applied for amounted to a sum of 5,361,000 francs, and the Commission was composed of M. de Mahy, president; Baron Boissy-d'Anglas, secretary; MM. Rivet, Peytral, Hovius, Fougeirol, De Lanessan, Dureau de Vaulcomte, Goblet, Pierre Alype, Georges Perin.

M. de Lanessan drew up the report of the Committee, which was issued to the Deputies on the 7th of July, 1884, and later a report was distributed containing the depositions of various persons who were examined as witnesses

M. Jules Ferry is stated to have informed the committee that the English Cabinet had not made any protest in the course of the negotiations, and had indeed admitted with a good grace that in protecting its countrymen in Madagascar the French Government did no more than exercise its strict right. He added that Admiral Miot, who was to leave Marseilles that day (April 9th) for Madagascar was instructed to ascertain what were the principal points in the island which it would be proper to occupy definitively, and that he was ordered in the meantime to occupy Passandava and Mojangà. In answer to questions respecting the occupation of Vohémar, M. Jules Ferry said that the instructions of the Admiral gave him great latitude; in fact, *carte blanche*. Finally M. Ferry informed the committee that if the negotiations with the Hovas were successful, the clause of the ultimatum demanding of them the formal recognition of the rights of France might be abandoned, inasmuch as the rights of France, being indisputable, had no need of recognition, but required only to be affirmed.

Admiral Peyron stated that the eleven ships of war already on the coast of the island were sufficient, and that in his estimation the expenses for both the troops and the fleet would amount to about 4,500,000 francs (£130,000).

The committee remained sitting for several months, and among other witnesses examined was Admiral Galiber on his return from Madagascar. This gallant officer stated that the British Government had strenuously endeavoured to bring about an understanding between France and the Government of Ranavàlona, but had failed. He accounted for this by declaring that the majority of the English residents in the island were Independent Methodists, who absolutely declined to be influenced even by their Government, and possessed the traditional English hatred of France.

Admiral Galiber :—" On arriving at Madagascar my first tour was made on the Sàkalàva coast in Passandava Bay. The Sàkalàva are very numerous, but cut up into a great number of tribes, independent of one another, and almost always at war between themselves. Their battles certainly are not very murderous, ending by one or two being wounded on one side or the other. I was much struck at seeing how completely these bellicose dispositions between the Sàkalàva disappeared as soon as they found themselves in face of the Hovas. When I was in Passandava Bay, all the population had taken refuge on the shore, abandoning their fields and villages. I demanded of their chief why they fled thus from their habitations, inviting him to return to guard their crops ; to all my questions he replied with a dismayed look, The Hovas! The Hovas! To restore calm and tranquility to these poor folk, I sent a few men to reconnoitre ; they met with some thirty Hovas thereabouts. The mere appearance of these few Hova spearmen had sufficed to put all the Sàkalàva to flight.

EVIDENCE.

Unless a man-of-war remains in the bay it is difficult to maintain the *morale* of the Sàkalàva."

The Admiral believed that the Hovas would accept the French protectorate were it not for the English, and that ten thousand men would be sufficient to march to Antananarivo. He did not himself advise any such advance into the interior, but approved of the policy of the Government in occupying definitively important points of the island, in order to convince the Hova ministers of the unalterable determination of France to maintain her secular rights. He pointed out the bad faith of the Hovas, which rendered it impossible to negotiate with them.

A mass of evidence was collected by the committee, given chiefly by naval officers and merchants, most of whom had been engaged in the cattle trade between Madagascar, Réunion, Mauritius, Egypt, and Marseilles, to which 15,000 oxen were shipped last year. The evidence seems to have been very contradictory, and we naturally find a good deal of self-interest manifested. For instance, M. Macé, who had an establishment on Nos-Vey (where, he reports, he had had the French flag hoisted for eight years) advised the Government to occupy St. Augustine's Bay and to establish a convalescent home there, as the climate there was salubrious, and the sick could be transported thither at less cost than to Réunion, &c.

Others in a like strain. MM. Mante and Borelli state that

Madagascar is a healthy station : "*En réalité, ceux qui disent que Madagascar est un pays malsain ne le connaissent pas.*"

Commander Boutet and most of the naval officers testified that it would not pay France to hold Madagascar by force.

The report of the Madagascar Special Committee in Paris was drawn up by M. de Lanessan, and a copy forwarded to Earl Granville by Lord Lyons on the 15th July, but the report was not discussed in the Chamber of Deputies until the following week.

The report began by affirming that since 1642, the date at which Richelieu granted to Captain Rigault a concession for ten years of the island of Madagascar, France had never ceased to claim possession of Madagascar, and that this claim had never been contested by any European power.

On the one hand, M. Georges Perin declared that it was "the national interest, and not the national honour, which was at stake in this affair." According to this honourable deputy, "this interest required that France should intervene in Madagascar solely in favour of her subjects molested and injured, that full and complete justice might be exacted from them, but nothing more. This justice can be obtained," said M. Perin, "by energetic and sustained naval action, which, by putting a stop to all traffic with the island of Madagascar, will famish the Hova Government and bring it promptly to conclude a treaty giving every satisfaction to French interests." M. Perin was convinced that unless this resolution were adopted, France would not only be forced into establishing herself at some points of the island, but into taking possession of the island in its entirety, a formidable business; that in accomplishing the conquest of the mainland serious resistance would have to be encountered; and he condemned an expedition which would cost France sacrifices of men and money out of all proportion to the benefits which could possibly be obtained. M. Perin was alone in this sensible, temperate counsel. On the other hand, the other members of the committee were unanimously of opinion that France should not limit herself to repressive action, but should enforce the exercise of her rights over Madagascar, that the mere chastisement of the Hovas by the destruction of their ports, which they had improperly established on the coast, and by the stoppage of their commerce, would only cause expenses as unproductive as they would be considerable. Such operations would require a great number of ships, during a long period, without effecting any positive result. Whilst, after the departure of the fleet, the Hovas would only recommence anew their molestations, and the French residents would be in more danger than before.

The members of the majority therefore affirmed the decision of the Chamber to enforce the rights of France over Madagascar. The negligence of former governments in sustaining their rights was no excuse for their abandonment. France had too long tolerated their denial and violation by insult and assassination by a barbarous people, encouraged for the last sixty years by the weaknesses of the French Government.

The committee accordingly recommended efficacious and lasting action.

It resulted from the depositions of those who best knew Madagascar that the tribes of the coast ardently desired the presence of the French amongst them, and that these tribes would furnish valuable auxiliaries [1] both for the defence of posts and for future advance. The first object would be to prove to the tribes so oppressed and plundered that France in establishing herself in Madagascar was

---

[1] The famous traveller and naturalist, M. Grandidier, stated to the committee: "Je crois que nous pourrions trouver parmi les Betsimisarakas et les autres tribus soumises aux Hovas, une foule d'individus qui, si nous sommes bons maîtres, accepteraient avec plaisir notre domination et feraient des soldats très passables. . . .

"J'ai déjà dit mon opinion au sujet des Sâkalàva, que je ne considère pas comme propres à faire des soldats réguliers ; mais, en tout cas, on ne pourrait jamais en réunir ni 30,000, ni même 10,000. Une des peuplades que nous pourrions nous rallier avec le plus de chances de succès, et qui pourrait nous être très utile, serait celle des Antanosses, mais elle n'est pas très nombreuse. Il n'y aurait pas grande difficulté à obtenir de leur roi Zomaner, moyennant des cadeaux, quelques centaines d'hommes qui pourraient former de bons soldats pour renforcer nos garnisons. Parmi les Betsimisarakas et les peuplades du Sud-Est, on pourrait aussi trouver de bonnes recrues."

decided to confine the Hovas within the limits of their territory, to prevent their interference in commercial transactions, their levying any duties, and any ill-treatment of the other tribes. For this purpose it would be necessary to found permanent establishments in the territory of these friendly tribes, who occupy all the coasts, and who would be all the more faithful, as they were interested in the maintenance of French anthority.

The military operations recommended included the blockade of the island and the destruction of all the Hova posts established on the coasts of Madagascar. The destruction of the posts had already been effected, and to maintain the blockade and to keep the Hovas at a distance from the coast, the committee proposed that the Government should maintain eleven ships in Malagasy waters with an effective strength of 2,224 officers and men.

The definite measures to be undertaken were stated to consist of the occupation of a number of points both on the coast and at certain distances from the sea. These points included (1) *Tamatave*, already in the hands of the French; (2) *Mojangà*, also held by the French; (3) *Mourouvai*, a village in the bay of Bembatoka, 50 kilomètres from Mojangà (Admiral Miot was instructed by the Colonial Minister to take possession of this port); (4) *Mavetanana*, a Hova post 100 kilomètres up the Betsiboka River, situated at its junction with the Ikiopa River ; (5) *Vohémar*, the possession of which would ensure the safety of (6) the Bay of *Diego Suarez*. Besides, it would be necessary to establish a route of communication between Vohémar and Antongil Bay, southwards to (7) *Tingtingue*, and (8) *Foule Pointe*. In addition, Admiral Miot was to occupy (9) *Passandava Bay*. The above points the Commission understood from the Government were either already occupied or about to be taken possession of. In addition, it was recommended that some points more to the south of the island should also be occupied, viz., (10) *Amboundro*, at the mouth of the River Mouroundava ; (11) *Tulear*, and (12) *Fort Dauphin*.

The credit which the committee proposed to grant amounted to 5,361,000 francs (£214,440). Perhaps the most interesting portion of M. Lanessan's report is to be found in the numerous appendices, consisting of various documents which the committee regarded as fully establishing the historical rights of France to the sovereignty of Madagascar. The first commencing with the order in council of His Most Christian Majesty Louis XIV., in which Cardinal Richelieu concedes to Captain Rigault the exclusive right of trading with Madagascar and its dependencies: and another (Appendix F) contains the correspondence, hitherto unpublished, in which the "pretensions" of England over Madagascar in 1815, and the abandonment of these "pretensions"[1] and the *retrocession* of Madagascar to France by England in 1817 are duly set forth.

The report of the Madagascar Committee was discussed in the Chamber of Deputies on the 21st July, 1884, when the Government bill was passed by a majority of 279, the numbers being 360 to 81.

M. Georges Perin, during the discussion, complained of the extension of the French operations in Madagascar as projected by the committee. It was no longer, he said, a question of occupying a few points in the north and north-west, as proposed by the Government in March. To-day, on the contrary, he said, you propose to occupy the whole circumference of the island. The committee, observed M. Perin, has laid down a regular plan of campaign for a war of conquest. The actual plan of the committee, he alleged, was in complete disaccord with the original plan of the Government. The committee proposes to occupy not only, as originally intended, some points on the north, north-east, and north-west, but to surround the island with a circle of posts sufficiently fortified and armed to resist attack. If the Chamber accepted the plan it had better put at the disposal of the Government three times the

[1] Mr., afterwards Sir Robert, Farquhar, then Governor of Mauritius, had claimed that, under the Treaty of Vienna, the French possessions in Madagascar were transferred to England under the phrase, "Mauritius and its dependencies." The English Government admitted that this claim was not well founded, and ordered Governor Farquhar to restore to the French all the posts which had been occupied by them in Madagascar before the war.

resources in men and money which were now asked for. He pointed out that Admiral Galiber's and Commandant Gaillard's statistics of mortality amongst the troops were terrifying, and that at Mojangà and at Tamatave there were at certain seasons fifty per cent. sick. Admiral Galiber had declared that his operations would have been completely stopped had he not been able to send his sick to Réunion.

Monseigneur Freppel (Bishop of Angers) advocated a crusade into the interior, and by a decisive *coup* the establishment of a French protectorate over the whole island: "Occupy the capital of the Hovas, to deliver them and free them from the tyrannical government which oppresses them, from a clique whose yoke they are unable to shake off, and leave them the free possessors of the soil. Establish a resident French general with a post of three or four hundred men, and extend your protectorate over the whole island of Madagascar. Such is, in my idea, the only solution of the question, without which you will accomplish nothing serious or lasting."

M. Jules Delafosse pointed out that until the invasion of the English missions, French influence had been preponderant in Madagascar; that previously it was the French who had been the counsellors of the Hova ministers and their best friends. It was certain that the English missionaries had conquered for the most part the island,

and were absorbing slowly but surely all Madagascar. The speaker hoped that, should the French advance to Antananarivo, they would hold the English missionaries responsible in their property and persons for the acts of war with which they mixed themselves up, and that they would be treated like belligerents. The Hovas, he added, notwithstanding appearances, were not so much a Government as a people of inland pirates, who had no financial institutions, but lived on exactions, confiscations, and the produce of their custom-houses. On that account it was necessary to attack and, he hoped, reduce them.

M. Bernard Lavergne expressed his apprehension that France was entering upon a course of action of which it was impossible to foresee the consequences.

Next followed M. de Lanessan, the author of the report, who of course defended it.

Admiral Peyron, the Minister of Marine, then gave some explanations respecting the amount and condition of the French forces at the disposal of Admiral Miot, the commander-in-chief of the Madagascar expedition.

M. Raoul Duval, in the course of a speech against the Bill, quoted the proclamation of the Governor of Réunion calling for volunteers for Madagascar, and cited especially the phrase: "The concessions of land shall not be taken back."

M. Réné Goblet asked the Government for explanations.

In reply, M. Jules Ferry affirmed that he had been the first to say to the Chamber that in this affair of Madagascar it was necessary to act with the greatest circumspection. " Previously to the resolution of the Chamber of the 27th March, we had," said M. Ferry, "confined ourselves to requiring the Hovas to recognize our rights; since the 27th March it has become our duty to exercise those rights. On this rests the plan of limited occupation which forms the first part of the conclusions of the committee, the only part which the Government has really adopted. When I appeared before the committee with the Minister of Marine, we said that it would be necessary to keep possession of Mojangà and Tamatave, and to find in the north at Vohémar, and perhaps also in the Bay of Passandava, points to be permanently occupied. We reserved, of course, the opinion of our commander-in-chief on the spot, but with the reservation of his being in accord with us, we thus limited the field of action for 1884." M. Ferry observed further on in his speech that the Government pronounced no opinion upon the second part of the conclusions of the committee; and that, to be quite frank with the committee, he must say that they appeared to him to go rather too far when they said that they were in accord with the Government in recommending that Ambondrou, Tuléar, and Fort Dauphin should be occupied. He added that the Government must also reserve its opinion as to the advantages and possibility of occupying Mavatanana, which is about sixty-two miles in the interior. M. Ferry pointed out that the best guarantee for the moderation of the plans of the Government was the smallness of the credit they asked for. As to the more extended views of the committee he expressed no opinion. The Government, he said, neither rejected them nor supported them; but as for the campaign of this year, no such views could be thought of; they were quite incompatible with the amount of the credit asked for. The bill was then passed by 360 votes to 81.

On the 14th August the bill came before the Senate, and was passed with only one vote against it. One of the members, M. Milhet-Fontarabie, stated that in his opinion the credits demanded were not sufficient, as it was quite impossible to say that the operations could be limited in their extent. M. Milhet-Fontarabie then traced the history of the French claim to Madagascar from the days when Governor Farquhar was ordered by the British Cabinet to deliver up Madagascar to the French Government; and he accused England of being the cause of all the difficulties which France had met with in the island. He called attention to the fact that the Hova troops were, at that time, commanded by an Englishman, Colonel Willoughby, and he considered that the French Government would be justified in bringing this matter to the notice of Her

Majesty's Government, who, he was quite willing to admit, were probably ignorant of the circumstance.

In replying, M. Faure, Under Secretary for Marine, mentioned that Colonel Willoughby was not an officer in Her Majesty's regular army, but merely a volunteer who had served in the Zulu campaign. The Government, said M. Faure, confined themselves to requiring the Hovas to recognize French rights. Since the 27th of March the French Government had exercised those rights under limited conditions: "You have the extent of them in the small credits which we asked for," . . . but under conditions of energy which the dignity of France requires.

The speech of M. Felix Faure was very well received by the Senate.

CHAPTER VIII.

BLOCKADE.

In all Captain Boyle's despatches to Admiral Sir William Hewitt at this period he was happily able to report a continuance of the cordial relations already established between the ships of the two European Powers. He found in Admiral Galiber a cordial readiness to afford explanations and assistance, and desired to put on record that nothing could exceed his courtesy and consideration. In February Mr. Graves had to report that the properties of the British subjects at Andevorante had been almost entirely destroyed by the Hovas, acting under the orders of the second in command of that place. This officer, however, was deposed by orders from Antananarivo and confined in prison.

On the 14th February Mr. Graves left Tamatave in H.M.S. *Tourmaline* for Mojangà, the nearest port to Mahabo, to inquire into a complaint made by the governor of the latter place that British subjects were selling arms and ammunition in contravention of the treaty. *En route*, Mr. Graves landed at Fénoarivo, where he appointed Mr. Baylis vice-consul, and the *Tourmaline* called at Mahanoro at the entrance to Antongil Bay to coal. After some delay in consequence of the non-arrival of the collier, Mojangà was reached on the 26th. At this time Mojangà was still occupied by the French, the corvette *Forfait* and two gunboats being in the harbour, whilst the fort on shore above the town was occupied by some marines and 250 Bourbon volunteers, together with an officer and twenty men, quartered in a French merchant's store in the town below. The town itself, Mr. Graves states, was quite undefended to the north-east and east, and appeared liable to be entered and burnt at any time by the Hovas, who were in considerable force at a camp some thirty miles up the river Boéni, near Mahabo. But under the protection of the guns of the French vessels the town must have been quite safe. Mr. Graves was unable to reach Mahabo, the French commandant informing him that the river was blockaded, and refusing permission for him to pass. The consul was therefore obliged to content himself with sending a letter to the governor asking for particulars to enable him to deal with the offenders, but no reply was obtainable. It appeared that about sixty British-Indian families lived at Mojangà, and nearly as many more up the river, but only seventeen registered themselves. Some of them said they were afraid of the French, that they would like to be registered if they were sure of British protection, but that they feared they would not for a long time be visited again by any British authority. Mr. Graves consequently explained to them the order in council as to registry, and assured them that a man-of-war or himself would revisit them within six months.

According to the French authorities, the British-Indians in Madagascar were in the habit of declaring themselves to be French or British subjects, as it suited them best at the moment; but Mr. Graves hoped, by exercising caution in keeping the register of British subjects, and occasionally comparing it with that kept by his French colleague, to prevent any further cases of the kind happening.

It was well understood that for some years previously many British-Indians at Mojangà had declared themselves to be Malagasy subjects in order to evade the law against slave-holding, and also to enable them to build stone houses, which was then forbidden to British subjects. None of the Indians on the occasion of Mr. Graves' visit possessed any papers in support of their claim to be British subjects; nor does it appear that the late consul, Mr. Pakenham, during his tenure of office ever visited Mojangà.

The morning after Mr. Graves' arrival an inquiry was held by the French commandant into the circumstances connected with an attack made some days previously by some Sàkalàva (*French allies?*) on the boats of a British-Indian which were descending the river with produce for export, in accordance with a permission issued by the commandant, in which affair, it appeared, the boats were

FRANCISATION.

captured and the Indians driven away. Some of the Indians owning dhows stated that they had been compelled to fly the French flag, though they would much prefer the British, and the French commandant admitted that these British subjects had received *francisation*, for which operation they paid no fees. According to French law this act is only permissible in a French colony.[1]

---

[1] It may be here observed that the question of slave-holding by British-Indian subjects has been, and is still, affected by the lack of British consuls on the Madagascar side of the Mozambique Channel. The west coast of Madagascar is entirely without a consular official of any rank whatsoever. The eastern coast has been, within the past year, fairly supplied by the appointments lately made of unpaid vice-consuls, but on the west coast there is not as yet one.

At Mojangà, the most important trading port on that side of the island, there were, and probably are, some two hundred or more British-Indian subjects engaged in trade, many of them owning dhows and other vessels trading to the African coasts. The absence of a British consul within reach of this place is resulting in these dhows and coasting vessels assuming the French flag and papers, which are readily furnished them free of cost; whereas to obtain British papers it is necessary to proceed to Zanzibar, where consular fees are exacted, thus losing for England a control which was beneficial for the police of these seas.

Our informant, who is well acquainted with the neighbourhood and the state of affairs, states that there is no resident merchant who could be recommended for the vice-consular post, and what is needed is a gentleman with a commission for Mojangà as vice-consul of that town, the north-west coast, together with the islands of Johanna and Mohilla under his jurisdiction. With these last-named islands a treaty of the most rigid kind has been lately ratified, but no steps have yet been taken to enforce its terms, and consequently the slave-trade is yet in full swing—witness the late captures made by H.M.S. *Osprey* and H.M.S. *Philomel*, as late as last December, 1884. Mr. Holmwood is nominally consul for those islands, under Sir J. Kirk at Zanzibar, but he goes there, we believe, but once or twice in three or four years, and therefore British interests are at present neglected. The French policy in these seas is so active that the tendency of a treaty with only an occasional triennial glimpse of a British representative, who then must say

At first the commandant, M. Wyvil, seemed inclined to be suspicious of Mr. Graves' presence at Mojangà ; but he appeared relieved on learning the object of his visit and the regulations as to registration of British subjects, who were, moreover, cautioned as to their observing strict neutrality during the hostilities. The American consular agent at Mojangà informed Mr. Graves that the customs there were said to have yielded 20,000 dollars since the French occupation on a seven per cent. *ad valorem* duty (in Tamatave it was 10 per cent.), and that there was much produce ready for export in the hands of British subjects up the river which they had been afraid to bring down. Mr. Graves subsequently visited Nossi-Bé, where he was informed that a dhow under British colours had been taken when endeavouring to land cargo on a part of the coast which was blockaded. Mr. Graves had received no notice that any blockade had been published.

unpleasant things to a slave-holding people, is to drive them into the arms of a more complaisant maritime power. It would seem therefore that, unless a more vigorous policy be introduced, within a few more years the French influence will be dominant in those islands, and the chain of French labour depôts be thus completed between Africa, Madagascar, and Réunion. It is a recognized fact that the French colonists look forward with expectancy to a fresh stream of black labour from Africa and Madagascar, to replace the immigration of Malabars, which has been stopped by the Indian Government. Any steps, therefore, taken to retain a hold on this line of labour traffic will tend to mitigate the horrors of the slave trade, which can only be effectually repressed by a system of boat cruising.

The sultan of Zanzibar, Burghash, is the only man in his dominions who affects to oppose the slave-trade at all ; and when it is considered that the very slaves which are caught by his police are placed summarily in his own slave-gang, the advantages to the slaves are somewhat equivocal.

Meanwhile the situation of the French in Madagascar remained unchanged, and the arrival of the new French Rear-Admiral in relief of Admiral Galiber was awaited with some expectancy.

Admiral G. Miot arrived and assumed command of the French forces in Madagascar on the 8th May, and the first step he took was to notify to Captain Boyle that he intended very shortly to place the ports of Mahanoro and Fénoarivo in a state of blockade. Captain Boyle replied that he did not acknowledge his note as a formal intimation, but simply as a friendly premonition of an impending blockade, subject to the conditions of international law; for at that time the French Admiral was waiting for other ships before he could commence the threatened blockade. There are, it appears, two species of blockade—(1) a *de facto* blockade only, and (2) a blockade by notification *accompanied by fact*. (Phillimore's International Law.) On the 16th May, Admiral Miot wrote to Consul Graves stating that Mahanoro would be blockaded the following day, and accordingly the French gun-boat *Capricorne* proceeded to Mahanoro on the 17th; and the officer commanding ordered the master of the British brigantine *Orénoque* to leave that port within five hours, although he had only half completed the loading of his vessel. On the 28th May, Admiral Miot informed the British consul that Fénoarivo would be blockaded from the 12th June.

A SENSIBLE PROPOSAL.

Upon this Mr. Graves called on the Admiral and proposed an arrangement, by which British vessels coming from Tamatave, which had there paid duties on their cargoes, should be allowed to discharge cargo at the blockaded ports. By this means the French customs revenue would be increased. The Admiral was prepared to accept this arrangement, but was obliged to refer home for instructions, as the order for blockading had come from Paris. In consequence of the blockade of Mahanoro, Mananzary to the south became a place of more importance, and its trade increased, whilst the number of British subjects was larger than before the war; Mr. Graves therefore appointed Mr. Henderson to be vice-consul of this port.

Immediately after the arrival of Admiral Miot at Tamatave, the Malagasy plenipotentiaries at Manjakandrianombana requested that a date might be fixed for the renewal of negotiations; and the first interview was fixed for the 13th May, on which date the seventh conference took place.

The Governor of Tamatave then read a communication from the Malagasy Government to the following effect: that, on examining the past negotiations, they (the Queen's ministers) saw clearly the generosity of France, in that she did not wish to touch the independence of Madagascar, or take her territory; they were therefore encouraged to renew their supplications. "We beg of you then, gentlemen, not to disdain the repetition of the request we make to you, plenipotentiaries and representatives of the French Republic; and these are the words which our Government at Antananarivo wish to bring to the notice of the Admiral who has succeeded Admiral Galiber; as to Mr. Commissioner, he already knows their purport. We beg you to take them into consideration, and our Government begs of you, gentlemen, to submit them to the Government of France, for it is convinced and it hopes that if you would be good enough to transmit them, all the more that the French Government is ready to show generosity to the Government of Madagascar, her ally for so long, that Government would not refuse to acquiesce to her request. *We shall be happy to do everything to satisfy France except in what affects the independence of Madagascar and of her territory."*

Admiral Miot.—" Listen attentively to the words I am about to read to you—The Government of the French Republic has solemnly resolved to settle all its affairs with Madagascar, and will spare no means in order to effect this end. You must know that the object of my coming here is not, in any way, to claim the rights of the Republic, nor to ask you to respect our treaties and our dealings with regard to those populations we love and protect (*i.e.*, the Sàkalàva); but I come to exercise those rights and to exact that respect. The unworthy attitude on your part towards Frenchmen is an intolerable outrage to the honour of France ; and the strong measures you make use of towards the people who have placed themselves under our protection add to your faults. Do not expect to be allowed to wave your flags over the northern territories, for in future they are truly under the protection of the French Republic. We will never abandon Mojangà, and we shall only leave Tamatave when we choose so to do. If you wish the war to cease, it can be done under the following conditions. 1. Indemnity and guarantees to our fellow-countrymen by the payment of 600,000 dollars (£120,000). 2. The guarantee to our countrymen of the rights stipulated in the treaty of 1868 by the abrogation of the law 85 ; or, an additional clause to the said treaty, by which our countrymen will have the right to take leases for long periods, renewable at will by the mutual consent of lessor and lessee. 3. An indemnity to all subjects of any nationality for damages caused by the present operations. Let your chiefs at Antananarivo be informed of the formal will of the Republic. Should you wish to treat on the bases above mentioned, we will consent to negotiate ; without these there can be no conference ; and it is certainly your own obstinacy which has provoked the last rupture. . . . If negotiations are to be renewed you must not limit the places we wish to occupy. Considering the long existence of our rights, we need not to ask of the Hovas rights which we already possess. Nor do we ask that the treaties we have made with the north should be respected. Our will from this day is to take and make good our possession, for which we do not want your consent."

"These are the instructions given me by M. Jules Ferry," exclaimed Admiral Miot, who at the same time exhibited M. Jules Ferry's autograph signature to the above terms, and the French plenipotentiaries declared the conference closed.
"Olli obstupuere silentes ;
Conversique oculos inter se, atque ora, tenebant."

The following day the Malagasy envoys wrote, consenting to treat on the points demanded by the French, so long as the independence of Madagascar was assured. To which communication a reply was made that the Republic did not wish to efface the Hovas from the map of Madagascar. Reference was again made to the capital, and the runners brought back an answer from Rainilaiarivony by the 27th ; upon which the 29th May was fixed for the re-opening negotiations.

The chief Madagascar envoy again read a document to the effect that the Government of the Queen of Madagascar did not hesitate to treat with the French upon the points indicated by the French Admiral, except with regard to anything affecting the independence of Madagascar. It was ready to come to terms with respect to the indemnity, the leasing of land, and other points claimed by France in satisfaction of her honour.

The ambassador also read a paper received from Antananarivo, by which the Hova Government agreed, in order to satisfy the honour of France, to retire from the territory occupied by Benao and Monga; "*provided* we shall be able to return after the expiration of a term agreed upon."

The Admiral said: "This is what we are going to do. We are going to occupy any place we choose in Madagascar, and if we have to do it by force you will have nothing more to do there, for we will drive you away; and if we succeed without force you will remain there with us. . . . This is settled. We wish to take possession of our property, and it does not belong to you. You are not of this country; you come from elsewhere. You are Hovas but not Malagasy."

The Governor.—You know very well that with regard to the antiquity of our arrival here, it is we, the Malagasy, who are the masters of the country from the time of our ancestors; this is why we are in possession of it until this day, for it has been our country from all time.

The Admiral.—You do not know this; it is we who know. . . . I repeat to you that on the 27th March the Chamber of Deputies decreed that France would maintain its general rights over Madagascar.

The Governor.—Your possessions were voluntarily abandoned by you in consequence of the aggression of the natives. As to the Queen of Madagascar, her possession is proved by the exercise of her supremacy which dates from very far back.

The Admiral.—The name is given her out of courtesy; from habit we call her "Queen of Madagascar," just as the title "Empress of India" is used; but this does not mean to say that all India belongs to her; it is only out of deference. . . .

The Admiral.—I wish to read to you a proposal for the clauses of a treaty :—

. .(1) From henceforward there shall be peace, friendship, and good understanding between Queen Ranavàlona III. and her successors.

The Governor.—Why do you withdraw the title of Queen of Madagascar?

The Admiral.—We do not withdraw the title of Queen of Madagascar, but we do not recognize her as "Queen of Madagascar," but only as "Queen of the Hovas." In fact, Queen Ranavàlona does not reign over certain territories in the south any more than I reign over France.

The Governor.—With regard to the titles we hold from sovereigns or from governments, if we are to be illegally deprived of them, we protest. Therefore, if it is wished to withdraw the title of "Queen of Madagascar," we cannot in any way consent, and cannot treat about it with you; since you yourselves, the French as well as the English, Americans, Italians, and Germans, have recognized it, as we have already declared to you.

QUEEN OF IMERINA.

The Admiral.—Very well; but when we called her "Queen of Madagascar" at first, it was merely a nominal title; but we do not for all that recognize her as "Queen of Madagascar," but only as Queen over the province of Imerina, for she only reigns over that part; as to the other parts, she conquered them by wars.

The Governor.—You know very well that every independent nation may conquer the territories which adjoin the kingdom, and this is what the Sovereign of Madagascar has done.

The Admiral.—In future, in any treaty we make with you we shall no more use the title of Queen of Madagascar unless we receive fresh instructions to that effect from our Government. France maintains her rights over Madagascar as well as the treaties she has entered into with the islands, and orders that no arrangements should be made as to the territories. Therefore let the Government of Queen Ranavàlona III. consent to withdraw all her soldiers from the northern territories between Cape Bellone and Cape St. Andrew, and to have nothing more to do there. Do not be ashamed, for in war there are always conquerors and conquered, and you will not fail to be conquered, therefore do not let any false shame stand in your way, but if you really desire to negotiate, and if you really do not wish for the bloodshed caused by our soldiers' march to Antananarivo, say frankly that you agree to make peaceful terms because you cannot hold out against such strength and power, and will agree to what we wish. Not long ago we were conquered by Germany, and we had to pay an indemnity of 100,000,000 dollars. With this before you, it would be best to come to terms quickly for fear France should increase her claims over all Madagascar. Unless you give in war must begin again. . . . The custom followed by plenipotentiaries in Europe, when it is wished to make a treaty in order to put an end to war, is to begin by signing the preliminaries, then they are discussed. This is the essential part of a treaty, and these are the principal clauses, viz :—

The Government of Queen Ranavàlona III. agrees :—

(1) To withdraw her garrisons from the territory north of Cape Bellone and Cape St. Andrew, and undertakes to have nothing further to do there.

(2) To pay a sum of 600,000 dollars as an indemnity for the war expenses, and to satisfy the demands of the French residents before the war.

(3) To compensate all persons of whatever nationality for losses caused by the present differences.

(4) To allow long leases of land to be made and renewed according to the pleasure of the contracting parties.

(5) To alter the treaty of 1868.

The Governor asked, "Why do you increase the difficulty of our coming to terms? We hoped that when you (Admiral Miot) came you would deal with us considerately."

The Admiral.—The difficulty will increase every day, and it is intended to make you agree quickly, lest you should lose the whole island. We had to be quick with Germany ; when we saw that we were about to be beaten, we came to terms speedily to put an end to the war. I hope you will see that it will be well for you to agree. Let it be known plainly in Antananarivo that the whole will be taken if you do not come to terms with us. In the beginning we came near to giving you Mojangà and Tamatave, but the people of France do not agree to that. Look out, for we shall come up to Antananarivo through Mojangà and drive you out of your position here at Manjakandrianombana.

This was the termination of the conference, and after a few days Admiral Miot was informed that the Hova Government would consent to treat regarding the territories of Benao and Monja, the indemnity of 600,000 dollars, and the long leasing of lands ; it would also repeal the obnoxious law No. 85. Beyond this the Government of Antananarivo could not go, and consequently Admiral Miot broke off the negotiations.

As there now seemed some prospect of an advance of the French on Antananarivo, Mr. Graves requested Mr. Pickersgill to report on the possibilities of the British subjects in the capital getting away in case of need. Mr. Pickersgill accordingly made careful inquiries without creating alarm, and reported that it would not be possible to obtain bearers for the foreign residents in case of any sudden emergency.

Mr. Pickersgill was of opinion that in the event of French troops advancing upon the capital, the European residents in the interior would be compelled, by lack of means of transit, to remain there until the war was over, not in Antananarivo, however, where the invading force would, doubtless, meet with a very determined resistance, but congregated in one of the adjacent villages outside the probable track of hostilities.

Admiral Miot informed Mr. Graves at the end of May that as soon as his reinforcements arrived he intended to drive the Hovas out of their camp in front of the town, and the British consul determined to visit Antananarivo and come to some understanding with the Prime Minister. He therefore proceeded *viâ* Vatomandry and Andevoranto to the capital on the 3rd June, leaving Captain Boyle, R.N., as acting vice-consul at Tamatave during his absence.

Meanwhile,[1] in Imerina great preparations were made in view of the projected invasion of Imerina, large camps of instruction were formed on the hills surrounding the city, and everywhere could be heard the sound of drums, and

[1] *The Madagascar Times*, May 21.

the cries of the spearmen exercising their weapons, whilst the drilling of recruits was energetically carried on.

There was a Kabary held on the 5th May, when the substance of the negotiations with Admiral Galiber was communicated to the nobles and officers, and Rainilaiarivony informed them that although the negotiations were broken off they need have no regret, for their hands were clean. One of the chiefs, Ravelonanosy, made the following characteristic speech: "Of this land no part can be given away, according to the compact which we made with Ranavalomanjaka; if we have to die, then death be upon us; if we are to lose, let us lose; for we are not a people with whom it is hard to live on good terms, but we are a people slow to go to war; therefore if matters have not been completed in a friendly manner, here we are to complete them; for when they get the worst of it in straightforward argument, are they to appeal to haughty superiority, as much as to say, 'If they cough it does not mean anything, but if we cough it is because we have swallowed hot pepper'? God forbid. Do not fear such expressions as 'Tell the Prime Minister to come here,' for the nation founded by Andrianimpoinimerina is still here to fight; there is not a man of us who is not a soldier, so let us eat and fare together; we ask to conclude a solemn compact to that effect, for we prefer to die in defence of this land of our fathers. As to the means, we all have plenty, both powder and balls, so let every man be prepared." Another chieftain, Andrianabiby, spoke as follows : " Those Frenchmen are like rats who go forth in search of food ; when they enter the barn they all go in by the same hole, but when they leave it, each one has his own road. They pretend not to take this land by force, but want to buy it by force ; if peace cannot be bought with money or wealth, then we will pay for it with our lives ; if a fence of our rice-field ever is stolen we raise a noise, and the land of our fathers is to be taken from us, and shall we remain silent ? God forbid. Let us all hasten to do our utmost to defend Madagascar. Is it not so, ye people ? "

Two questions were then put to the assembly by the Prime Minister. If the French further desire or consent to negotiate, shall we accept the offer ? The people replied, Yes ! In the event of the French refusing to negotiate further, but preferring to fight, shall we fight ? The unanimous reply was, Yes !

The Prime Minister then made a long stirring speech. " It is not that we are seeking to take what belongs to others," he said, " but simply to defend what belongs to us." He then concluded by ordering that within a certain time every able-bodied man should hold himself in readiness for war. The various chiefs and officers then spoke, assuring the Queen's Government that they assented to the order of the commander-in-chief.

On the 18th May, Lieut-Colonel Digby Willoughby, who had been for some time in the employ of the Malagasy Government, and was given the rank of Adjutant-General, left the capital for Manjakandrianombana. He took reinforcements with him, and these troops before leaving were addressed by the Prime Minister in inspiriting language.

The Foreign Enlistment Act is very strict in forbidding any British subject from entering into the military employment of a belligerent government; this individual infraction of the rule was noticed subsequently in the Senate by M. Milhet de Fontarabie, but the Under Secretary of Marine explained that the Colonel Willoughby spoken of was not an officer of the regular army, but merely a person who had served as a volunteer in the Zulu war; where, it will be remembered, this gentleman raised a troop called "Willoughby's Horse." By his joining a belligerent force in the field against the troops of a friendly power Mr. Willoughby has placed himself beyond the protection of the British flag, and rendered himself liable to severe penalties, for which the French will doubtless press when they have an opportunity.

When the news reached Antananarivo of Admiral Miot's conditions, as expressed at the conference of May 29th, great indignation was felt by the people, and in the *Malagasy Gazette*, published on the 6th June, the following royal proclamation was published :—

"I, Ranavàlomanjaka, through the grace of God and the will of my people Queen of Madagascar and defender of its laws, declare unto you my subjects, that negotiations with the French have come to an end, for we can no longer endure their doings, for they say that this land of our ancestors is not ours but theirs, and has been theirs for a very long time; if we give it up to them, that is what they want, say they; but if we do not give it up to them, then they will take it by force, and we shall be deprived of our independence. In consequence of these unbearable threatenings, the words which we have long expressed must now become fact, namely, that every one shall stand up like a man and fight the enemy. It is not we who wish to fight, but our rights are threatened to be wrested from us by violence, and now the day for action has come. Remember that it is not merely my land and kingdom that are being invaded, but the land of our ancestors, the land where are the graves of many of our fathers and mothers, husbands, wives, and children; and those who do not rise to the strength of manhood now are friends of the French and not mine. Be diligent then in learning the art of war, for the day draws nigh when I shall examine your ability therein, and none shall I exempt from instruction. If there be any that you see not learning, be he who he may, bring him to the seat of judgment, and I shall fine him in money equivalent to the price of his head, for he is a traitor. Let each one beware of causing tumult, and be not excited by others to disorder, for order and unity are our strength in this business. Should tumult or disorder arise, then I shall make that town in which it arises responsible for it. Behold also the foreigners that are now in my land and kingdom ; take good care of them and of their possessions, for they are our friends, and have nothing to do with those who are fighting against us. Observe well these my words, and let each one show himself a man both in thought and deed, in order that the world may see that our courage is not mere talk."

"RANAVALOMANJAKA, Mpanjaka ny Madagaskara."

The French invasion by this time had exercised a powerful and living influence in sustaining the hatred both of France and French Catholicism in the Malagasy mind.

Consul Graves reached Antananarivo by the 13th of June and was received by the Queen at an audience on the 16th, when he addressed her as follows :—

"YOUR MAJESTY,—It is with great pleasure that I find myself in your presence this day. I had hoped to be able to visit this your capital at a less distant period from the date of my arrival in Madagascar, but I have in the meantime visited many of the towns on the coast held by your garrisons, at which I am glad to be able to state I was received with all courtesy by the governors in your Majesty's name.

"I was much struck on my journey here from the coast with the beauty of the country through which I passed ; its natural riches, its wealth of forests and pasture; but I could not avoid a feeling of regret that those riches had not been more developed by the hand of man, that those pastures were not covered with flocks and herds, the timber of those forests, which in some places appeared to have been recklessly destroyed by fire, was not being hewn into shape to be sent to countries where it would be so valuable, and which in return would send you many articles which Madagascar does not produce. I could not but feel sad at the thought of what a difference there might have been if the enlightened policy initiated by your Majesty's great predecessor, Radama I., under the advice, I believe, of a gentleman sent out by my government, of encouraging the introduction of foreign skill and capital, had been continued by his successors ; but I am indeed glad to hear that your Majesty, under the prudent guidance of his Excellency the Prime Minister, is prepared to do what the wise rulers of all countries and all ages have done, that is, to offer inducement to foreigners to help you by the introduction of their skill and capital, which may be wanting to your Majesty's subjects, in developing the natural resources of this island, and at the same time to increase the revenues of your government. As your Majesty is well aware, steam and the telegraph have annihilated distance, and now every country is able to send its natural products to the market which is best suited for them. Two countries in the far east, which through natural antipathies of race and religion till quite recently endeavoured to shut out foreigners from their dominions, have now been induced to open them to foreign trade, and I do not think that they have ever regretted their change of policy. I have spoken plain words, for I think it my duty to do so, both as the representative of a friendly nation, and as one who, if you will allow, will be myself a friend to you and your people. In conclusion, I beg to thank your Majesty for the good and wise words spoken by you in the last *Government Gazette* with regard to my countrymen : good because they order your subjects to keep the treaty engagements entered into by the government, and wise because they forbid them to commit acts which might unhappily turn friends into foes ; and I would beg to assure your Majesty that I also will spare no effort to compel my countrymen to observe the treaty between the two countries, and in this I feel sure I shall be seconded by Her Britannic Majesty's vice-consul in this city, Mr. Pickersgill, and the different British vice-consuls on the coast."

The Queen replied : " It is a great pleasure to us to see you, representative of our good friends, safely arrived in my capital. I take the words which you have just uttered as a fresh proof of the good friendship and the earnest wish your government entertain, towards us. I am delighted to assure you that I am always ready to do my best in opening my country to civilization and commerce with other nations, fully convinced that by so doing it tends not only to increase the wealth of our dominions, but good understanding between us and the Treaty Powers will ensue. I trust that the English nation, which has shown good feelings towards us for a very long period, will be willing as ever to help us morally in carrying out our views."

Four days afterwards Mr. Graves was present at a review of some infantry with field guns; the men, who were armed with Remington rifles, went through their drill very well, and marched and skirmished very fairly. These men had, it appears, been kept over the usual service time on account of the war. With the exception of the sight of the children from the schools being drilled in public, no one would imagine, writes Mr. Graves, from the appearance of the capital, that the country was engaged in a war. Nearly every one with whom Mr. Graves conversed expressed a desire that the war might be finished, in order that the country might progress, and this desire appeared genuine, although no inconvenience on account of the war had yet been felt by the governing class or the people of the interior.

Mr. Graves remained at the capital until the 1st of July,

when he returned *viâ* Mahanoro to Tamatave. On passing through Mahanoro he learnt that the French gunboat *Capricorne* had fired a couple of shell at the Malagasy fort there on the 25th June.

As soon as the consul left the city, orders were issued for the assembling of a great Royal Kabary on the plain at Mahamasina, which took place on the 3rd of July. It is well described by M. Tacchi in the *Madagascar Times*, from which the following account has been abridged.

For several days the town and neighbourhood were crowded with people flocking in from the country and every one was anxiously expecting the Queen's manifesto.

Mahamasina is a large plain at the foot of the mountain or which the city of Antananarivo is built. Very careful arrangements had been made for the order and marshalling of such a vast concourse of people, who assembled in their thousands, and a platform was erected for the sovereign and her ministers, from which the manifesto was delivered.

Cross-roads, some ten feet wide, were kept open in every direction by fences, and large prominent arches at each entrance enabled the people to steer their way in and out of the crowd without disorder or inconvenience. Doctors were stationed at intervals, their positions being denoted by a little white flag bearing a red cross. By ten o'clock the people were already crowding to their places, and some twenty to thirty thousand were already on the field, while every house and terrace, wall and balcony, overlooking the plain was covered with women. The different armies now began to pour upon the field. In the distance could be seen a field of steel approaching, glittering in the sun and resembling the waving of a moving cornfield; these were the warriors of the Aukaratra mountains. As they approached, it was seen that they were naked to the loins. Troops of spearmen do not march in such close order as ordinary troops, as the spear is carried in the attitude of hurling or thrusting, and their march is quite different. Their movements consist in falling a few paces backwards, like a man about to throw, and then in running forward with the body poised on one foot and the other leg raised as if hurling the spear. With different variations of these movements they advance with a symmetry and regularity never yet attained in their European drill, the drums beating time ; and at regular intervals they bring down their shields against the handles of their spears with a rattle resembling the dashing of the shingle on the sea-shore, followed by a simultaneous war-cry—a yell unearthly, which makes the blood run cold. Countless multitudes of these spearmen thronged in, some being led by old men over eighty years of age, others by a man whose size and height would make him conspicuous above the crowd. Alternating with the regiments of spearmen were bands of children of all ages armed with spear and shield, one band especially attracting notice as consisting of children between six and ten years of age. Their spears were about five feet long, and their shields of wood about fifteen inches in diameter.

All the schools of Antananarivo were drawn up in arms and the palace school made a very good show in their scarlet uniforms. There were also countless regiments of recruits armed with muzzle-loaders, flint-locks, and native-made guns.

The regular city regiments, consisting of 5,000 troops, marched on to the field at half-past eleven, and took up their positions along the central enclosure and along the different avenues dividing the plain. They were dressed in white tunics, dark blue cotton trousers, and brown helmets, and were all armed with breechloading rifles, which looked exceedingly bright and clean. At twelve o'clock the Queen left the palace, and it required more than an hour to pass through the city and descend to the plain.

The Queen arrived in a gilt palanquin carried by twelve bearers, and was received by the Prime Minister and Commander-in-chief, who was mounted on a white horse.

Her Majesty then mounted the platform and took her seat on the throne under the canopy. Ranavàlomanjaka III. was dressed in European costume, a robe of white silk trimmed with pink satin. She wore her hair plaited, and on her head was a light gold coronet. On a small table to her right was a large Bible, and on a similar table at her left was a scarlet and gold crown.

The Great Kabary.

The *Kabary* had now commenced. The Prime Minister, drawing his sword, saluted, the whole army presented arms, the bands played the national anthem, and the cannon in the battery on the heights of Ambodin Andohalo fired a salute of twenty-one rounds.

The saluting over, the troops came to "the shoulder," the trumpets and bugles sounded a flourish, and the Queen rose from her throne. In a few minutes a perfect silence ensued amongst the expectant multitude, and, waving her small golden sceptre over her people, Ranavàlona in a clear ringing voice addressed the people:—

"O ye people devoted to your fatherland, and ye soldiers strong (in battle), my heart is glad as I stand among you. I see that both I, your Queen, and this land of our ancestors are indeed dear to you; and when I have summoned you to assemble, you have come at the appointed time; therefore I express my satisfaction to you; life and the blessing of God be upon you.

"And I have to say to you, O my soldiers (for we all form part of the army now, both I and my people), that since those Frenchmen have invaded our land, I have done everything to bring about a termination of the war.

"Although we have already paid sums of money twice, it was my intention to give whatever would not involve my sovereignty or impair the independence of Madagascar, this land of our ancestors; for I particularly dislike, and it grieves me indeed, that your blood should be shed.

"But they were not willing, O my army, and want one third of Madagascar for themselves, and for us to pay £120,000, as also to indemnify all the losses of other nations during the war; and yet it was not we that destroyed that property, but the French alone bombarded and destroyed; they struck the first blow and did not even give notice of war, but even assailed women and children; and that even is not all they want, but I and my ancestors have been insulted, and they will not acknowledge me as Queen of Madagascar, but only as Queen of Imerina.[1]

"That then, it appears, is what France wants from us before the war will cease. I have announced that to you

---

[1] "Nous sommes en présence d'une nation constituée; la constitution n'est pas aussi serrée que celle d'une nation Européenne moderne; elle ressemble plutôt à ce qui existait chez nous au temps de la féodalité; l'Emirne représentant le domaine royal, régi directement par le souverain, et les autres provinces gouvernées par des chefs dont le vasselage, affirmé en théorie tend à devenir fictif selon la distance plus ou moins grande qui les sépare de la capitale. Cependant, le gouvernement central a presque partout des agents; il dispose des ports, dont il perçoit des douanes; il envoie des expéditions contre les tribus révoltées et les soumet. Les rois de Madagascar sont plus maîtres de leur royaume que ne l'etait du leur Philippe de Valois, Jean-le-Bon ou Charles V."—M. Saillens, p. 20.

and you have refused to accede. I have heard your refusal to accede to the above French demands, and these are my words to you. I join you, my people, in refusing the claims of any one to take the land, and I protest against Andrianimpoinimerina being insulted, for from father to son shall four of my ancestors have presumed to reign, and shall I Ranavàlomanjaka be dethroned? I and you, my people, will not have it! For is it not so, O my people?

"We now ask you, O people, to defend our just cause, for God gave this island of Madagascar to my ancestors and to yours, and your ancestors joined Andrianimpoinimerina and Lehidama in offering their bodies as a bulwark to this kingdom. And it was left as an inheritance to us Malagasy, but the French will take it away by force, they say; therefore I declare unto you:

"I shall fulfil, O my people, the share in the defence of the land which belongs to me as Queen. I have done so, but still I will do more, for, though I am a woman, I have the heart of a man, and I stand up to lead you forth to prevent and oppose those who seek to take our land; for God forbid, O ye people, that we should become the servants of foreigners. Is it not so, ye people?

"I am confident, O my people in arms, that we are all united as one in holding fast to this beloved land of our ancestors, and in acting so as to frustrate the evil designs of our enemy. For is it not so, O ye people?

"Further, I have to say to you I am extremely gratified to see the unity of combination in learning the art of war. Go on learning, and await my commands, for I shall not let the enemy come upon you unawares; for our courageous friends have gone to guard the coasts where the enemy will land.

"And I have to say to you, O people, that you may all know at once, there are no Frenchmen here, but they are foreigners entertaining good friendship toward us who remain here now; so let every one take good care not to interfere with their persons or property.

"However, my people, whatever be our strength, or however great our numbers, all this is in vain without the help of God; let every one of us therefore ask for His help for deliverance in this our just cause.

"And these are my last words to you, O my army, though our bodies be annihilated, we shall not be ashamed nor confounded, but our name and our fame will live for ever, because we rather chose to die than yield up our fatherland and the good which God has given us. For is it not so, O ye warriors?"

It required some little time for the Queen's words to be circulated among the crowd; but by the time Ranavàlona reached her last "Is it not so, ye soldiers?" the excitement and enthusiasm were at a climax, the people shouted, waved their spears and shields, and the sight was one never to be forgotten.

It was now the turn of the people to reply to Her Majesty. First came the representatives of the civilians and the different noble clans of the Hovas; their speeches consisted of assurances to the Queen that they were ready to fight. Their indignation about the Queen being called Queen of Imerina was very great. One spectator said, "We have seen your Majesty's caution in not wishing to endanger the lives of the people and in trying to make it up by paying money, &c.; but we won't have any more trying to make it up." At this expression the enthusiasm of the people was so great that the speaker's voice was no longer heard. Next spoke Rainilaiarivony, standing with his drawn sword in front of his young sovereign.

The Prime Minister's Speech.

"On this occasion of your appearance in Mahamasina, O Ranavàlomanjaka, before the people who are as your father and your mother, it is not a question of how many persons God left this kingdom to be ruled by, for you alone inherited it from your ancestors. You have come here before the people to thank us, to express your satisfaction at our preparations for war. But we, on the other hand, would say: It is not for you, the Queen, to thank us, but we, the people, come to thank you, O Lady, and may God's blessing be upon you. What! You have stated how, in order to preserve peace, you have relieved your conscience by offering money or anything that will not involve your sovereignty or impair the independence of Madagascar; you, the Queen, have informed us of that; and we, the people, when we consider this and are informed of what grieves and troubles you, we thank you. Long life, prosperity, and the blessing of God be upon you, O Ranavàlomanjaka!

"Your presence here this day, O Lady, makes us sad, for the enemy have spoken annoying and provoking words; but, nevertheless, we are rejoiced to see you come amongst us, for you have no more regrets; you say I do not like to shed blood if it can be prevented. We are glad indeed to hear that, and thank you, O Queen.

"And now these are our words, O Lady. We have paid money three times to those Frenchmen, once at Fénoarivo, once when the £48,000 indemnity was paid, and once the *Toalc* Arab dhow indemnity. All that is not enough, and still, not to have any after regrets, your Majesty has consented to be yielding, for the sake of peace, but they are still inexorable. What! and now they say you are not Queen of Madagascar, but only Queen of Imerina. We say therefore, O, Lady, that what you are doing is right, and we are ready to offer up ourselves in your service. God sees the hearts of our soldiers, and knows that our words will be supported by our arms. Our soldiers say, If we die in the defence of our fatherland, it is not death, but fame and glory: our flesh may be killed, but our fame will endure.

"And see again the way in which your people come to your call! How many days since you summoned them, and see their numbers, even greater than at your coronation! O Lady, hear our words. Rest assured. Ah, ah! they said, after three or four shells have been fired, Madagascar will give in immediately. Not only that, but they incite the Paris Government by saying that the English and other nations obtain privileges, while Frenchmen have none at all. However, we cannot blame the Paris Government for that. But still, they believe the *misrepresentations of their agents*, and are urged to attack us. Therefore we say, O Lady, rest well assured. We have seen their doings at Mojangà, at Anorontsanga, at Manjakandrianombana and Mahanoro, and at other ports, and you can fulfil the desires of your heart and remain at ease. What! and you, O Queen, shall say, 'I will go forth and lead you.' Those words rejoice our hearts indeed, O Lady; but still Andrianimpoinimerina and Lehidama your ancestors reigned in peace, and do thou also, O Lady, govern, rule, and reign at ease, for we are here to fight.

"Those brave ones to whom you have referred in your proclamation are sufficient to hold the country, much more the whole army. Therefore we say, O Lady, What is their blood, and what is our blood? Are we not both flesh and blood? As to this land which gave us birth, as to this portion of earth which God has allotted to us, yield not at all as far as the defence of this land is concerned; and fear nothing, for we have our army. Is it not so, ye warriors?

"We will not be the servants of these Frenchmen, for we prefer death rather than to serve them. Our forefathers, who knew not the true God, resented when their country was interfered with, and that is how their kingdom was founded; but we believe in the true God, O Lady, and I am not ashamed to say it. They do not appeal to reason at all in seeking an understanding, but continue to force us, especially by such expressions as 'They will spill our blood.' That is simply foul cursing, but we use no foul words towards them. They call us barbarians, but they who consider themselves as civilized have never published a declaration of war, but have fired on women and children; there is their civilization for you! What they call their right and justice stands out before all the world.

"They made a treaty with us in 1868, in which they acknowledged the Queen as Queen of Madagascar, but now again they go back on their own treaty.

"We paid a sum of money, and the very land for which we paid £48,000 is what they claim now. The affair was completed before the Emperor Napoleon III., and signed in the Government books ; and it is there stated that they will make no further claims whatsoever on our kingdom of Madagascar—and now again see what they are doing.

"I might continue with examples, but I will confine myself to words which will reassure you. These are the words of your soldiers: Do whatever it delighteth your heart to do, for in what concerns the upholding of this kingdom, and especially the sovereignty of your Majesty, we will see to that. For is it not so, O ye soldiers ?

"We are indeed exceedingly rejoiced to see our Queen come forth and offer to lead us to battle, but in return we say, Remain here at Antananarivo ; we are ready to withstand the enemy.

" There are foreigners here who are friends to you, therefore be assured, O Lady, that we shall observe the law towards them as far as is possible. Had you not told us, the people know that they are your friends, and be assured that we shall take care of them. And as regards the French making war upon us, especially in what concerns the command of the army, its organization and discipline, rest assured, for here am I Rainilaiarivony, and every one will have his part.

" The man who stands before your Majesty was born to defend this land and to serve his Queen. That is not an empty expression, for God sees into my heart. Come death, come loss, before the land shall be taken from us. Our war is a just war, and we do not fear ; if we die, we have right on our side, and God knows it. And the fame of those who die in the defence of their country will never perish.

"We must all die whether we fight or not, how much more so when our country is taken from us? But if we die in good actions, erect a stone, your Majesty, to our memories and trust in your army. Is it not so, O soldiers?

" Rainidriamanpandry (Governor of Tamatave) and those with him who are guarding the country on the coast say, ' Fear not, Ranavàlomanjaka, for we will not allow the enemy to come up.'

" Yesterday letters came from Mojangà. The French attacked by night, and, when our soldiers fired on them, they all jumped into the sea. And yet, your Majesty, they are a renowned nation ! But where we have justice and right on our side it is as your Majesty's father used to say, 'Truth is like a single hair which will knock down a bullock.' For when, think we, can Madagascar stand against France? But those who have right on their side have God. It is certain that God has had already great compassion and mercy on us, for it is now more than a good year since they opened war on us, and by His ordering here we are the same as ever. We have full confidence, O Lady, for we lean on God.

"It is not our little children that we shall force to fight, for why should we push forward the young ones? Let them first learn and grow in wisdom: for we are here, your Majesty, to do that. Is it not so, O soldiers?

"Fear not to reign then, O Lady, for your ancestors founded this kingdom, and we have sustained it. God has prospered you, therefore do not fear, but reign and rule in peace. For is it not so, O soldiers?"

After the Prime Minister had finished his speech the Queen again rose and said : "Since those are the words of you and your soldiers, I am confident ; life, prosperity, and the blessing of God be upon you."

Her Majesty then expressed a desire to see some of the schools go through their spear exercise. Some of the schools from the Betsileo Province then came forward chaunting their war-songs. The boys were about twelve years of age and were very proficient. Her Majesty now descended from the platform, and mounting a white horse rode round the plain of Mahamasina to review [1] the troops amid the cheers of the people. The Prime Minister then

---

[1] In emulation of Queen Elizabeth's famous review of her troops at Tilbury in the autumn of 1588, three centuries ago :—

"For our oath we swear
By the name we bear
By England's Queen and England free and fair,
Hers ever and hers still, come life, come death :
God save Elizabeth."

declared the Kabary at an end, the royal salute was given, and the troops and people dispersed.

The attack on the camp of the Malagasy near Tamatave to which the Prime Minister alluded was a reconnoissance made by the French towards Manjakandrianombana on the morning of the 28th June. Admiral Miot seems to have given up all ideas of an advance towards the interior, since later reconnoissances proved that the defences of the Malagasy position at Manjakandrianombana were far stronger than he had been led to believe; the outposts extending to Ampasimandrorora.

The French commander-in-chief informed Mr. Graves that he intended to blockade Fénoarivo and Mohambo, ports eight miles apart, with the same vessel. The consul was therefore doubtful whether a blockade of that nature could be considered effective. A French gunboat anchored off Fénoarivo on the 15th June, and between that date and the 25th July she only remained in all some eight days, while during her absence a German and a Danish vessel were able to enter the port and land goods. Yet Admiral Miot still maintained that the effective blockade had not been interrupted, and an English vessel attempting to discharge cargo on the 17th July was ordered out of the port by the French transport *Scorff*.

At the end of August the situation in Madagascar remained unchanged. It was reported that the Hovas had been harassed by the French shells and had withdrawn the greater part of their troops to some hills two miles in the rear of their fortified camp; but in all probability the withdrawal was only of invalids, for the Hovas suffer from the malarial fever of the coast nearly as badly as Europeans.

The French garrisons also by no means escaped the fever, and there was a good deal of sickness among the soldiers who had recently arrived from Tonquin; whilst the boy volunteers from Réunion were totally unfitted to withstand the malaria and existence on soldiers' rations.

On the 21st or 22nd August the *Allier* was patrolling the anchorage of Mahanoro with a boat which received some gunshots. The boat then returned to the ships, upon which a flag of truce was sent on shore to inform the foreign residents that the fort would be bombarded the following morning. This measure was carried out, the *Allier* discharging thirty shell against the fort; not one of these projectiles reached the town, which by the strict orders of Admiral Miot was untouched.

On the day following the last bombardment of Mahanoro a vessel, *The Coleridge*, hailing from Mauritius, put into Mananzary, where an American, styling himself Captain and Brevet-Major L. de R. du Vergé and U.S. consul for St. Paul de Loanda and south-west coast of Africa, landed with a staff of two secretaries, five companions and a servant. This small party proceeded to Antananarivo, but the object of their mission has not yet transpired.

Admiral Miot subsequently ordered two points in Passandava Bay to be occupied, Ambodimadiro and Ampassimena.[1] The latter of these was attacked by the Hovas, who were repulsed by the Réunion volunteers composing the garrison. Some skirmishing also appears to have taken place at Ambatolampy, near Mojangà.

Early in November two Friends of the Foreign Mission Association reached Tamatave from Mauritius, and at first they were refused permission to land on their way to the capital. As soon, however, as Admiral Miot heard that they were Friends, he changed his tone entirely. "Yes, he knew the Friends by report. If he let them go to the capital would they refrain from encouraging the Hovas in fighting?" They replied that as Friends they could not do otherwise. Would they give him their word not to do so? They would. He then consented to allow the missionaries to proceed.

The Admiral afterwards observed, "The Friends are peacemakers, and if they like to go up to Antananarivo and help to make peace between the Hovas and us I shall be glad. *I wish for peace!*"

Later news from Madagascar has been received by the

---

[1] It was reported that the French intended occupying Baramahamay, Ampasimbitika, and Anorontsanga.

Minister of Marine, from which it appears that after landing at Vohémar, a French column, composed of three hundred Europeans and nine hundred Antankaras (friendly Sàkalàva) attacked and carried the fort of Ambaniou to the south of Vohémar. Two hundred Hovas were killed in defending the position, whilst only four of the assailants were wounded.

On December 17th, when the Chamber commenced the debate on the colonial budget, M. Raoul Duval asked for explanations with regard to the intended action of the Government in Madagascar.

M. Pieyre (a Legitimist) said he was for striking a rapid and heavy blow in Madagascar, because that would be the best place for the transportation of hardened convicts. Admiral Peyron informed the Chamber that five points were now occupied by the French, but that a complete blockade was impossible. Measures were about to be taken to relieve the troops now in the island, who had been there a long time. The cost of the Madagascar expedition amounted, up to the present time, to upwards of twelve million of francs, which was more than double the credit voted for that purpose.

This is the plain unvarnished story of the French claims over Madagascar. It is written in no spirit of jealousy of our neighbouring ally, for it is sincerely to be hoped that a *modus vivendi* may yet be found which, without offence to any national susceptibilities on either side, may result in France obtaining all the benefit of an alliance with Madagascar in its best sense, without the loss which is entailed on a hostile and, in our present view, arrogant occupation. May Heaven help the right!

POSTSCRIPT.

SINCE the foregoing pages were written the author has had the gratification of reading the proofs of M. Saillens' valuable work, "*Nos Droits sur Madagascar*," in which he candidly exposes the historical rights of France over Madagascar, and gives a dispassionate and severely critical analysis of the so-called French grievances against the Hova Government. Some few of his pregnant remarks and illustrations have been added as notes or embodied in the preceding story; but M. Saillens' *bilan*, or summing up, is so very much to the point that it must be given at length, for it thoroughly expresses the disinterested opinion of European and Transatlantic observers who have closely studied the various phases of the Madagascar Question.

"What interest has France," asks M. Saillens, "in making war with the Hovas? Is it for colonization? But only a small portion of the country is habitable, that part which they occupy, the plateaux of Ankova. The coasts are altogether unhealthy; stricken with fever, our soldiers, sailors, and colonists are decimated every year. Are we to undertake the sanitation of this vast country, when we have not yet been able to sanitate an island much nearer to us, eminently fruitful, and three parts uncultivated, Corsica?

"To undertake the conquest of these highlands, to subdue the Hovas in their mountains, an army of twenty thousand men must be employed, a twenty years' war must be expected. A guerilla warfare of skirmishes and surprises, war to the knife, similar to that which the savage Corsicans carried on with the Genoese invaders. It is the vendetta at a thousand leagues from home: for a people which has tasted independence will not readily surrender it without a blow. It is one thing to conquer the inert masses of the Indo-Chinese populations without will or energy, indifferent to what master governs them; and quite another this fiery proud tribe, similar in many respects to the people fighting against them, who have never submitted to any one, and who, established among their mountains, will not willingly suffer their ancient liberty to be snatched from them.

"Indeed, for them independence is expansion. They are the most gifted by nature of all the tribes of the island which, speaking the same language, having probably the same origin, are evidently destined by nature to form one nation. We went to war for Italy on this principle, shall we proceed to fight against it in Madagascar, and do we not fear to create precedents which may, one day, be turned against ourselves?

"Better to shrug one's shoulders and not honour the Malagasy by making them of so much importance; for it is not a question of little or great causes; there are just causes and others which are not so. Principles have the same importance whether they apply to a people, a tribe, or only a man.

"In fact, we are not at all persuaded that the conquest of Madagascar has real advantages for France. Colonies nearly as extensive, and far less unhealthy, have not to this day enriched our treasury, and but moderately increased our commerce, although, for that matter, they have served well enough as a field of enterprise and traffic for other powers, and such may be the case for long years to come. The future benefits are not worth the sacrifices now to be made in human lives and money. The convincing proof is that England—who is experienced in colonies, who has had Madagascar several times in her hands, who could have taken possession of it under Radama I. without trouble, and under Radama II. could have accepted the offer of Protectorate which was made to her—England has not concerned herself about it. She has doubtless calculated on this conquest being too dear and producing too little. She even willingly abandoned to Radama I. a large tract of country (about one hundred square miles) which she had obtained from the natives at Port Loquez, in exchange for the treaty which abolished the slave-trade (23rd October, 1817).

"The only causes of the present war are, first and foremost, the jealousy of the French Jesuits, who cannot forgive the Protestants for having been the first to arrive, and for having obtained the preponderating influence at the court and in the country. The second is the extreme desire which our colonists of Réunion have exhibited on all occasions, for the last forty years, that this conquest should be accomplished. This desire, as we have said, contrasts with the former opposition presented by that same colony and her sister, the Isle of France, to our projects in Madagascar.

"It is true that the subsistence of these two islands comes in a great proportion from the great African island; that if Madagascar were closed to them their very existence would be threatened. But is it necessary to conquer Madagascar in order to oblige her to feed Réunion and Mauritius; cannot treaties be made? And this supply of provisions, is it not much more compromised by a state of continual hostility, which will render agriculture difficult in Madagascar, and consequently diminish the working of her products?

"It must be asked whether the colonists of Réunion have not other motives than those they openly proclaim. Their zeal in this affair does not appear to us perfectly disinterested. They offered to the Home Government to send to Madagascar some companies of volunteers, and they have, in fact, armed and equipped some companies which now second our regular troops out there. But it occurs to us that our colony of Réunion requires *coolies*; that her plantations suffer from lack of labour, and that it has become most difficult, not to say impossible, to import them from British India, as was the practice formerly. Réunion requires *coolies*, and it is well known what sort of servitude is expressed by these words, which is only the modern synonym, more or less mitigated, for that of *slaves*. Not being able to obtain Hindoos, Réunion hopes to obtain Malagasy. We merely indicate this fact, *en passant*, judging it superfluous to emphasize it by any further comment.

" On the whole, we believe that a violent policy will not give to us any real advantage, it will only alienate from us for ever the heart of this people, so sensible to good treatment and kindness.

" We believe in the policy of peace and we recommend it with all our might. The Hovas are disposed to make concessions to us. On the tenure of landed property, in particular, we have a right to expect much from them. They will open their ports to us, they will consent, possibly, to neutralize a portion of the disputed territory.

" Let us be conciliatory, let us triumph by generosity, let us invade this people by progress, by civilization and commerce; let us not identify our flag with that of a religion, which is not, after all, more French than Malagasy. These are the best means which we can employ in order to make of Madagascar that which she was formerly called, and that which she will be one day, for the benefit of the dark continent, an Oriental France."

The look-out is indeed hopeful when we find a Frenchman pointing out boldly and clearly to his fellow-countrymen their mistaken policy. The frank and candid tones of M. Saillens' exposition of the situation in Madagascar are refreshing after the euphemistic phrases of the Chauvinist writers across the Channel. It is time that the French public should be no longer hoodwinked by highly-coloured descriptions of the rich territories to be acquired by France.

M. Saillens has torn aside brusquely the veil of pretended patriotism and zeal which has shrouded hitherto the petty self-interests of the Réunion planters. Their deputy, M. Dureau de Vaulcomte, has vaunted the courage and resources of the Creoles whom he represents, but Admirals Galiber and Miot have already considerably rubbed the gilt from off the backs of the Réunion volunteers.

It is not fighting that the colonists want, it is the acquisition of an inexhaustible depôt of black labour.

SUPPLEMENTARY CHAPTER.

THE MALAGASY MISSION.

BY F. W. CHESSON, HON. SEC. OF THE MADAGASCAR COMMITTEE.

THE Malagasy envoys, the objects and results of whose mission to Europe, and especially to France, Captain Oliver has fully detailed in the foregoing pages, left Paris for London on Sunday, November 27, 1882. They quitted that city very abruptly in consequence of an incident which even now is by no means clearly understood in this country. They were most anxious to enter into a satisfactory arrangement with France, and to terminate a dispute which, if prolonged, they knew could not fail to be attended with the most injurious consequences to their country. In the ultimatum placed before them for their signature they were required not only to acknowledge a French protectorate on the north-west coast of Madagascar, and to undertake that throughout the island foreigners should be granted leases of land for a period of ninety-nine years, but also that the Malagasy Government should formally recognize a general claim of France to exercise jurisdiction over the whole island. On the two first points a compromise of some sort might perhaps have been arranged by a judicious diplomacy, but it was simply impossible for the envoys to affix their signatures to a document which virtually signed away the independence of their country. There can be little doubt that if the French people had known at the time the real nature of the issue between M. Duclerc and the envoys, they would have shown much less sympathy than they did with the action of their Foreign Office. The passage in the note to which the envoys took the gravest exception was as follows :—

"It is, however, well understood that these assurances cannot in any way question the general rights which France from all time has claimed over Madagascar, which rights the government of the Republic, under the present circumstances, is bound expressly to reserve, while sincerely hoping that the friendly and confiding spirit of the Hova Government towards us will allow us to refrain from calling them up again."

It is unnecessary to expose the monstrous nature of the claim thus made, as this has been most ably done by Captain Oliver in his narrative of French dealings with Madagascar. It is sufficient to say that the general rights of sovereignty which the Republic, through the pen of M. Duclerc, claimed to exercise over Madagascar is as historically unfounded as it is morally unjust. The envoys, even if they had not been actuated—as they undoubtedly were—by motives of patriotism, dared not make a concession which experience shows can only be wrung from a nation in the hour of its greatest extremity; and that the French Foreign Office was fully conscious of its inability to justify its conduct in the eyes of the French people, was subsequently shown by the suppression in the French Yellow Book of the passage in the ultimatum to which the envoys offered such unqualified resistance. The crisis was reached on the day already mentioned—November 27, 1882. As the envoys stubbornly refused to betray their country, M. Revoil on the day in question went to the Grand Hotel, which was the Malagasy head-quarters in Paris, and in the name of the French Ministry ordered the Malagasy flag to be hauled down. The envoys accepted the situation, and crossed the Channel on the same night, glad enough, no doubt, to be able to retire from a position which had become more and more intolerable. Mr. J. N. Richardson, M.P. for Armagh, who, accompanied by Mr. Sibree, visited the envoys shortly before they came to London, gave the public some idea of the state of semi-captivity in which he found them. M. Revoil had been constantly in their company from the moment they landed at Marseilles. This gentleman, Mr. Richardson said, was with the envoys during the three-quarters of an hour he and his companion were kept waiting at the entrance to their apartments, and it appears that most of that time was occupied with an altercation between them and their custodian as to whether the English visitors should be admitted to an audience. Such a state of tension could not long continue, and when it was brought to a termination the envoys did not attempt to conceal their feelings of relief.

On November 28th, the present writer first saw the chief envoy, Ravoninahitriniarivo, the Malagasy Minister for Foreign Affairs, and nephew of the Prime Minister, together with his colleague, Ramanarika. The father of the second envoy was educated at Manchester, and had consequently been able to impart to his son in childhood a knowledge of the English language. At the close of the interview, Ramanarika said to his visitor in earnest tones: "If you will help us this time, I cannot tell you what progress we will make."

On the same day a deputation from the Madagascar Committee waited on Lord Granville.[1] Sir Charles Dilke, the Under Secretary, was also present. A more influential body of persons has seldom attended at the Foreign Office to place before the Secretary of State the views of the public on a grave public question. Mr. A. McArthur, M.P., the chairman of the committee, forcibly stated the objects of the deputation. He disclaimed on the part of his

[1] See Appendix, p. 271.

colleagues any desire to ask for any privileges or immunities which they would deny to the French or any other nation; and urged the Government to use their influence to prevent war. The memorial of the Committee pointed out that there were five times as many English as French subjects in the island, and that our trade was quadruple that of the French. It also showed that France did not believe in her own protectorate. The levying of taxes is a vital act of sovereignty. It was therefore impossible to reconcile the conduct of the French "in freely paying the duties exacted by the Malagasy government on the north-west coast with their present contention that the Queen has no right to exercise authority in that part of the island." Equally pertinent was the statement of the memorialists that "they could not contemplate without alarm the prospect of Réunion and other French colonies making the north-west provinces of the island the scene of a traffic in African labour, which experience has clearly shown to be another form of slave-trade." In conclusion, they argued that the case was manifestly one for arbitration, and that our interests in the question entitled us to suggest to both parties that they should submit the dispute to the decision of a friendly Power. Mr. W. E. Forster, in the course of some weighty remarks, said that "his ground for taking so deep an interest in the matter was the fact that the kingdom of Madagascar was the one native power which stood before every African race as having made real progress in civilization and Christianity;" Sir Henry Barkly urged the value of Madagascar to Great Britain as a source of food supply for Mauritius ; Bishop Ryan laid stress on the fact that, notwithstanding the present claims of France, she had, again and again, recognized the Malagasy sovereigns as the rulers of the whole island ; and Admiral Sir John Hay dwelt on the increased difficulties which a French protectorate of Madagascar would cause to the British navy in the suppression of the slave-trade. The duty of bringing before Lord Derby some details of the work of the missionary societies in Madagascar devolved on Mr. Arthur Marshall, a director of the London Missionary Society, Mr. J. N. Richardson, M.P., of the Friends' Missionary Association, and the Rev. F. A. Gregory, of the Society for the Propagation of the Gospel. They showed that the Malagasy had been redeemed from barbarism chiefly by English effort.

Lord Granville, in his reply, recognized the influential and representative character of the deputation, and made graceful allusion to the fact that it included several members of Parliament who sat on the opposition side of the House. He made two statements of great importance. He said that "in 1853 and 1854 there were discussions between the two governments which resulted in the understanding that neither would take action with regard to Madagascar without previous consultation with the other;" and with regard to the proposed French protectorate over a large portion of the island, he remarked that "he was not aware of any treaty which gave such a right to France." Lord Granville occupied a difficult position. It was desirable that he should be perfectly frank as to the Foreign Office view of the French claims, and at the same time equally careful not to wound the *amour propre* of the French Government. This he did with great judgment and tact, and the friends of the Malagasy greatly appreciated his manifest desire to promote a peaceful settlement of a complicated and difficult question.

It will be seen that the deputation brought before Lord Granville the various considerations which moved large sections of the English people to sympathize with the Malagasy in their troubles. Some critics objected to this, because, they said, that the philanthropic feelings and the selfish interests of England were offensively mixed up together. Surely this was hyper-criticism with a vengeance! The deputation would have justly exposed itself to blame if it had not made a complete statement of its case to Lord Granville. Moreover, it is puerile to pretend that there is any incompatibility between philanthropy and legitimate commerce, especially in Madagascar, where

ABOLITION OF SLAVERY. 255

these two agencies working in combination have succeeded in banishing the slave-trade from the island. Unfortunately in this country there are many persons of stunted sympathies, who are unmoved by injustice when the sufferer happens to have a black skin; and recent events have made it painfully apparent that this narrow-minded class is by no means confined to members of one political party.

It is certain that the French policy in Madagascar has been materially influenced by the planters of Réunion, who depend almost wholly upon servile labour for the means of carrying on the industries of their island. For many years past they have been in the habit of obtaining natives from the Sàkalàva coast; and so long as the Malagasy themselves kept up the slave-trade, there was no danger of their losing access to so convenient a market. But when Queen Ranavàlona proposed to enforce the treaties which enabled her to prohibit the embarkation of her subjects on foreign vessels without a passport, the pro-slavery party in Réunion feared that a vital blow was about to be struck at the labour traffic on the north-west coast of Madagascar. The English Government unwittingly precipitated the crisis by stopping coolie immigration between India and Réunion — a measure rendered necessary by the systematic cruelty and injustice with which the planters treated the Indian subjects of the Queen. One of the noblest acts of modern times was the abolition of slavery in the French colonies by the Provisional Government of 1848. Senator Schœlcher, the author of that policy, is still living, and it is grievous to know that the security of the great measure which he carried nearly forty years ago should now be jeopardized by a Republican government whose pride it should have been to guard the illustrious traditions which it had inherited from the days of Lamartine and Arago.

On December 14, 1882, the envoys were entertained at a splendid dinner at the Fishmongers' Hall. Mr. J. Hampden Fordham, the Prime Warden, presided; and the Lord Mayor and several civic dignitaries were present. Mr. Fordham, on welcoming his Malagasy guests to the hall, assured them that they had the hearty sympathy of the citizens of London, who "earnestly hoped that in the councils of that great nation which was our nearest neighbour, a just and pacific policy, which was the truest interest of every government, might prevail." This struck the true keynote of the national feeling. The chief envoy made a telling reply, which was translated by Mr. W. C. Pickersgill, the interpreter to the mission. His Excellency paid a tribute to France as well as to England. He said: "Through the help and teaching which have come from you English, and from the French also, we have struggled to leave our ignorance behind us, and have come to the foot of civilization's ladder. We are no longer lying asleep in the mire below; and I tell you most truly, gentlemen, that our ambition is to climb that ladder, and we fail to see what right any other nation has to prevent us from climbing it in peace." The envoy assured the citizens of London that the Malagasy did not want to quarrel with France, whom they regarded as one of the great and wise nations of the world, but that their anxious desire was to carry out faithfully the treaties they had made with her and with other Powers. Speaking in a homely but pleasant vein, Ravoninahitriniarivo remarked that "the courtesy and friendliness" of the great city of London would be, in the language of the Malagasy proverb, "like kine that are born in summer pasturages—at once both pleasure and profit."

The envoys subsequently visited the provinces, and were entertained by the civic authorities at Birmingham, Manchester, Liverpool, and Nottingham. They were delighted with their reception, especially at Manchester. At Nottingham they were entertained by the Duke and Duchess of St. Albans. They also spent a day at Reading, where they were the guests of Mr. George Palmer, M.P. The visits they paid to manufactories and workshops impressed them with a sense of the greatness and power of civilization, and inspired them with the desire to introduce into their own country the capital and enterprise which had achieved such stupendous results.

In the latter part of February, 1883, the envoys sailed

for the United States, and remained in that country from March 3rd to March 31st. Their interview with the President took place on the 7th of that month. They had no difficulty in negotiating a treaty with the United States, and it was ratified at the State Department on March 13th. The treaty recognized Queen Ranavàlona's sovereignty as embracing "the whole of Madagascar." The land question was settled by the concession to American subjects of leases perpetually renewable. In a remarkable passage the Malagasy Government declared that they were desirous of promoting the development of the natural resources of the kingdom as well as of advancing the various useful, mechanical, and agricultural industries for which the country was fitted. The Government therefore promised that if American citizens desired either to engage in industrial pursuits, or to instruct the people in the useful arts, applications on the part of such persons for facilities to carry out these objects would be favourably entertained. Such a treaty reflected great credit upon the Washington Government, and also upon Colonel Robinson, the American Consul at Tamatave, who took a leading part in the negotiations.

The American Treaty authorized the Malagasy Government to regulate, or, if they thought fit, even to prohibit, the importation of intoxicating drinks into the island. This went far beyond the provision on the same subject which was introduced into the English treaty. The Malagasy authorities were authorized to stop the importation by British subjects into Madagascar of any spirits which on examination proved to be deleterious to the public health ; but it was stipulated that the operation of testing should be performed exclusively by Europeans, nominated in equal proportions by the Malagasy and the English. Lord Edmond Fitzmaurice, Under-Secretary for Foreign Affairs, took an enlightened interest in a clause which marks an important advance in the relations of England with semi-civilized countries. It is satisfactory to know that the treaty with Siam invests the government of that country with a similar power of dealing with the evils of the liquor traffic.

On the return of the envoys to London, they made immediate preparations to pay their long-delayed visit to Germany. On the eve of their departure, *i.e.*, on April 17, 1883, the Madagascar Committee, headed by Mr. A. McArthur, M.P., Sir Harry Verney, M.P., Sir T. F. Buxton, M.P., Mr. G. Palmer, M.P., Admiral Gore Jones, and the Rev. Malcolm Maccoll, waited upon their Excellencies at the Alexandra Hotel. Mr. McArthur, in introducing the deputation, expressed a hope that the mission of the envoys would be as successful at Berlin as it had been at Washington. Ravoninahitriniarivo, in reply, gave a glowing account of his American tour. The Americans, he said, while clinging to their ancient friendship for France, had been hearty in their manifestations of sympathy with Madagascar, and equally emphatic in declaring that the French by their present policy were tarnishing their national honour. The Malagasy, it may be added, were amazed at the power of public opinion in the United States.

A few days after this interview the envoys arrived at Hamburg, where they were the guests of Herr Albrecht Oswald, a German merchant, who has extensive commercial relations with Madagascar. They met with a most hospitable reception. At a dinner held in their honour, the guests included the Royal Prussian envoy, the Imperial Austro-Hungarian consul, and several members of the Hamburg Senate. The chief envoy spoke modestly of the progress which the Malagasy had been able to make, remarking that "it could only be rightly estimated by those who knew the hole of the pit out of which they had been dug." He aptly quoted this Malagasy proverb: "If a person will neither milk the cow nor hold the calf, but only lick the cream, he is not dealing fairly." His audience had no difficulty in making the application for themselves, but he naïvely added: "It is a great pleasure to us to assure you that no one from your land is doing, or attempting to do, that in Madagascar." At Berlin the envoys were able to conduct to a successful issue the negotiations for a new treaty with Germany. They were graciously received by several members of the Imperial family, but they did not see Prince Bismarck.[1]

In June the envoys returned to Paris for a short time, and in July they left for their own country. Before they sailed they met the Directors of the London Missionary Society, who took the deepest interest in their mission. The French Government entertain a strong prejudice against the missionaries of this society—a prejudice which all who know anything either of the personal character or of the labours of men like Ellis, Shaw, Cousens, Price, Jukes, Moss, or Sibree, must regard as inexplicable. Mr. Arthur Arnold, M.P., who has seen missionary influence at work in various parts of the world, says that, "as a rule, it is a power exercised in support of the weak, and a protest, not always effectual, against the rapacity and licentiousness which are too often displayed by Europeans of every country when they are beyond the reach of law." This statement is perfectly true, and it is especially true in Madagascar, where the missionaries, while they have done all that Christian teachers could lawfully do to protect the natives against wrong, have at the same time been careful to avoid the political arena. Such ought ever to be the attitude of missionaries, whatever form of Christianity they profess, and in whatever land their lot may be cast.

[1] It is only right that the valuable help which Dr. Karl Blind has rendered to the Malagasy cause in the German press should receive a word of acknowledgment.

The envoys took with them a letter from Her Majesty to Queen Ranavàlona. They greatly appreciated the efforts which Lord Granville had made to promote peace; and they also expressed a lively sense of the kindness they had received from Sir Francis Seymour, whose official duties brought him into frequent contact with them. In addition to the letter referred to, they were the bearers of a beautifully illuminated address to their own Sovereign, the gift for the most part of a number of British subjects who had resided in Madagascar, and who, in this graceful form, thanked Her Majesty for the protection and hospitality they had enjoyed in her territories.[1] The Hon. Secretary of the Madagascar Committee performed his last official act in connection with the mission of the envoys by placing this address in their hands; and he is not soon likely to forget the earnestness with which Ravoninahitriniarivo assured him of the gratitude which the Malagasy would ever cherish towards their English friends. The envoys, a few hours later, left England for South Africa. They were offered a safe-conduct, but they naturally declined to return to their own country in a French steamer. St. Augustine's Bay, on the south-west coast of Madagascar, is only three days' sail from Natal; and on their arrival at Durban they found a vessel which was about to leave for that part of

---

[1] The address included the signatures of Sir Archibald Anson, Mr. Joseph Sewell, Mr. A. Kingdon, the Rev. J. Sibree, &c.

the island. They embarked without delay, and as the French blockade was not rigorously maintained, they succeeded in landing on the coast, and in then making their way to the capital.

It is gratifying to know that on their arrival at Antananarivo the warmth of their reception showed that their arduous and patriotic efforts to serve their country in distant lands were fully appreciated by the Malagasy Government and the people.

APPENDIX.

SOATSIMANAMPIOVANA.

PÈRE FINAZ, who accompanied M. Lambert, habited as a layman, in the capacity of secretary, under the *alias* of M. Hervier (the name of his mother), to Antananarivo in June, 1855, thus describes Soatsimanampiovana at that date. (See *Père de la Vaissière*, vol. I. p. 235.)

"Soatsimanampiovana, not far from the forest of Angavo, is the fine country house of M. Laborde. We made our entry there on the 10th June at noon. A military band playing in our honour various familiar pieces, whilst a choir of young girls sang Malagasy songs in welcome of the travellers. The whole place was holding a *fête* for our reception. But what impressed us most of all was the patriarchal hospitality of our host. What an excellent man is dear M. Laborde! How nobly and sincerely he welcomed us! In perfect community of ideas and sentiments with us on the subject of the great project (*i.e.*, the conspiracy against the throne of Ranavàlona), it seems as if we three had been old friends of long standing. We love one another like three brothers. (*The two slave-dealers and the Jesuit priest!*)

"Soatsimanampiovana means 'beauty without change.' Its position is most agreeable. The country house is situated opposite a neat village, the residence of fifteen hundred workmen, whom M. Laborde directs, and with whom he has indeed created veritable marvels of industry. Some ten years since these localities were nothing but an uninhabited desert. Now amidst vast reservoirs of water formed by dams with sluices furnishing the various manufactories with abundant water power, there stands a blast furnace of cut stone for mineral smelting, and besides a cannon foundry, where there are now twenty field-pieces, ready for delivery, and a mortar which is now being bored. From here we pass to a pottery and glass factory, whilst the buildings constructed for silk manufacture and soap-making are at a little distance. Further on, in a retired corner, is the arsenal for congreve rockets.

"It is one man who has created all this, and who carries on the works by artisans whom he has himself instructed.

"When M. Laborde arrived in the country, another Frenchman, named M. Droit, had already tried to establish a gun factory in the village of Ilafy, near Antananarivo. M. Droit was a native of Franche-Comté. Coming to Mauritius, he there married the daughter of a Hova named Ramboavao, long resident in that island, where he was known under the name of Joly-cœur. (See Ellis's *Hist.*, vol. I. p. 157.) M. Droit left Mauritius in 1829 for Anjouan (one of the Comoros), and from thence, at the instigation either of his wife or of her grandparents, he went up to Antananarivo, where he preceded M. Laborde. He was exiled thence about 1835, for having refused to implicate himself in the treasonable affair of the French vessel *Le Voltigeur* (sold to Ranavàlona, and sent by her into St. Augustine's Bay to surprise the Sàkàlava chiefs). He accordingly sought refuge with Ramanetaka at Mohilla, where he died on the 1st January, 1837. We shall find, later on, Madame Droit entrusted by France to undertake the office of governess to the two daughters of Ramanetaka. A clever smith, Droit succeeded in manufacturing muskets, but he was unable to bore them conveniently. M. Laborde, at the Queen's desire, assisted M. Droit, and was soon able not only to accomplish the proper boring of the muskets, but to cast and bore ordnance as well. The establishment at Ilafy being badly situated, too far from timber and water supply, M. Laborde moved the works to the spot where they now are erected at about eight leagues from the capital."

Dr. H. Lacaze, who visited Soatsimanampiovana in 1868, after its abandonment, thus described the aspect of the place at the time that M. Garnier was negotiating the treaty. (*Souvenirs de Madagascar*, par M. le Dr. H. Lacaze, p. 39.)

"At 10 o'clock we perceived at a little distance a number of houses with their roofs off and considerable buildings in ruins. This sight announced our arrival at a place of exceptional importance such as we had not been accustomed to since leaving Tamatave. We were at Soatsimanampiovana, the former dwelling of M. Laborde. This establishment is built in the midst of hills round which winds a small brook with numerous lakes, whose surface glistened from afar.

"A large house in timber roofed with thatch, surrounded by trees with red blossoms, the *Zahama*, a species of laurel, enclosed within a red clay wall, crowns the summit of a hill. . . . After breakfast we made the tour of the establishment and its surroundings, and M. Poncet (a very black little man, who had belonged, *as a slave*, to M. Laborde since his infancy), who spoke French well, made an excellent cicerone. He had assisted in the creation of the places which we were about to visit and could give us most interesting details concerning them. The house is large and built of solid timber, surrounded by verandahs. It has not been inhabited for some time, and signs of neglect and dilapidation are visible on all sides. Débris of trellis, mills for various grain, an immense kitchen with a fireplace where there were still enormous cooking pots worthy of Homeric feasts.

"In the rooms and the saloon were pictures representing the battles of Napoleon and scenes of Malek-Adel. Outside the enclosure were numerous outbuildings. Soatsimanampiovana is entirely the creation of M. Laborde during the reign of Ranavàlona I. He made there not only an industrial town but also a pleasure retreat. On a hill, in the vicinity of that on which the residence is situated, is to be seen a large village, now abandoned, as well as a small palace for the Queen, whose officers, soldiers, and suite occupied the cottages surrounding it. The roofs have been removed, and for the most part there only now remain the red clay walls. In the plain below there is visible a fine house with storeys which was built for Radama II. when he was yet a prince, besides extensive buildings and a large water conduit leading to the various wheels. These houses and manufactories were constructed solely from native resources, and included a foundry, a gun factory, lime-kilns, brick-yards, glass and pottery ovens, &c. To-day they are nothing but magnificent ruins. It was in 1841 that M. Laborde created this vast establishment ; and escutcheons surmounted by *a crown* bear the above date with the *name of the Queen* and the initials J. L. During many years the court was accustomed to stay here, and the large concourse of work-people, of from 5,000 to 6,000 men (*all slaves*), occupied in transporting ore and timbers, with the fêtes, contributed to give life and animation to a country otherwise unattractive, and to-day remaining silent and deserted.

" M. Laborde, exiled in 1857, after the conspiracy in which he was accused (*convicted?*) of having taken part, was obliged to leave all, and a few years have sufficed to transform into ruins this monument of the intelligence and industry of one man. It is sad to traverse these fine edifices. Some aqueducts in granite conducted water to the wheels of the mills ; the large foundry is entirely constructed of grey granite and covered in with tiles ; the doors and windows are arched in a style not to be surpassed in civilized countries. Leaving Europe when young, and cast by shipwreck on the coast of Africa, M. Laborde by his sole intelligence, with the help of some Manuals, became architect and engineer, and by the force of his genius was able to inculcate into the rude native workmen the skill necessary to aid him in creating all these industries. Since the departure of the builder and manager, all is fallen, and to-day it would seem as though an age of vandalism had passed over the ruins.

" The soil throughout this region is red, composed of ochreous tuff and loam, so compact that solid walling can be constructed with it fit for houses and their surroundings. The neighbouring mountains are, it would appear, rich in iron and copper ores. Wood is employed as fuel, and as it is obtained from afar it needed a legion of *slaves, not receiving any pay*, to enable M. Laborde to construct the establishment and work his factories without loss.

" On a neighbouring hillock adjoining the royal palace is the tomb of M. Laborde's brother, a monument in quartzose granite, square and about three mètres in height, surmounted by a column and a lightning conductor. On the opposite side of the valley, on the left bank of the stream, is the tomb of Rainisoka, the grandmother of Radama, and of some relation to the Queen. Game is plentiful throughout these lakes. Not far from M. Laborde's house is a magnificent piece of water, enlarged and artificially dammed for the preservation of a water supply in dry seasons, so that the mills should never want for power."

ULTIMATUM, PRESENTED BY REAR-ADMIRAL PIERRE AND M. BAUDAIS, TO THE QUEEN OF MADAGASCAR, 1st JUNE, 1883.

THE French Government, animated by a sincere desire to re-establish as soon as possible with the Government of Her Majesty, Queen Ranavàlona II., the relations of peace and friendship which have for a long time united them, but determined to employ all means to preserve intact the conventional situation which it has acquired in Madagascar, has given order to the undersigned to make known to the Government of Queen Ranavàlona the conditions on which

APPENDIX. 269

depends, henceforth, the maintenance of the good relations which France desires to preserve with this Government.

1. The Government of the Queen shall effectively recognize the rights of sovereignty, or the protectorate which the treaties concluded with the Sàkalàva chiefs confer on us, over certain territories. These territories extend from Baly Bay to the west as far as Antongil Bay to the east, passing by Cape Amber.

2. The law, No. 85, in complete contradiction with Art. IV. of the treaty of 1868, shall be repealed, and the Queen shall engage to give formal and immediate guarantees, at a time and place appointed by the Commissioners of the French Republic provided with full powers from their Government to settle this question, in order that in future the right of ownership or letting on long lease can be exercised in perfect liberty by all French subjects.

These conditions will form the subject of a special convention, to sign which the Government of Her Majesty, Queen Ranavàlona II., shall engage to send, within a period of fifteen days, a plenipotentiary to the place pointed out by the French Commissioner. This plenipotentiary shall possess full powers necessary to accept the revision which the Commissioner of the French Republic may propose if expedient of all or part of the treaty of 1868.

3. The Government of the Queen shall agree to pay, within thirty days from the date of acceptance of the present ultimatum at Tamatave, into the hands of the Commissioners of the French Republic, the sum of one million of francs, that is, 200,000 dollars (£40,000), as an indemnity due to French subjects. The undersigned, as soon as the present ultimatum is accepted, will make known to the Government of Queen Ranavàlona the conditions which they require in guarantee of the execution of the clauses enumerated above.

These conditions are not presented to the Government of Queen Ranavàlona II. to be discussed, but to be accepted by *yes* or *no* within an interval of eight days. This period has been thus allowed for : three days to go from Tamatave to Antananarivo (120 miles) ; the same for return from Antananarivo to Tamatave ; *two days for consideration.*

The undersigned have received from their Government formal orders not to leave the slightest ambiguity as to the terms fixed upon.

If therefore the acceptance should be ambiguous or incomplete, or if it should not reach, before midnight on the 9th and 10th of June, the Commissioner of the Republic, who will transmit it to the commander-in-chief of the Naval Division of the Indian Ocean, Rear-Admiral Pierre will have, with regret, to open fire on the defences of the town of Tamatave, taking possession of them, and destroying all the Government establishments of Her Majesty Queen Ranavàlona on the east coast of Madagascar.

The custom-house of Tamatave will be occupied, and the dues collected by the French authorities, until they amount to the sum claimed, and until complete satisfaction as before mentioned shall be obtained.

Ulterior measures will be taken towards obtaining a guarantee that the right of ownership shall be obtained by our countrymen.

The results of the operations of the Naval Division on the north-west coast are such as to show the Government of Her Majesty, Queen Ranavàlona II., the efficacious means at the disposal of the Rear-Admiral, commander-in-chief, for carrying out similar effects.

On behalf of the Government of the French Republic, the undersigned hereby hold the Government of the Queen Ranavàlona II., as well as the Prime Minister, personally responsible for any attempts that may be made, throughout Madagascar, against the French as well as against foreigners of whatever nationality. Any attempt made directly or indirectly on their lives, liberty, property, family, or goods of their families, shall be made good by indemnities of which the undersigned will fix the amount, and the payment of which shall be exacted immediately.

If the Government of the Queen, after having accepted the conditions of this present ultimatum, shall cause any premeditated delay in the accomplishment of one or more of its pledges, or if the plenipotentiary at any time should try to plead the insufficiency of his powers, hostilities will commence without further summons.

The undersigned have a firm hope that the Government of Queen Ranavàlona, in accepting these conditions, of which it is impossible to deny the moderation, will relieve them from having recourse to the employment of force, and nothing will give them greater satisfaction than to avoid the useless shedding of blood.

(*Signed*) PIERRE.
(*Signed*) BAUDAIS.

(See also No. 25 Diplomatic Document.)

APPENDIX. 271

The *Times* of November 29, 1882, contained the names of many members of the deputation, including Mr. Alexander McArthur, M.P., the Right Hon. W. E. Forster, Sir H. D. Wolff, M.P., Admiral Sir John D. Hay, M.P., Sir Harry Verney, M.P., Sir W. McArthur, M.P., Sir H. T. Holland, M.P., Sir J. Clarke Lawrence, M.P., Mr. Alderman Fowler, M.P., Mr. J. W. Richardson, M.P., Mr. Alderman Lawrence, M.P., Dr. Cameron, M.P., Mr. Dillwyn, M.P., Mr. Broadhurst, M.P., Mr. Talbot, M.P., Mr. Cropper, M.P., Mr. G. Palmer, M.P., Mr. Thomasson, M.P., Mr. Arnold Morley, M.P., Mr. T. R. Hill, M.P., Mr. T. Lea, M.P., Mr. W. Fowler, M.P., Mr. H. Lee, M.P., Mr. Summers, M.P., Mr. Gorst, M.P., Mr. Mackie, M.P., Colonel Gourley, M.P., Mr. A. Grant, M.P., Sir Henry Barkly (late Governor of Mauritius), Sir William Muir, General Tremenheere, Bishop Ryan, The Revs. Canon Gregory, Canon Money, Prebendary Tucker, F.A. Gregory, J. Guinness Rogers, J. O. Whitehouse, J. Sharp, C. E. B. Reed, and Newman Hall, Messrs. Donald Matheson, J. G. Alexander, Edmund Sturge, C. E. Mudie, J. Bevan Braithwaite, J. Herbert Tritton, S. R. Scott, J. Kemp Welch, J. H. Fordham, Arthur Marshall, Joseph Hoare, F. W. Chesson, H. Escombe (M.L.C., Natal), J. E. Teall, A. Kingdon, &c. There were also present representatives of the Society for the Propagation of the Gospel, the London Missionary Society, the Aborigines Protection Society, the Friends' Missionary Association, the Anti-Slavery Society, the British and Foreign Bible Society, and the Evangelical Alliance.

INDEX.

ABDALLAH, 66.
Abdally ben Ally, 66.
Accession, Ranavàlona III., 159.
Admiral Cécile, 17.
—— Galiber, 177.
—— Miot, 208, 241.
—— Peyron, 94, 244.
—— Pierre, 112, 139, 142.
—— Jauréguiberry, 78.
—— Le Timbre, 85.
Administration, 34, 157.
Admiralty despatches, 124.
African slaves, 12, 15, 16, 25, 153, 246, 251.
Alakaosy, 57.
Algeria, 136.
Algiers, 20,
Alype, Pierre, 188.
Ambassadors to Europe, 90.
—— Paris, 94.
—— London, 102.
—— America, 148.
—— Germany, 150.
—— Italy, 150.
Ambassiandro, 74.
Ambitious schemes of M. Lambert, 15.
Ambodin-Andohalo, 39, 49.
Ambohimanga, 56, 78.
Ambohimirimo, 152.
Ambohitsorohitra, 40.
Ambongo, 64.
Ambositra, 132.
Amour du clocher, 1.
Amparibé, 11.
Ampasibitika, 71.
Ampassambitika, 243.
Ampasimena, 73, 87.
Anaty-Rova, 155.
Ancestral idols, 155.
Andohalo, 49,
—— Promulgation of Law at, 49.
Andoka, 57.
Andriamananizao, 157.
Andriambelo, 155.

Andriamifidy, 87, 157.
Andrianibiby, 220.
Andrianimpoinimerina, 153, 160, 232.
Andrianisa, Mr., 91, 127.
Andrian Mihaza, 7.
Andrian Souly, 80.
Andriantasy, Plenipotentiary, 175.
Angareza, King, 65.
Angoulake River, 66.
Ankara Province, 61, 76.
Ankaratra mountains, Spearmen from, 228.
Antananarivo, the capital, 1.
—— Embargo on steamer named, 86.
Antankara, French allies, 244.
Antanosses, 194.
Antine, 68.
Antongil Bay, 113.
Arab dhows, trading under French colours, 57.
Arnoux, M., 6.
Arrival of M. Baudais at the capital, 2.
Arvoy, M. d', 24.
Attack on Tafondro, 64.
Attacks on Tamatave, 121, 133.
—— Manjakandrianombana, Camp of, 241.
Avaratr' Ilafy, 13.
Azy mainty molahy, 40.

BAKARY, 51.
Baker, Mr., 12.
Baly Bay, 15, 64.
Banishment of conspirators, 26.
Baragnon, M., 99.
Baramahamay, 243.
Bardet, Mr., 173.
Barkly, Sir H., 253.
Baron Jeanne, 7.
Baron, Mr., F.L.S., 156.
Baudais, M., 1, 59, 72.
Bavatoubé Peninsula, 24.
Beautemps-Beaupré, Le, 113, 121.
Beforona, 132.

INDEX.

Behamaranza, 87.
Bekirondro, 57.
Belitsara River, 66.
Bellanger, M., 67.
Bémanéviky, 115.
Bembatoka River and Bay, 115.
Bellones, Cape, 215.
Beravony, Queen, 80.
Berlin, 150.
Betanimena, 6, 10.
Betsileo, 34.
Betsimisaraka, 6.
Billot, M., 94.
Binao, Queen, 87, 100.
Bismarck, Prince, 101, 150.
Blockade of east coast, 208.
Boisy d'Anglas, Baron, 188.
Bombardment of Mojangà, 116.
—— Tamatave, 6, 121.
—— Hivondro, 121.
—— Foule Point, 122.
—— Fénoarivo, 174.
—— Vohémar, 172.
—— Mahanoro, 173, 242.
Bombay, 7, 173.
Bona Mousa, 66.
Bouéni tribe, 51.
Bourbon, 59.
Boursaint, La, 121, 172.
Boutet, Commandant, 172.
Boyle, Captain, R.N., 176.
Brooklyn, The, United States' corvette, 177.
Brooks, Mr., 11.
Brossard de Corbigny, Baron, 31.
Brun, Charles M., Minister of Marine, 111.
Brutail, Frère, 132.
Buet, Charles M., 47.
Buisson, Lieut., 51.
Burning the national idols, 153.

CABINET of Berlin, 101.
Cameron, Missionary, Architect, Engineer, 11.
Campan, M., Chancelier of French Consulate, one of the Laborde heirs, 47.
Canham, M., 11.
Capricorne, The, 208.
Captain Johnstone, 114.
—— Boyle, 176.
Cassas, M., Consul and Commissioner of France in Madagascar, 47.
—— Removed to Hongkong, 48.
Cazet Père, Préfet-apostolique at Antananarivo, 39.
Cécile, Admiral, 17.
Challemel-Lacour, M., 112.

Chamber of Deputies, Debates in, 182, 192, 244.
Charges against Government of Madagascar, 4.
Charges against Mr. Shaw of poisoning, 124.
—— of imprudent conduct, 124.
—— Captain Johnstone, R.N., 114, 130.
—— acting consul, 126; correspondence, 128.
Chart of Concession to M. Lambert, 28, 32.
Chesson, Mr., 98, 248.
Chick, Mr., 11.
Chiefs, Sàkalàva, acknowledge Radama II. as sovereign, 66.
—— French treaties with, 68.
Christianity acknowledged by the Government of Madagascar, 33, 154.
Christians, Persecution of, 27, 152.
Clarendon, Lord, 12.
Clément Laborde, M., 40, 43.
Cloche, La, 92.
Clochetterie, La, 48.
Cloué, M., 61.
Codification of laws, 49, 158.
Colonel Middleton's mission, 31.
Commission, Special, to examine credit for Madagascar Expedition, 188.
Commissioners for France, 2, 82.
Committee, Madagascar, 102.
Committee, Special, appointed by Chamber of Deputies, 188.
Commotion at Antananarivo, 85; at Tamatave, 119.
Company, the French, Madagascar, 7, 29.
Complications possible, not imminent, 117.
Compristo, M., 59.
Comte de Louvières, Death of, 70.
Conferences at Paris, 94.
—— at Ambodimanga, 175.
Congo River, 2, 112.
Congony River, 115.
Consul Cassas, 47.
—— Graves, 176.
—— Laborde, 70.
—— Meyer, 49.
—— Pakenham, 30.
Consular officers, 120, 126, 176, 218.
Concession, Chart of, to Lambert, 28.
Conflicting evidence, 57, 191, 194.
Conspiracy, 25.
—— of Rasata, 153.
Conspirators expelled, 26.

INDEX. 275

Corbigny, Baron de, 69.
Cordelière La, 64.
Coronation of Ranavàlona II., 154.
—— of Ranavàlona III., 159.
Correspondence between Ravoninahitriniarivo and the French Commissioners, 82.
—— Adriamifidy and the same, 87.
—— Prime Minister and Admiral Pierre, 118.
Correspondence, The Pierre-Johnstone, 122, 128.
Coup d'état attempted, 25.
—— its failure, 26.
Credit for Madagascar Expedition, Vote for, 201.
—— Debate on in Chamber, 182.
—— —— in Senate, 201.
Cremazy, M., 154.
Creuse La, 121.
Cyprus, 183.

D'ARVOY, M., 24.
Death of Admiral Pierre, 142.
—— Count de Louvières, 70.
—— Ranavàlona II., 151.
—— Consul Pakenham, 126, 140.
Death, Threats of, 85.
Decrais, M., 94.
Debates in the Chamber of Deputies, 182, 192, 244.
—— in the Senate, 201.
De Freycinet, M., 78.
De Langle, Fleuriot, Admiral, 64.
De Lastelle, M., 7.
De Louvières, Count, 70.
De Mahy, M. Minister of Marine, 188.
De Vaulcomte, Bureau, 188.
Decidée, La, 51.
Declerq, M., 60.
Decrais, M., 94.
Debates in Chamber of Deputies, 182.
—— in House of Commons, 134.
—— in Senate, 201.
Depositions of witnesses, 194.
Deputation to Lord Granville, 102.
D'Éscamps, H. M., 9, 62.
Désirée Laverdant, M., 10.
Desprez, Lieut., 68.
Destruction of idols, 155.
—— of posts and flagstaves, 87, 115.
De Vogue, Major, 242.
Diego-Suarez, 76, 113.
Dispensary, Mr. Shaw's, 124.
Disputes between France and Madagascar, their origin, 4, 246.
Divination, 152.
Donald Currie, Sir, steamer Taymouth Castle, 123.

Drotie, M., 13, 250.
Drouyn de Lhuys, 70.
Dryad, H.M.S., 114.
Duclerc, M., President of Council, 91, 94.
Dupleix, M., 1.
Dupré, Commodore, 69.

EARLY career of Laborde, 7.
East coast, Blockade of, 208.
Education, Improvements in, 34, 157.
Effect of climate, 166.
Egypt, 191,
Ellis, Rev. W., 21, 69, 150, 261.
Emancipation of Mozambique slaves, 34, 158.
Embargo on the Antananarivo, 87.
—— on the Stillman, 87.
Embassy decided on, 88.
Engagés, 15.
English Consuls — Pakenham, 30 ; Graves, 176.
—— Vice-Consuls, Johnstone, 126; Pickersgill, 176.
—— Government, Action of, 136.
—— missionaries, 199.
Enterprise, Colonial French, 1.
Enthusiasm of people, 220, 240.
Envoys, Hova, 89.
Euryalus, H.M.S., 71.
Evacuation, 97, 125.
Excitement of Hovas, 233.
Exeter Hall, 143.
Expulsion of conspirators, 26.
Expulsion of French residents, 131.

FACTORIES, 10.
Fallières M., President of Council, 111.
Farquhar, Sir Robert, 197.
Féhérègne, 66.
Felix, Père, 131.
Fénoarivo, Bombardment of, 121.
Ferry, Jules M., 111.
Fianarantsoa, 132.
Fiche, 6.
Finaz Père, 21.
Fisatra, 162.
Fishmongers' Hall, Banquet at, 256.
Fitzmaurice, Lord E., M.P., 259.
Flag, Hova, 53, 74.
Fleuriot de Langle, 64.
Flore, La, 111, 121.
Forfait, Le, 82, 87, 121.
Forged deeds, 40.
Forster, Mr. W. E., 252.
Fort Dauphin, 174.
Foule Point, 122.
France and Germany, 110.

276 INDEX.

Francisation, 206,
French claims, 59, 249.
—— commissioners, 2, 82.
—— consuls, 7.
—— flag hoisted, 123.
—— government, 78, 91.
—— grievances, 4.
—— outposts, 133.
—— residents expelled, 132.
—— rights of sovereignty and protectorate, 59.
Freppel, Monseigneur, 198.
Freycinet, M. de, 78.
Fougeirol M. 188.
Functions consular stopped, 123.

GAILLARD, M., 116.
Galiber, Admiral, 177.
Galos M., 70.
Gambetta, 74, 78.
—— Sudden death of, 111.
Garnier, M., 70.
Germany, 101, 150.
German subjects, 101.
Gladstone Mr., 134, 140.
Glass manufactory, 11.
Goblet, M., 188.
Gourbeyre, Commodore, 6, 14.
Granville, Earl, 93, 248.
Graves, Hicks, Mr., 176.
Gregorian calendar, 43.

HAMBURG, Envoy at, 260.
Happy, The, 16.
Hasina, 95.
Hastie, Mr., 42.
Hay, Admiral Sir John, 253.
Hayes, Lieut., 179.
Heads of French and English on poles, 14.
Hell, Admiral Baron de, 59.
Hervier M., 21.
Hivondro R., 6, 121.
Holmwood, Consul, 206.
Hova, 79.
Hovius, M., 188.

IBART, King, 68.
Iboina, 51, 113.
Ida Pfeiffer, Mdme, 25.
Iharoka River, 131.
Ikiopa River, 11.
Illness of the British consul, 89.
Ill-will imputed to Madagascar Government, 3, 4.
Imerina, Queen of, 215.
Imperial auspices, 28.
Inaccurate account, 97.
Incendiarism, 122.

Indemnity, 32, 59, 65.
Infringement of French rights, 78.
Inheritance, The Laborde, 5.
Instructions of the Minister of Marine, 113.
Insurrection at Nossi-Bé, 63.
Interpellation of M. Lanessan, 182.
Isonierana palace, 11.

JAURÉGUIBERRY, Admiral, Minister of Marine, 78.
Jean Réné, 6.
Jehenne, Captain, 61.
Johns, Mr., 12.
Johnstone, Captain, 114, 128, 129.
—— Promotion of, 130.
Jones, Admiral Gore, 71.
Jongoa, 57.
Jouen, Père, 15, 21, 62.
Jules Dupré, 32.
Jules Simon, 112.
Juliette Fiche, 162.

KABARY, Assembly, The Grand, 230.
Kabary ground of Andohalo, 49, 82.
Kingdon, Mr. 103.
Kirk, Sir John, 142.
Knowles, Lieut., 120.

LABORDE, M., Consul, 71,
—— Early career of, 7.
Laborde claims, 5.
—— Inheritance, The, 5.
—— heirs, 37.
La Cloche, 92.
Langle, Fleuriot de, Viscount, 64, 70.
La Bourdonnaye, 1.
Lambert, 15.
Land leases, 107.
Lanessan, M., Deputy, 182.
—— Reporter, 59, 64, 188.
Laverdant, Désirée, 10.
Lavergne, Bernard, M. 199.
Law of England, 107.
—— of Guernsey and Jersey, 108.
Laws, Code of, 49, 158.
Law No. 85, 49.
Laymeriza, King, 66.
Le Batz, Père, 132.
Lédoulx, M., 142.
Le Gros, M., 11.
Lehidama, 160, 232.
Lesseps, Seignac M., 86.
Le Timbre, Captain, 87.
—— Admiral, 87.
Liquor Traffic, 146, 258.
Lister, Mr., 146.
London, Arrival of Hova Envoys in, 102.

INDEX. 277

London Missionary Society, 261.
Lord Lyons, 104.
Louisiana, State of, 1.
Louis Philippe, 62.
Louvières, Count de, 70.
Lyons, Lord, Ambassador at Paris.

MACARTHUR, Mr. A., M.P., 102, 251.
Machicora, 68.
Madagascar Company, 28.
—— Government, 157.
—— Independence of, 149.
—— Kings of, 5, 68, 95, 152, 153, 160, 157, 232.
Madagascar, Queens of, 6, 8, 9, 53, 68, 93, 95, 151, 222.
Madagascar Times, 92.
Magnéas, 68.
Mahabo, 154, 204.
Mahagolo, Bombardment of, 64.
Mahambo, Bombardment of, 121.
Mahamasina, Plain of, 160.
Mahanoro, Bombardment of, 173, 227, 209.
Mahavanona, 87.
Mahafaly, 68.
Mahela, Bombardment of, 174.
Mahy, M. de, Minister, 111.
Mananzary, 132, 174, 242.
—— Bombardment of, 209.
Manjakandrianombana, Camp of, 121, 133.
Mansion House, Speech at, 140.
Mantasoua, 13.
Manouis, 67.
Marambitsy, 51, 96.
Marie Angélique, 65.
Mananhar, 169.
Marks, Mr., 40.
Maroantsetra, 169.
Maromby, 131.
Marontsangana, 76.
Marseilles, 191.
Mascareigne steamer, 15.
Mascarene islands, 8.
—— Plantations, 15.
Masindrano, 132.
Mauritius, 15, 197.
Mayotte, 54, 57, 93.
Mediation, Offers of, 109.
Messalina, Modern, 9.
Mexico, 2.
Meyer, M., 53.
Miles, Colonel, 134.
Milhet de Fontarabie, Dr., Senator, 201.
Ministers, Malagasy, 157.
Miot, Admiral, 208, 241.
Mivavis, 65.

Moenidoso, 68, 208, 241.
Mohambo, 241.
Mojangà, 51, 115.
—— Bombardment of, 116.
Monja, Queen, 100.
Montcalm, 1.
Mouroundava River, 196.
Morontsanga, 115, 116,
Mozambique, 13, 15, 59.
—— slaves, Emancipation of, 34, 158.
Mullens, Dr., 115.

NAPOLEON I., 1.
—— III., 65.
Negotiations in Europe, 94.
—— Madagascar, 175.
Nièvre, La, 121.
Night attacks, 133.
Northcote, Sir Stafford, 135.
Nossi-Bé, 60, 76, 81.
Nossi-Cumba, 60.
Nossi-Faly, 76.
Nossi-Mitsiu, 74, 75.
Nos-Vey, 191.
Note Verbale, 107.

OFFERS of Mediation, 108.
Offices, Good, refused, 109.
Orénoque, The, 208.
Origin of French dispute, 3, 246.
Osprey, H.M.S., 206.
Ouringi, Chief, 68.
Ousséni, 66.
Outrage at Marambitsy, 51.
Outzinzou, Queen, 64.

PAKENHAM, CONSUL, 71, 89.
—— Death of, 127.
Palmer, George, M.P., 257.
Palmerston, Lord, 103.
Panga, Queen, 62.
Parrett, Mr., 8, 72.
Passandava Bay, 60, 115.
Passot, Lieut., 61.
Perin, Georges, 188, 192.
Peyron, Admiral, Minister of Marine, 94.
—— Statement by, 189.
Peytral, M., 188.
Pfeiffer, Mdme. Ida, 8.
Philomel, H.M.S., 206.
Phrase, to press, inadmissible, 109.
Pickersgill, Mr., Missionary, 72.
—— Consul, 176.
Pierre, Admiral, 111, 112, 115, 128, 142.
Pique gunboat, 59, 115.
Plenipotentiaries, French, 94, 209.
—— Malagasy, 90, 174, 200.

Plot, 22, 153.
Plunkett, Hon. Mr., 93.
Plymouth, 125.
Poisoning, Charge of, 124.
Powder-mills, 11.
Préfet-Apostolique, 39.
Press to, untranslatable phrase, 109.
Prêter, Literal translation of, 109.
Prévoyante La, 61.
Priests, Jesuit, 65.
Prime Minister, The Queen's husband, 34, 163.
—— Speech of, 234.
Printing, 11.
Proclamation of the Queen of Madagascar, 222.
Property, Rights of, 33, 49, 216.
Protectorate, 59.

QUAI D'ORSAY, 79.
Quarterly Review, 91.
Queen Beravouny, 80.
—— Binao, 87, 100.
—— of Imerina, 215.
—— of Madagascar, 232.
—— Ravanàlona I., 8, 9, 163.
—— II., 9, 150.
—— III., 150.
—— Outzinzou, 64.

RABAUD, M., 99.
Rabibisoa, 91.
Rabodo, 160.
Raboky, 65,
Radama I., 5, 95.
Radama II., 68, 152, 153.
Rafàrasòa, 151.
Raffray, Vice-Consul, 110.
—— Mayor of Tamatave, 123.
Rahaniraka, 30, 90.
Raharo, 25.
Rainidriamanpandry, Governor of Tamatave, Plenipotentiary, 174.
Rainiharo, 153.
Rainiketaha, 30.
Rainilaiarivony, 73, 162.
Rainilambo, 157.
Rainimaharavo, 157.
Rainimahazire, 157.
Rainimiadana, 157.
Rainitsimbazafy, Home Minister, 157.
Rainivoninahitraniony, 163.
Rainizanamanga, Plenipotentiary,175.
Rakoto-Radama, Prince, 163.
Ralaitsirofo, Minister of Justice, 157.
Rallier, Commander, 139.
Ramàhatra, Judge, 151.
Ramaniraka, Ambassador, 90, 102, 251.

Ramarosana, 175.
Ramasy, 51.
Ramboasalama, 152.
Ramòma, 150, 153.
Ramonja, 150.
Ramòrabé, 150.
Ranavàlona I., 6, 8, 9, 68, 151.
—— II., 53, 71, 95, 151.
—— III., 151, 222, 223, 225, 230.
Rasata, 153.
Rasoherina, 95, 153, 160.
Rasoherimanjaka, 1.
Ravoninahitriniarivo, 102.
—— Minister for Foreign Affairs, 157.
—— Ambassador, 90, 102.
—— Speeches of, 256, 260.
Razafindrahéty, 151.
Razahamanana, Premises of, 41.
Razàkaratrimo, 150.
Razanakombana, Minister of Law, 157.
Rebellion excited, 92.
Red-books, 168.
Removal of flags, 97.
Réné, Jean, 6.
Renegade, 14.
Repulse of attacks, 133, 243.
Retrocession of Madagascar by England, 197.
Réunion, Island of, 12, 15, 139.
—— Volunteers of, 242, 247.
—— Deputy for, 185.
—— Planters of, 255.
Review of troops, 240.
Revoil, M., 99, 250.
Revolution, 32.
Riaux, Francis, author and historian, 7.
Ribiby, 68.
Richardson, J. N., M.P., 250.
Richelieu, Cardinal, 196.
Rights, French, 59.
—— General, 100.
—— Historic, 182.
Rivet, M., 188.
Robert Drury, 8.
Robin, M., 14.
Robinson, Colonel, United States consul, 88.
Roman Catholic mission, 39.
Rontaunay, 6.
Rosiers, M., 67.
Roux, M., 99.
Rowlands, Mr., 11.
Royal Proclamation, 222.
—— Reception, 223.
—— Speeches, 225, 230.
Royal city of Ambohimanga, 76.
Royal summer retreat, Tsinjoarivo, 156.

INDEX. 279

Rupture of Conferences and of Relations at Paris, 101.
Rupture at Ambodimanga, 176, 182, 217.
Ryan, Bishop, 253.

SAFY-AMBALA, 65, 80.
Safy-Lessouky, 65.
Saillens, M., 45, 100, 245.
Sàkalàva, 51, 54.
—— allies, 205.
Sambrano, R., 87.
Savoie, M., 8, 9, 10.
Seals of Foreign Office, 42.
Seizure of Hova flags, 87, 116, 117.
Shaw, Mr., 123.
Signatures, Verification of, 30, 40.
Signing the charter, 30.
—— the treaties, 32.
Sikidy, 152.
Simon, Jules, 112.
Slaves, 12, 15, 206, 207.
—— Emancipation of, 34, 158.
Slave-trade, 15, 206, 207.
Society of Friends, 243.
Souhalala, 80.
Soumagne M., Vice-Consul, 71.
Sovereigns, The five, 160.
Squabble, Undignified, 92.
St. Albans, Duke and Duchess of, 257.
St. Andrews, Cape, 216.
St. Vincent, Cape, 60.
Stillman, the barque, Embargo on, 87.
Suez Canal, 111.
Summons, Formal, 122.
Superbie, M., Representative of the French residents, 118.

TACCHI, Mr., 92, 147, 227.
—— Interpreter, 147.
—— Owner and Editor of the *Madagascar Times*, 227, 22.
Tahiti, 20.
Tahiuksuaka Mountains, 66.
Tafondro, Attack on, 63.
Tamay, 65.
Tamatave, 114, 118.
—— Bombardment of, 121.
Taymouth Castle, The, 123.
Tazo, General, 166.
Thibaudin, General, 112.
Threats against the French, 84.
Times, The *Madagascar*, 92.
Tintingue, 179, 196.

Timber palace of Isonierana, 11.
Tissot, M., Ambassador at Albert Gate, 105.
Toale, The, 51, 52, 96.
Tofotra, 65.
Tonquin, 112.
Toulon, 110, 111.
Tourmaline, H.M.S., 176.
Treaties with France, 32, 33, 64, 65, 66, 68.
Treaty with United States, 148.
Tricolor, Removal of, 85.
Tsiahouan, 64.
Tsiazompaniry, Palace of, 83.
Tsimandroho, 61.
Tsimiaro, 61, 74.
Tsitampikis, 65.
Tsioumeka, Queen of the Sàkalàva, 59.
Tullear Bay, 67.
Tunis, 112.

ULTIMATUM, 113, 118.
Understanding between England and France, 103.
United Kingdom Alliance, 147.
United States, Treaty with, 148, 258.
—— Ratification of Treaty with, 148.
—— Visit to, 148.
—— Return from, 149.

VAISSIÈRE, Père de la, History of Madagascar, 62.
Vallon, Captain, 53.
Vaudreuil, La, 114, 115.
Vaulcomte, Dureau de, 188.
Versions, Different, of French and Madagascar dispute, 97, 99.
Victoria, Queen, Letter to, 41.
Vienna, Treaty of, 197.
Vohémar, 61, 76.
Voluntary hired labourers, 16.
Voluntary removal of flags, 97.

WADDINGTON, M., French ambassador, 141.
Water mills, 6.
Webber, Père, 21.
Wills, Rev. James, 166.
Wrangling correspondence, 37, 47, 58.
Wyvil, M., 207.

YELLOW Books, 97, 99.

ZANZIBAR, 15, 79, 134.

UNWIN BROTHERS,
THE GRESHAM PRESS,
CHILWORTH AND LONDON.

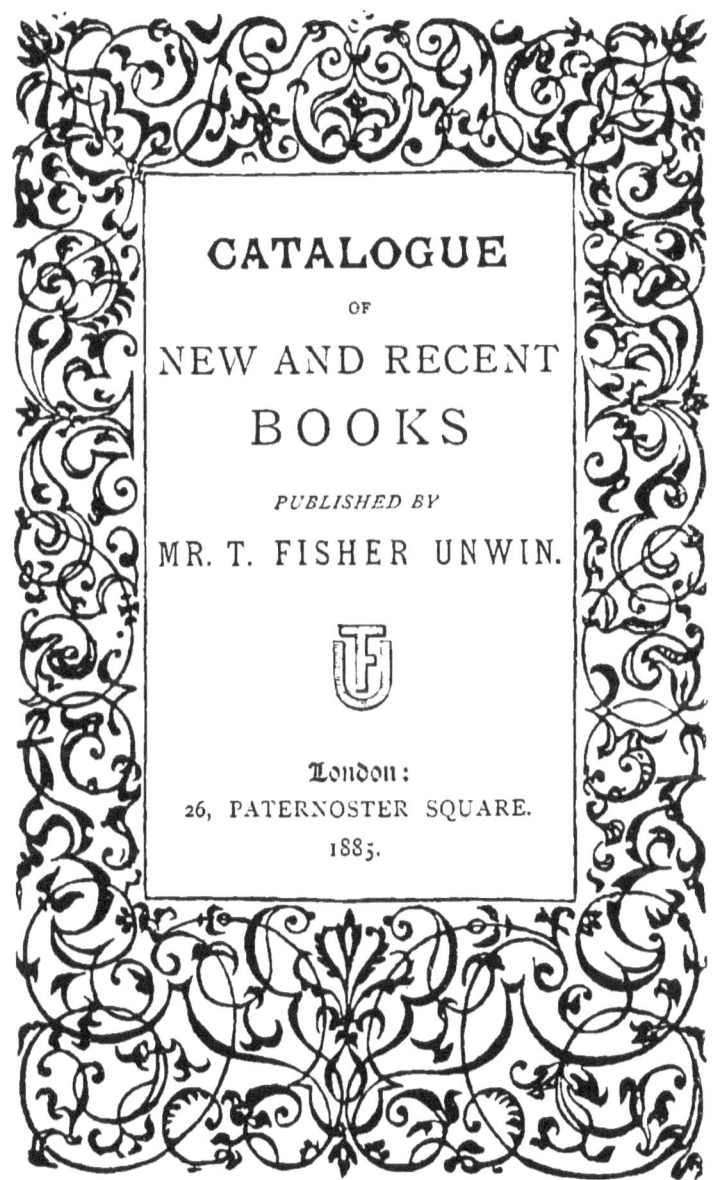

CATALOGUE
OF
NEW AND RECENT BOOKS

PUBLISHED BY

MR. T. FISHER UNWIN.

London:
26, PATERNOSTER SQUARE.
1885.

New Work by the late Editor of " THE EXPOSITOR.*"*

"EXPOSITIONS,"

DEDICATED TO BARON TENNYSON (*Poet Laureate*).

BY REV. SAMUEL COX, D.D.,

Author of "A Commentary on the Book of Job," "Balaam, an Exposition and a Study," "Salvator Mundi," &c.

Contents.

1. The Purchase of Opportunities.
2. The Sanitary Order of the Moral World.
3. The Divine Root of the Human Pedigree.
4. The Children of Wrath.
5. Abraham.
6. Religion and Reward.
7. The City of the Soul.
8. Nor any other Creation.
9. The Law of Retribution.
10. } The Prayer of the Remnant.
11. }
12. Forgiveness not Impunity.
13. Dives and Lazarus.
14. The Transfiguration.
15. Faith, a Condition of Salvation.
16. Faith and Unfaith, the Two Marvels which astonished Christ.
17. Righteousness which is by Faith
18. Faith, a Condition of Pleasing God.
19. The Scope of Prayer.
20. The Sin unto Death.
21. Child of the Devil or Child of God.
22. The Mission of Christ.
23. Destruction from the Face of the Lord.
24. The Son of Man the Saviour of the Lost.
25. The Sin of Iscariot.
26. The Repentance of Iscariot.
27. Fear cast out by Love.
28. Spiritual Husbandry.
29. The Sterner Parables.
30. The Moral of the Banned Fig Tree.
31. David's Friend.
32. The Friend of Jesus.
33. The Death of Ezekiel's Wife.

Demy 8vo., Cloth, about 500 pages, 7/6.

EXTRACT FROM PREFACE.

"Here are some thirty expository lectures or discourses such as I used to contribute to *The Expositor* while I was its editor. Since that pleasant task was taken from me, I have received at least two hundred letters from the clergy and ministers of every branch of the Christian Church in Great and in Greater Britain—as well as from laymen of all sorts and conditions—telling me, often in terms that could not but deeply touch my heart, of help and comfort they had received from my expository work, and begging me to devise some form in which it might be carried on. Many of them assured me that they did not speak for themselves alone, but also for numbers of their brethren whom they knew to be no less anxious on the latter point than themselves."

March 31, 1885.

CATALOGUE
OF
MR. T. FISHER UNWIN'S
PUBLICATIONS.

FRANCE AND TONGKING: A Narrative of the Campaign of 1884, and the Occupation of Further India. By JAMES GEORGE SCOTT (SHWAY YOE), Author of "The Burman: His Life and Notions." Map and Two Plans. Demy 8vo. [*Ready*   0   16   0

£ s. d.

"Mr. James George Scott, who has acted as special correspondent for several journals in the far East, has written a work on the French campaign in Tonquin, which will be published very soon. Mr. Scott is still with the French army in that country."—*Athenæum*, Jan. 13, 1885.

THE TRUE STORY OF THE FRENCH DISPUTE IN MADAGASCAR. By Captain S. PASFIELD OLIVER, F.S.A., F.R.G.S., &c., late Royal Artillery, Author of "Madagascar and the Malagasy," &c. With a Chapter by F.W. CHESSON, Hon. Secretary of the Malagasy Committee. With a Map. Demy 8vo. ... ...[*Ready*   0   9   0

"It will contain a review of the most interesting events in the early relations of France with the great African island, and an account drawn from official documents of the quarrel which has led to the present hostilities. It will be illustrated by a map which will show the principal places occupied or bombarded by the French. Captain Oliver, who has twice visited the island, was presented with the Star of Madagascar by Radama II., but this Order is no longer given to Foreigners."—*Daily News*, Jan. 16, 1885.

TO CANADA WITH THE EMI-GRANTS. By J. EWING RITCHIE (CHRISTOPHER CRAYON), Author of "East Anglia," "British Senators,"&c. Twelve Illustrations. Cr. 8vo. [*Ready*   0   7   6

THE ART OF WAR IN THE MIDDLE AGES, A.D. 378-1515. Being the Lothian Prize Essay for 1884. By C. W. C. OMAN, B.A., Fellow of All Souls College, Oxford. With Maps and Plans. Crown 8vo., cloth ... ... [*Just Out*   0   3   6

"An interesting book."—*Saturday Review.*
"All soldiers should read it, and no student of history but wil find it useful."—*United Service Gazette.*

Mr. T. Fisher Unwin, 26, Paternoster Square.

CHARLES DICKENS AS I KNEW
HIM: The Story of the Reading Tours in Great Britain and America (1866-1870). By GEORGE DOLBY. Third Thousand. Crown 8vo. 0 6 0

"Is pleasant and unpretentious . . . His account of his experiences is interesting in a very high degree. It will be welcome to all lovers of Dickens for Dickens' sake."—*Athenæum.*

"Will certainly be read with interest by all who admire the great writer . . . The book will be welcomed by all who are eager to learn everything relating to one who has left behind so deep an impression on the hearts of mankind."—*Daily Telegraph.*

"He has told his story in the most effective manner, accompanying a plain and clear narrative with abundant touches of the peculiar humour which no friend of Dickens should be without."—*Daily News.*

" George Dolby knew the 'Chief' full well,
 And as he knew him drew him ;
 So read the tale he has to tell—
 'Charles Dickens as I Knew Him.'"—*Punch.*

"The book is one which will well repay reading. . . . A book which gives us so many pleasant pictures of one of the most interesting figures in modern literature."—*Saturday Review.*

UNITED STATES NOTES: A History
of the various Issues of Paper Money by the Government of the United States, and of the distribution of the Surplus in 1837. With Appendix on the Legal Tender Question. By JOHN JAY KNOX, late Comptroller of the Currency. With Photo-Lithographic Specimens, and Forms of the various Notes. Demy 8vo., cloth ... [*Ready* 0 12 0

"A very minute historical sketch of the treasury and other notes issued by the Government. . . . The book should be carefully studied by those who would understand the subject."—*New York Herald.*

"The book has solid merits, and will be found highly serviceable by students of our financial history. It would be difficult to name any other work in which the currency operations of the Treasury and the proceedings of Congress in relation thereto are so minutely and impartially described."—*The Nation* (New York).

THE AMBASSADORS OF COMMERCE.
By A. P. ALLEN, An Old Traveller. With Illustrations by STURGESS. Crown 8vo., cloth
 [*Ready* 0 3 6

New and Recent Books.

AN ARTISTIC GIFT-BOOK.

ON TUSCAN HILLS AND VENE-
TIAN WATERS. By LINDA VILLARI, Author of
"Camilla's Girlhood," "In Change Unchanged,"
"In the Golden Shell," &c. With Ten Illustrations
by Mrs. ARTHUR LEMON. Square Imp. 16mo. ... o 7 6

" Her style is easy and pleasant, and ever and again her remarks are happy. . . . Very delightful is the account of the Abetone."—*Literary World.*

" Next to the privilege of visiting these localities, this book is the best thing, and no expense has been spared in making the volume an artistic success."—*Bookseller.*

FAIRY TALES FROM BRENTANO.
Told in English by KATE FREILIGRATH KROEKER.
Pictured by F. CARRUTHERS GOULD. Twenty-two
Illustrations. Square Imp. 16mo. ... ... o 5 o

" The extravagance of invention displayed in his tales will render them welcome in the nursery. The translation,—not an easy task,—has been very cleverly accomplished."—*The Academy.*

" The illustrations are delicately executed, and the binding is one no child, who *is* a child, could look upon without delight."—*Whitehall Review.*

" An admirable translator in Madame Kroeker, and an inimitable illustrator in Mr. Carruthers Gould. . . . The stories deserve both the German and the English poet's encomium, and the illustrations are simply irresistible."—*Truth.*

THE POISON TREE: A Tale of Hindu
Life in Bengal. By BANKIM CHANDRA CHATTER-
JEE. Translated by M. S. KNIGHT. Introduction
by EDWIN ARNOLD, M.A., C.S.I. Crown 8vo. ... o 6 o

" I am glad to recommend this translation to English readers as a work which, apart from its charm in incident and narrative, will certainly give them just, if not complete, ideas of the ways of life of their fellow-subjects in Bengal."—*Extract from Preface.*

" The healthiness and purity of tone throughout the book. . . . In reviewing novels, it is seldom that we regret very seriously the limitations of our space ; but we are genuinely sorry that we cannot speak at greater length of a book which presents so many points of interest."—*Academy.*

" Admirably translated into English by Mrs. Knight."—*Scotsman.*

THE WRECKERS OF LAVERNOCK.
By ANNIE JENKYNS. Crown 8vo.... ... ... o 5 o

" In delineation of character the authoress is extremely clever."—*Schoolmaster.*

Mr. T. Fisher Unwin, 26, Paternoster Square.

A SMALLER BIBLIA PAUPERUM,

conteynynge Thyrtie and Eyghte Wodecuttes Illvstratynge the Lyfe, Parablis, and Miraclis off Oure Blessid Lorde and Savioure Jhesus Crist, with the Propre Descrypciouns theroff extracted frō the Originall Texte off IOHN WICLIF, somtyme Rector of Lutterworth. With Preface by the late Verie Rev. ARTHUR PENRHYN STANLEY, D.D., Dean of Westminster. Square 8vo. Bound in Parchment, old style ; brass clasps 0 10 6

" A very interesting volume, elegantly bound in a cover copied from an old book in the British Museum."—*Bibliographer.*

" The illustrations are grotesque and quaint specimens of early art, and the whole book with its mysterious history, and its evident function as an instructor of the illiterate, is extremely suggestive and interesting."—*Literary World.*

THE ART GIFT-BOOK OF THE SEASON.

THE SEVEN AGES OF MAN. From

Shakespeare's " As You Like It." ARTISTS' EDITION. Illustrated with Seven Photogravures from Original Paintings by the most eminent American Artists. *List of Illustrations:* The Infant, by F. S. CHURCH ; The Schoolboy, by WILLIAM ST. JOHN HARPER ; The Lover, by THOS. HOVENDEN ; The Soldier, by GILBERT GAUL ; The Justice, by A. B. FROST ; The Lean and Slippered Pantaloon, by W. F. SMEDLEY ; Second Childishness, by WALTER SHIRLAW. Large 4to., elegantly bound, bevelled boards, gilt edges 0 10 6

POPULAR EDITION of the above, Illustrated with Woodcuts by the following eminent Engravers : E. HEINEMANN, HENRY WOLF, C. H. REED, FRANK FRENCH, GEO. P. WILLIAMS and FRED. JUENGLING. Square pott 16mo., cloth elegant, bevelled boards, gilt edges 0 5 0

" The comparison is interesting and instructive throughout, and justifies this lengthened notice of two very pretty books."—*Saturday Review.*

" It is simple justice to say that as a gift-book the volume will be prized for its beauty as a production of somewhat ambitious designs."—*Scotsman.*

" Strongly contrast the old and new style of engraving. . . . The various artists have all been well-chosen."—*Graphic.*

New and Recent Books.

LIFE AND WORK IN BENARES and KUMAON, 1839-77. By JAMES KENNEDY, M.A., Author of " Christianity and the Religions of India." Introduction by Sir WILLIAM MUIR, K.C.S.I., LL.D., D.C.L., Late Lieut.-Governor, N.W.P. Eleven Illustrations. Crown 8vo., cloth 0 6 0

"Of what he saw and did he writes agreeably, without obtruding the autobiographical form. . . . The volume is better worth reading than others of much higher literary pretensions.' —*Academy.*

THE UNKNOWN GOD, and other Sermons. Preached in St. Peter's, Vere Street, by the Rev. ALEXANDER H. CRAUFURD, M.A., formerly Exhibitioner of Oriel College, Oxford, Author of "Seeking for Light." Crown 8vo., cloth [*Ready* 0 6 0

THE REALITY OF FAITH. By the Rev. NEWMAN SMYTH, D.D., Author of "Old Faiths in New Light," "The Religious Feeling," "The Orthodox Theology of To-day." Third and cheaper Edition. Crown 8vo., cloth... ... ... 0 4 6

"They are fresh and beautiful expositions of those deep truths, those foundation truths, which underlie Christian faith and spiritual life in all their varied manifestations. . . . We thank the publisher for bringing out these singularly suggestive and instructive discourses in so good a form."- *Christian Age.*

THE QUESTION OF QUESTIONS: Is Christ indeed the Saviour of the World? By THOS. ALLIN. Crown 8vo. 0 5 0

"We cannot but accord it a hearty welcome. . . . Carefully and vigorously worked out. . . . We commend Mr. Allin's careful and eloquent statement."—*Church Reformer.*
" Mr. Allin's book will have a welcome from those who desire wise and simple guidance in their study of this important question."—*Literary World.*

PAYING THE PASTOR, Unscriptural and Traditional. By JAMES BEATY, D.C.L., Q.C., Member of the Canadian Legislature. Crown 8vo. 0 6 0

"Is well got up, and in every respect calculated to repay careful perusal. . . . We recommend it as greatly helpful in mastering New Testament doctrine on this important and practical question."- *Ecclesiastical Observer.*
" Skilfully put."—*Presbyterian.*

Mr. T. Fisher Unwin, 26, Paternoster Square.

EUPHORION: Studies of the Antique and the Mediæval in the Renaissance. By VERNON LEE, Author of "Ottilie," &c. In 2 vols. Demy 8vo., cloth extra 1 1 0

"The book is bold, extensive in scope, and replete with well-defined and unhackneyed ideas, clear impressions, and vigorous and persuasive modes of writing. . . . Large questions have been scrutinized in a comprehensive spirit, and are treated with both breadth and minuteness, according to the scale of the work. This will be apparent from a list of articles in the two volumes. After an introduction comes 'The Sacrifice,' 'The Italy of the Elizabethan Dramatists,' 'The Outdoor Poetry,' and 'Symmetria Prisca.' . . . 'The Portrait Art,' 'The School of Boiardo.' . . . Lastly comes the longest essay of all, ' Mediæval Love,' filling nearly one hundred pages. This is certainly a masterly performance, going over a wide field, and showing at every stage abundant discrimination."—*Athenæum*.

"It is a distinct advance on Vernon Lee's previous work. The impressions it records are as vividly individual as ever, the knowledge which informs it is fuller and riper. It deals with a period incomparably more interesting than the 'teacup times of hood and hoop,' through whose mazes her first work led us so pleasantly ; and it has more unity and continuity than ' Belcaro.' Its title is most happily chosen, since the studies all converge upon that mystic union of the mediæval Faust with the Helen of antiquity from which the Renaissance sprang."—*Pall Mall Gazette*.

"Every page of 'Euphorion' give evidence of immense reading in Renaissance and in mediæval literature, and the author possesses the sure instinct so needful in a student of old books, which leads her to the passages where intellectual booty is to be found. . . . Deserves a most cordial welcome as a fresh and original contribution to the history of civilization and art; written in graceful and often eloquent English."—*Spectator*.

THE AMAZON: An Art Novel. By CARL VOSMAER. With Preface by Professor GEORGE EBERS, and Frontispiece drawn specially by L. ALMA TADEMA, R.A. Crown 8vo., cloth 0 6 0

"It is a delineation of inner life by the hand of a master. It belongs to the school of Corinne, but is healthier and nobler, and in its thought and style fully equal to Madame de Staël's famous work. We do not wonder at the European recognition of its great merits."—*British Quarterly Review*.

"Throughout the book there is a fine air of taste, reminding one a little of Longfellow's ' Hyperion.' "—*The World*.

"It is a work full of deep, suggestive thought. M. Vosmaer, in writing it, has added another testimony to his artistic greatness and depth."—*The Academy*.

New and Recent Books.

ARMINIUS VAMBÉRY; His Life and Adventures. Written by himself. With Portrait and 14 Illustrations. Fourth and Popular Edition. Square Imperial 16mo., cloth extra ... ... o 6 o

"A most fascinating work, full of interesting and curious experiences."—*Contemporary Review.*

"It is partly an autobiographic sketch of character, partly an account of a singularly daring and successful adventure in the exploration of a practically unknown country. In both aspects it deserves to be spoken of as a work of great interest and of considerable merit."—*Saturday Review.*

"This remarkable book is partly an autobiographical sketch of character, partly a record of a singularly bold and successful attempt to explore a country which at the time when Professor Vambéry undertook his journey was practically *terra incognita*. . . . Professor Vambéry's Autobiography is *omnium consensu* a work of very great interest and merit."—*Life.*

"We can follow M. Vambéry's footsteps in Asia with pride and pleasure; we welcome every word he has to tell us about the ethnography and the languages of the East."—*Academy.*

"Professor Vambéry, of Pest, has just published a book in England that tells the story of his life; a book that forms, under every aspect, most agreeable reading. It is not only a deeply interesting account of his adventurous career, but it is also written in a light and attractive manner, so that the reader's attention does not flag for a moment."—*Die Gegenwart.*

"The character and temperament of the writer come out well in his quaint and vigorous style. . . . The expressions, too, in English, of modes of thought and reflections cast in a different mould from our own gives additional piquancy to the composition, and, indeed, almost seems to bring out unexpected capacities in the language."—*Athenæum.*

"There is something in his travels which reminds us of the wanderings of Oliver Goldsmith. . . . The English public will find their interest in him increased rather than diminished by this graphic account of his life and adventures."—*British Quarterly Review.*

"Has all the fascination of a lively romance. It is the confession of an uncommon man; an intensely clever, extraordinarily energetic egotist, well-informed, persuaded that he is in the right and impatient of contradiction."—*Daily Telegraph.*

"The work is written in a most captivating manner, and illustrates the qualities that should be possessed by the explorer."—*Novoe Vremya, Moscow.*

"We are glad to see a popular edition of a book, which, however it be regarded, must be pronounced unique. The writer, the adventures, and the style are all extraordinary—the last not the least of the three. It is flowing and natural—a far better style than is written by the majority of English travellers."—*St. James's Gazette.*

*** *Over Eighty other English and Foreign periodicals have reviewed this work.*

Mr. T. Fisher Unwin, 26, Paternoster Square.

THE EPIC OF KINGS. Stories retold from the Persian Poet Firdusi. By HELEN ZIMMERN, Author of "Stories in Precious Stones," "Life of Lessing," &c. With Etchings by L. ALMA TADEMA, R.A., and Prefatory Poem by E. W. GOSSE. Popular Edition, Crown 8vo., cloth extra   0 7 6

"Charming from beginning to end. . . . Miss Zimmern deserves all credit for her courage in attempting the task, and for her marvellous success in carrying it out. . . . Miss Zimmern has indeed mastered a pure simple English which fits the antiquity of her subject, and the stories are told in a manner which must provoke the envy and admiration of all who have attempted this singularly difficult style of composition."—*Saturday Review.*

Also an Édition de luxe, on Dutch Hand-made Paper, Super Roy. Quarto, limited to 200 copies. Artist's Proofs on Japanese Paper, signed and numbered, bound in Parchment extra 3 3 0

Later Impressions, limited to 300 copies, on English Super Roy. 4to., the Etchings on India Paper, unsigned, bound in Cloth extra 2 2 0

*** A limited number of these editions may still be had.

GLADYS FANE: The Story of Two Lives. By T. WEMYSS REID. Fourth and popular edition. In 1 vol. Crown 8vo., cloth extra 0 6 0

"'Gladys Fane' is a good and clever book, which few readers who begin it are likely to put down unfinished."—*Saturday Review.*

"The author of the delightful monograph on 'Charlotte Brontë' has given us in these volumes a story as beautiful as life and as sad as death. . . . We could not 'wear in our heart's core' the man who could read aloud with unfaltering voice and undimmed eyes the last pages of this prose story, which is almost a poem, and which
        'Dallies with the innocence of love
        Like the old age.'"—*Standard.*

"Mr. T. Wemyss Reid, the talented editor of the *Leeds Mercury*, has in 'Gladys Fane' developed wonderful power as a writer of fiction. 'Gladys Fane' is no ordinary tale; the conventionalities of the present-day novel writer are not observed, but Mr. Reid gives us what should be the aim of all who produce light literature, something *novel.*"—*Guardian.*

"She is thoroughly original; her portrait is carefully finished; and it may safely be said that if Mr. Reid has a few more characters like this in reserve, his success as a novelist is assured. . . . It is a sound piece of work, and, above all, it is very enjoyable reading."—*Academy.*

New and Recent Books.

SUMMER: From the Journal of HENRY D. THOREAU. Edited by H. G. O. BLAKE. With an Index. Map. Crown 8vo., cloth, 382 pp. ... 0 7 6

This volume will contain passages selected from Thoreau's Journals, comprising his observations and reflections during the summers of many years. Some of these are descriptive, with that fine photographic accuracy which marks Thoreau's pictures of natural scenes. Other passages contain those subtle reflections on society, religion, laws, literature, which also characterize whatever Thoreau wrote, and which pique the curiosity and stimulate the minds of his readers. The book has a full index. Thoreau himself seems to have contemplated a work of this kind, for in his Journal he writes of "A book of the seasons, each page of which should be written in its own season and out-of-doors, or in its own locality, wherever it may be."

HENRY IRVING: in England and America, 1838-1884. By FREDERIC DALY. With a Vignette Portrait, specially etched from a Private Photograph taken by S. A. WALKER, by AD. LALAUZE; printed on hand-made paper by M. SALMON, of Paris. Second thousand. Crown 8vo., cloth extra 0 5 0

"Mr. Frederic Daly has brought together an interesting mass of facts which will be acceptable to the admirers of the eminent actor. Mr. Daly writes with judicious moderation, and without excessive adulation, thoroughly appreciates the deservedly high position occupied by the subject of his biography."—*Athenæum*.

"Mr. Daly is a strong though by no means undiscriminating admirer of Mr. Irving. This easy and well-written narrative gives a good idea of the popular actor's career."—*Contemporary Review*.

"Conscientiously full, thoughtfully considered, and gracefully written "—*Daily Telegraph*.

"It refers succinctly to Mr. Irving's literary efforts, essays, and addresses, and concludes with a survey of Mr. Irving's personal characteristics. . . . An interesting and useful volume. . . . A portrait of Mr. Irving, etched by M. Lalauze, is admirable in execution."—*Saturday Review*.

"Written with discriminating taste."—*The World*.

"Mr. Daly sets forth his materials with a due sense of proportion, and writes in a pleasing vein."—*Daily News*.

SETTLING DAY: A Sketch from Life. By SOPHIE ARGENT. Crown 8vo., cloth 0 3 6

"A charming story of real life, and one that is as true to human nature as it is true to facts."—*Congregationalist*.

"A pleasant and wholesome little novelette. . . . It is agreeably written."—*Society*.

Mr. T. Fisher Unwin, 26, Paternoster Square.

THE FUTURE WORK OF FREE TRADE IN ENGLISH LEGISLATION. I. Free Trade in Land. II. Financial Reform. III. Monopolies. (*The Cobden Club Prize Essay for 1883.*) By C. E. TROUP, B.A., Balliol College, Oxford. Crown 8vo., cloth 0 3 6

"Lucid in style, and based on a thorough comprehension of economic science, the book deserves the attention of all who are interested in the questions of which it treats—questions which are likely to assume prominence in the not-distant future."—*Scotsman*.

"Leaves no doubt in the reader's mind that Mr. Troup fully earned his prize by treating the whole subject in a spirit of discrimination as well as with undoubted ability."—*Leeds Mercury*.

A LOST SON. By MARY LINSKILL, Author of "Hagar," "Between the Heather and the Northern Sea," "Cleveden." "Tales of the North Riding," &c., &c. Crown 8vo. 0 6 0

STOPS; or, How to Punctuate. With Instructions for Correcting Proofs, &c. By PAUL ALLARDYCE. Third edition. Demy 16mo., parchment antique or cloth 0 1 0

"Is a clear and useful little book, which is written with more literary skill than is usually shown in such manuals. Mr. Allardyce will no doubt do more important work."—*Athenæum*.

"At the end Mr. Allardyce gives the useful example of how to correct a proof—an art which some of those who live by the pen never master thoroughly."—*Saturday Review*.

"We have hardly any words but those of praise to give to his very thoughtful, very dainty little book."—*Journal of Education*.

"We can conceive no more desirable present to a literary aspirant."—*Academy*.

THE HOUSE PURCHASER'S GUIDE: Practical Hints for all Householders. By FREDERICK SNELLING. Demy 16mo., Cloth limp 0 0 9

New and Recent Books.

CENTENARY SERIES.

1. **JOHN WICLIF**, Patriot and Reformer : his Life and Writings. By RUDOLF BUDDENSIEG, Lic. Theol., Leipsic. Parchment covers, Antique printing 0 2 0
Paper Covers 0 1 0

"Mr. Fisher Unwin has printed in delicious old text, with a frontispiece and vellum binding worthy of an old Elzevir, Mr. Rudolf Buddensieg's brief extracts from Wiclif's writings. . . . These are full of interest, and the little volume will be useful for reference."—*Graphic.*

"The matter is equal to the manner, consisting of a summary of the career of the great Reformer, drawn up by an acknowledged master of the subject, and of a judicious selection of characteristic passages from Wiclif's works."—*St. James's Gazette.*

"No better summary of the conclusions could perhaps be given than that which Dr. Buddensieg has epitomized."—*British Quarterly Review.*

"A charming book got up in the 'old-style,' bound in parchment and well printed on thick paper, containing a scholarly and appreciative account of Wiclif's life."—*Nonconformist.*

"Beautifully printed in the old-fashioned manner, and bound in imitation of vellum, this book is a thing of beauty. The specimens of Wiclif's writings are deeply interesting."—*Sword and Trowel.*

2. **THE TABLE TALK OF DR. MARTIN LUTHER.** Fcap. 12mo., Antique Paper, Parchment boards 0 2 0

This is an entirely new selection and translation by Professor Gibb, from the ever-popular *Tischreden oder Colloquia* of "The Monk that shook the world," and forms an appropriate *souvenir* of the 4th Centenary now being held throughout Christendom.

"His words are half-battles."—*Richter.*

"'The Table-talk.' The most interesting now of all the books proceeding from him."—*Carlyle.*

"Deserves the very highest praise. Great discrimination has been shown in the choice of extracts, and considerable skill in the grouping of them under appropriate heads."—*Congregationalist.*

3. **DOCTOR JOHNSON**: His Life, Works and Table Talk. By Dr. MACAULAY, Editor of *The Leisure Hour* ... ... 0 2 d
Paper Covers 0 1 0

This little work will form an interesting *souvenir* of the great lexicographer, as described in its title. The first part will be a newly-written life by Dr. Macaulay, and the remaining part of the book will be short extracts illustrative of his writings and conversation.

Mr. T. Fisher Unwin, 26, Paternoster Square.

OUR MODERN PHILOSOPHERS:
Darwin, Bain, and Spencer; or, The Descent of Man, Mind, and Body. A Rhyme, with Reasons, Esssys, Notes, and Quotations. By " PSYCHOSIS." Crown 8vo., cloth extra, 236 pp. ... ... o 4 6

" He is a powerful writer. . . . Many of his stanzas are happy illustrations of wit and wisdom."—*Literary World.*
" This is a clever, amusing, and instructive book."—*The Christian.*
" This work is highly creditable to the learning and industry of its author."—*Glasgow Herald.*

THE LAW AND THE PROPHETS:
Being the Hulsean Lectures for 1882. By F. WATSON, M.A., Rector of Starston, and some time Fellow of St. John's College, Cambridge. Demy 8vo., cloth ... ... o 6 o

" It is worthy of careful and critical review. . . . The book will be read with great interest by those who are interested in questions that it treats."—*British Quarterly Review.*
" Mr. Watson's lectures must be awarded unqualified praise. The lectures themselves are admirable, and nothing less can be said of the subsidiary additions, which are very valuable as confirmatory of the main arguments and theses."—*Clergyman's Magazine.*

THE CHRIST OF HISTORY.
An Argument grounded on the Facts of His Life on Earth. By JOHN YOUNG, LL.D., Author of " The Life and Light of Men," " The Creator and the Creation," &c. Seventh and Popular Edition. Crown 8vo., cloth ... ... o 3 6

OFF DUTY:
Stories of a Parson on Leave. By CHARLES WRIGHT. Crown 8vo., cloth... ... o 2 6

"'So genial in its conception, and so modest in its pretentions.'
—*Christian Million.*
" It is a pleasant miscellany of prose and verse, with sunny gleams of humour."—*Christian Leader.*
" A playful little volume, full of cheery chat, often running away from the flats of prose into airy verse—with racy anecdote, wise suggestion, and sound good sense underlying even its fun."
—*Greenock Daily Telegraph.*
" The idea of the book is well conceived and carried out. . . . The book is just the one for the sea-side or holiday resort, and only needs to be read to be thoroughly enjoyed."—*Banbury Guardian.*

New and Recent Books.

LIGHT IN LANDS OF DARKNESS:

A Record of Mission Work in
GREENLAND, LABRADOR,
EGYPT, SOUTH AMERICA,
SYRIA. ARMENIA,
PERSIA, ETC., ETC.

By ROBERT YOUNG, Author of "Modern Missions" With an Introduction by the RT. HON. THE EARL OF SHAFTESBURY, K.G. Illustrated. Crown 8vo., cloth extra. Second edition 0 6 0

This volume may be considered as a second series of Modern Missions (see page 18). It has been issued in response to the general demand for a completion of the record of *all* Protestant Missions throughout the world.

HALF-HOURS WITH FAMOUS AMBASSADORS.

By G. BARNETT SMITH, Author of "The Life of Gladstone," &c. Crown 8vo., cloth extra, with Steel Portrait 0 7 6

*** Including Talleyrand, Sir R. M. Keith, Gondomar, The Chevalier D'Eon, Metternich, Harley, Alberoni, and Lord Malmesbury.

"More entertaining than many a sensational novel."—*Echo.*

THE ADVENTURES OF ROBINSON CRUSOE.

By DANIEL DEFOE. Newly Edited after the Original Editions. With Twenty Illustrations, by KAUFFMAN, printed in colours. Fcap. 4to., cloth extra 0 7 6

"This is irrefutably the edition of 'Robinson Crusoe' of the season. It is charmingly got up and illustrated. The type and printing are excellent."—*Standard.*

MOLINOS.—Golden Thoughts from "The

Spiritual Guide" of MIGUEL DE MOLINOS, the Quietist. With a Preface by J. HENRY SHORTHOUSE, Author of "John Inglesant." 136 pp., large Fcap. 8vo., cloth extra or parchment ... 0 2 6

Readers of "John Inglesant" will be glad to have the opportunity of renewing their acquaintance with this Spanish Mystic of the Seventeenth Century, through the medium of a careful selection and translation of the best things in his "Guide."

Mr. T. Fisher Unwin, 26, Paternoster Square.

PILGRIM SORROW. By CARMEN SYLVA (The Queen of Roumania). Translated by HELEN ZIMMERN, Author of "The Epic of Kings." With Portrait-etching by LALAUZE. Square Crown 8vo., cloth extra 0 5 0

"For this nature of literature the Queen appears to have a special gift. . . . And never has she been happier than in her *Leidens Erdengang*, which lies before us to-day. The fundamental idea of this cycle of stories is wholly symbolical. . . . The next story . . . is a piece of exquisite writing . . . It is said that for the very charming motherly figure of Patience, the Queen's own mother, the wise and good Princess of Wied, has furnished the prototype. . . . The last story of the cycles, called *A Life*, changes into an elegiac tone, and depicts an existence spent in the search of Truth. Though slightly veiled, it is impossible to ignore its autobiographic character. We have here the soul of the Queen laid bare before us."—*Literary World* (Review of the German edition).

"If to write poetry upon a throne be rare of itself, it is certainly still rarer to find Queens giving artistic form to those moments of existence that approach the mysteries of human life. Already, in her "Sappho," the German poetess, who now occupies a throne, has treated of the relationship of man to the eternal, but the antique garb somewhat veiled her purpose, while here (in "Pilgrim Sorrow") she moves amid modern as well as universal life, and is thus able to reveal the whole depth of her feeling and lament. For what has inspired her poetic phantasy is the ever-unanswered question : Wherefore and whence is sorrow in the world? The treatment is throughout symbolical. . . . It deserves to be counted among the modern monuments of our literature."—Review of the first German edition in the *Augsburger Allgemeine Zeitung*, Nov. 2, 1882.

OTTILIE: an Eighteenth Century Idyl. By VERNON LEE, Author of "Belcaro," "Prince of the Hundred Soups," &c. Square 8vo, cloth extra ... 0 3 6

"A graceful little sketch. . . . Drawn with full insight into the period described."—*Spectator*.

"Pleasantly and carefully written. . . . The author lets the reader have a glimpse of Germany in the 'Sturm und Drang' period."—*Athenæum*.

"Ottilie von Craussen is a charming character."—*Leeds Mercury*.

"A graceful little picture. . . . Charming all through."— *Academy*.

"Of exquisite literary workmanship; it is full of interest."— *Galignani's Messenger*.

"It is a prose-poem which cannot fail to exercise on most readers a refining and purifying influence."—*Scotsman*.

"To all who relish a simple, natural, and most pathetic story, admirably told, we recommend this eighteenth century idyl."— *St. James' Gazette*.

New and Recent Books.

THE TEMPLE : Sacred Poems and Private Ejaculations. By Mr. GEORGE HERBERT. Small Crown. *New Edition*, with Introductory Essay by J. HENRY SHORTHOUSE, Author of "JOHN INGLESANT."

This is a fac-simile reprint by typography of the Original Edition of 1633. *No pains have been spared to make this an exact replica as regards paper, size, print, and binding.*

4th Edition, Sheep, imitation of Original Binding	0 5	0
Paper boards, Old Style, uncut edges	0 5	0
Imitation Morocco	0 6	0

"This charming reprint has a fresh value added to it by the Introductory Essay of the Author of 'John Inglesant.'"—*Academy*.

TALES OF MODERN OXFORD. By the Author of "Lays of Modern Oxford. Crown 8vo., cloth extra 0 6 0

POEMS AND HYMNS. By the Rev. G. T. COSTER, of Whitby. Fcap. 8vo., cloth extra, gilt edges 0 5 0

A CUP OF COFFEE. Illustrated. Fcap. 8vo., boards 0 1 0
"This pleasant gossiping monograph . . . . light and genial throughout."—*Daily Chronicle*.

THE HISTORY OF RASSELAS, Prince of Abyssinia. By SAMUEL JOHNSON, LL.D. A new edition, small crown 8vo. 0 1 0

Mr. T. Fisher Unwin, 26, Paternoster Square.

MEDITATIONS & DISQUISITIONS
ON THE FIRST PSALM : On the Penitential and the Consolatory Psalms. By Sir RICHARD BAKER, Knight, Author of "The Chronicle of England," &c. &c. A verbatim reprint in modern spelling. With Introduction by Rev. A. B. GROSART, LL.D., F.S.A. Portrait and Autograph. Crown 8vo., cloth 0 6 6

"We have long known the comments of Sir Richard Baker, and we have often wondered how they escaped reprinting. . . . He turns his text over and over, and sets it in new lights, and makes it sparkle and flash in the sunlight after a manner little known among the blind critics of the midnight school. Deep experience, remarkable shrewdness, and great spirituality are combined in Sir Richard. It is hard to quote from him, for he is always good alike, and yet he has more memorable sentences than almost any other writer."—*The Sword and Trowel.*

THOMAS CARLYLE, The Man and His
Books. Illustrated by Personal Reminiscences, Table Talk, and Anecdotes of Himself and his Friends. By WM. HOWIE WYLIE. Third edition revised and corrected. Crown 8vo., cloth extra ... 0 7 6

Reviewing the latest volumes on Carlyle, the *Spectator* of November 12, 1881, says :—"The best specimen is that by Mr. Howie Wylie, previously reviewed in these columns, a work which we know to have been read with pleasure by at least one warm and intimate friend of Carlyle, and to which, after perusing others of its kin, we return with a somewhat heightened estimate, from the point of view of the critic."

"One of the most masterly biographies—a bit of work, indeed, which it would be hard to surpass for sympathy, delicacy, liberality of view, and wealth of friendly insight."—*Contemporary Review.*

SUNSHINE AND SHADOWS : Sketches
of Thought, Philosophic and Religious. By WILLIAM BENTON CLULOW, author of "Essays of a Recluse." New and enlarged edition, with Portrait and Appendix. Crown 8vo., cloth extra... 0 5 0

"Should be a great favourite with the small class of readers who love condensed and concentrated expression, and who value a book in so far as it sets them thinking for themselves. Such readers will regard 'Sunshine and Shadows' as great spoil, as a companion in rambles, a book to be pencilled in the margin, to be taken down at odd moments as a refreshment. Readers who love Landor and Hare and Pascal will welcome Mr. Clulow's work and prize it highly."—*Bradford Observer.*

New and Recent Books.

FOOTPRINTS: Nature seen on its Human Side. By SARAH TYTLER, Author of "Papers for Thoughtful Girls," &c. With 125 Illustrations. 3rd and cheaper edition. Crown 8vo., cloth extra, coloured edges 0 3 6

" A book of real worth."—*Spectator.*

MODERN MISSIONS: Their Trials and Triumphs. By ROBERT YOUNG, Assistant Secretary to the Missions of the Free Church of Scotland. With many Illustrations, and a Mission Map. Third edition. Crown 8vo., cloth extra 0 5 0

"Tells the great story of the trials and triumphs of *Modern Missions*. It was a happy idea to endeavour to include that story, as briefly told as might be, in one small volume, so that Christian people of every Church might read within its four hundred pages the tale of what has been done in every land and by all sorts of Christians for the evangelisation of mankind. This book should certainly be placed upon the shelves of parish, congregational, and Sunday-school libraries. It is brief and comprehensive."—*Christian World.*

GERMAN LIFE AND LITERATURE. In a Series of Biographical Studies. By A. H. JAPP, LL.D. Demy 8vo., cloth 0 12 0

" This volume, as a whole, is admirable, each chapter being characterised by thoroughness, impartiality, fine critical discernment, an always m inly literary ab.lity, and, above all, a moral healthiness of tone. In fact, we are not acquainted with any English work, or, for that matter, with any Continental or American work, which we could place with so much confidence in the hands of a young student of modern German literature as the volume under review, and as special proof of our assertion we would select the essay on Goethe. . . . For this work we must express sincere gratitude to the author."—*Spectator.*

THE HUMAN VOICE AND THE CONNECTED PARTS: A Popular Guide for Speakers and Singers. By Dr. J. FARRAR. With Thirty-nine Illustrations. Crown 8vo. cloth extra. 0 3 6

" A very careful and minute exposition of vocal phenomena. Its utility is enhanced by a large number of diagrams."—*The Scotsman.*

" A work that is sure to be found of real practical value."—*British Quarterly Review.*

Mr. T. Fisher Unwin, 26, Paternoster Square.

THE "LIVES WORTH LIVING" SERIES
OF POPULAR BIOGRAPHIES. Illustrated.
Crown 8vo., cloth extra ... ... per vol. o 3 6

1. Leaders of Men.
2. Wise Words and Loving Deeds.
3. Master Missionaries.
4. Labour and Victory.
5. Heroic Adventure.

---

1. **LEADERS OF MEN**: A Book of Biographies specially written for Young Men. By H. A. PAGE, author of "Golden Lives." Crown 8vo., cloth extra, with Portraits. Fourth edition ... o 3 6

The Prince Consort.
Commodore Goodenough.
Robert Dick.
George Moore.
Samuel Greg.
Andrew Reed.
John Duncan.
Dr. John Wilson.
Lord Lawrence.

"Mr. Page thoroughly brings out the disinterestedness and devotion to high aims which characterise the men of whom he writes He has done his work with care and good taste."—*Spectator.*

"No one knows better than Mr. Page how to put within moderate compass the outstanding features of a life that has blessed the world so as to present a striking and impressive picture. This is just the volume to enlarge the views and to ennoble the aims of young men, and to such we specially commend it."—*Literary World.*

"Here is a book which should be in the hands of every boy in the kingdom in whose mind it is desirable to implant a true ideal of life, and a just notion of the proper objects of ambition ; and we may congratulate Mr. Page upon having carried out his task with all possible care and skill. 'Leaders of Men' is every way an admirable volume." —*Court Circular.*

---

2. **WISE WORDS & LOVING DEEDS**: A Book of Biographies for Girls. By E. CONDER GRAY. Crown 8vo., cloth extra, with Portraits. Fifth edition ... ... o 3 6

Mary Somerville.
Lady Duff Gordon.
Sarah Martin.
Ann Taylor.
Charlotte Elliott.
Madame Feller.
Baroness Bunsen.
Amelia Sieveking.
Mary Carpenter.
Catherine Tait.

"A series of brightly-written sketches of lives of remarkable women. The subjects are well chosen and well treated."—*Saturday Review.*

New and Recent Books.

"LIVES WORTH LIVING" SERIES.

3. **MASTER MISSIONARIES**: Studies in Heroic Pioneer Work. By ALEXANDER H. JAPP, LL.D., F.R.S.E. With Portraits and Illustrations. Crown 8vo. Third edition 0 3 6

"An extremely interesting book. The reader need not be afraid of falling into beaten tracks here."—*The Guardian.*

"A collection of sketches from the practised pen of Dr. Japp, of men who have rendered good service to their race. All are graphic and very interesting."—*Nonconformist.*

"It brings before the reader a vivid conception of all the grandest chapters in pioneer effort throughout the world. There are many who must have felt the want of just such a handy book as this, and these will be grateful to Dr. Japp."—*Glasgow Mail.*

"A really excellent and readable book."—*Literary Churchman*

4. **LABOUR AND VICTORY.** By A. H. JAPP, LL.D. Memoirs of Those who Deserved Success and Won it. Third edition, Crown 8vo., cloth extra 0 3 6

Sir James Outram.
Thomas Edward.
Sir James Simpson.
William Ellis.
Bishop Selwyn.
Sir Titus Salt.
Thos. Davidson.
Friedrich Augusti.

"There must assuredly be a large number of readers to whom these stories of the lives of such men will prove very acceptable."—*Spectator.*

"We should be glad to see this volume in the hands of thousands of boys and young men."—*Leeds Mercury.*

5. **HEROIC ADVENTURE**: Chapters in Recent Exploration and Discovery. Illustrated. Third edition. Crown 8vo., cloth extra 0 3 6

** *Containing in a popular form an account of the travels and adventures of great explorers of modern times, including Schweinfurth, Prejevalsky, Commander Markham, Vambery, Serpa Pinto, and Nordenskiöld.*

"Gives freshness to the old inexhaustible story of enterprise and discovery by selecting some of the very latest of heroes in this field."—*Daily News.*

Mr. T. Fisher Unwin, 26, Paternoster Square.

I'VE BEEN A-GIPSYING: or Rambles among our Gipsies and their Children in their Tents and Vans. By GEORGE SMITH, of Coalville, Author of " Gipsy Life," " Canal Adventures by Moonlight," &c. *With an Appendix showing the Author's plans for the Compulsory Registration of Gipsy Vans, and the Education of Gipsy Children.* New and Revised and Popular Edition. 12 Illustrations ... ... o 3 6

Her Majesty the Queen has been graciously pleased to accept, and to thank Mr. Smith for, a copy of the above work.

The Rt. Hon. Sir Stafford Northcote, M.P., thus writes to the author :—"Accept my best thanks for your book, which cannot fail to be most interesting, both on account of the subject and of the author. Your good works will indeed live after you."

"Mr. Smith's sketches of his visits to the gipsies are graphic and varied, and will, we trust, serve to excite a wider interest in the perplexing question of their amelioration, to which the author has already given yeoman's service."—*Contemporary Review.*

THE ROMAN STUDENTS; or, On the Wings of the Morning. A Tale of the Renaissance. By the Author of " The Spanish Brothers," &c. With Illustrations by G. P. JACOMB HOOD. Cheaper edition. Imperial 8vo., cloth extra ... o 4 6

"One of the best stories of the year."—*British Quarterly Review.*

AMERICAN DISHES, and How to Cook Them. From the Recipe-book of an American Lady. Crown 8vo., cloth extra ... ... o 2 6

" A smart little tome . . . Fisheries and fish being at present in the ascendant, I should recommend all culinary students to turn to the section of the lady's book devoted to fish recipes and general instructions how to choose and prepare the denizens of the deep for the table . . . She is great also in fish-balls . . . Consult her pages likewise for baked beans, hominy, potato puffs, rye meal, squash biscuits, and minced cabbage. In soups she is strong."—G. A. S., in *Illustrated London News.*

DICK'S HOLIDAYS, and What He Did with Them. A Picture Story Book of Country Life. By JAMES WESTON. Profusely Illustrated. Imperial 4to., Cheaper edition, cloth extra ... ... o 3 6

"This is precisely the book that sensible parents must often have been wanting. . . . This delightful book."—*Academy.*

" A delightful collection."—*Graphic.*

New and Recent Books.

NEW AND CHEAPER EDITIONS.

GUDRUN, BEOWULF, and ROLAND. With other Mediæval Tales. By JOHN GIBB. With 20 Illustrations. Second and cheaper edition. Crown 8vo., cloth extra 0 3 6

"This volume will be certain to charm youthful readers ; and a safer or more acceptable gift-book it would be difficult to find. . . . Without some such work these precious prototypes of Anglo-Germanic romance would have remained sealed volumes for all youthful readers ; they therefore owe a debt of gratitude to him who has translated, condensed, and put them into a popular prose form for their perusal."—*Academy.*

THE HOUSE BY THE WORKS. By EDWARD GARRETT, Author of "Occupations of a Retired Life," &c., &c. With Frontispiece. Third and Cheaper edition. Crown 8vo., cloth extra ... 0 3 6

" The girls with their Quaker and Moravian training, the worthy and benevolent Mrs. Pendlebury, and society generally, rich and poor, in Perford, are depicted with skill."—*Daily News.*

"The picture he gives us here of the Enticknapp household, with its Moravian and Quaker traditions, is one nearly perfect of its kind for sobriety of taste and freedom from all sentimental exaggerations."—*Graphic.*

THE PRINCE OF THE HUNDRED SOUPS : A Puppet Show in Narrative. Edited, with a Preface by VERNON LEE, Author of " Belcaro," " Studies of the Eighteenth Century in Italy," &c. With Four Illustrations in Sepia, by SARAH BIRCH. Cheaper edition. Square 8vo.,cloth 0 3 6

" There is more humour in the volume than in half-a-dozen ordinary pantomimes."—*Spectator.*

" The preface is really more interesting than the ' Prince of the Hundred Soups,' and that—as we hope our readers will find out for themselves—is saying a good deal."—*Academy.*

" For myself, I can say that it had upon me the appetising effect of that dish in Horace which 'replaced the sated guest upon his elbow ;' for though, when I took it up, I was utterly weary and dazed with the number of books I had gone through, yet I devoured it from cover to cover with a new zest."—*Truth.*

Mr. T. Fisher Unwin, 26, Paternoster Square.

INDUSTRIAL CURIOSITIES: Glances Here and There in the World of Labour. Written and Edited by ALEXANDER HAY JAPP, LL.D., F.R.S.E. Fourth edition. Crown 8vo., cloth extra o 3 6

"Would make an excellent prize or present-book, especially for boys with a taste for miscellaneous information. Anyone, however, whose notion of a book is not limited to novels ought to be able to read it with pleasure, and can hardly do so without profit."—*Academy.*

"Dr. Japp travels through a variety of subjects, always entertaining and instructive."—*Spectator.*

"Nowadays boys are so fed upon story books and books of adventure that we welcome a book which tells them something about the facts of the world they live in."—*Graphic.*

PLANT LIFE: Popular Papers on the Phenomena of Botany. By EDWARD STEP. With 148 Illustrations drawn by the Author. Third edition. Crown 8vo., cloth extra ... . o 3 6

OPINIONS OF THE PRESS.

"The author has produced a little volume well suited to attract the attention and stimulate the curiosity of the student. By clothing the dry details of morphological construction with information as to the life history of plants, and by calling attention to the varied adaptations of form to function, he has followed in the wake of that numerous band of naturalists who have at once done so much to extend the bounds of botanical science, and to make it attractive to the amateur."—*Athenæum.*

"More delightful reading for the country at this season of the year authors and publishers have not provided for us."—*Pall Mall Gazette.*

"An unpretending book, whose contents cover a very great extent of botanical ground."—*Science Gossip.*

ILLUSTRATED CATALOGUE OF THE ROYAL SOCIETY OF PAINTERS IN WATER COLOURS, 1885. With Facsimiles of Sketches by the Artists. Demy 8vo. [*Just Ready* o 1 o

New and Recent Books.

NEW AND RECENT POETRY.

A MINOR POET: And other Verses. By
AMY LEVY. Crown 8vo., paper board style, uncut
edges ... ... o 3 6

"A distinct advance in power on Miss Levy's former verse.
. . . It will be hard if her verse does not win many friends by its
sympathy and tenderness."—*Cambridge Review.*
"Some of her more ambitious pieces remind one of George
Eliot's poems."—*St. James's Gazette.*
"Her idea of the character of 'Xantippe' is certainly original,
and several of her shorter pieces are simple, heartfelt, and har-
monius."—*Whitehall Review.*
"Deserves to be singled out from the mass of every-day verse
for special commendation. The book is very much above the
average of such productions."—*Derby Mercury.*

MEASURED STEPS. By ERNEST RADFORD.
Crown 8vo., cloth ... ... o 4 o

"He is very happy in his 'Translations from Heine,' fully
entering into the poet's humour, and deftly reproducing the half-
sarcastic, half-pathetic spirit in which Heine so often wrote."—
Whitehall Review.
"Mr. Radford is himself a poet of no mean ability, and with a
good deal of Heine in his composition."—*Sheffield Independent.*
"He has imported into his deeper verse the beauty of a half-
regretful subtlety and the interest of a real penetration. He can
think with fineness and record his thoughts with point."—
Frederick Wedmore, in The Academy.

POEMS AND BALLADS. By PRYCE
GWYNNE. Square Crown 8vo., cloth extra ... o 3 6

COLLEGE DAYS: Recorded in Blank Verse.
Printed on Dutch hand-made paper. Fcap. 8vo.,
parchment ... ... o 5 o

A RIVER HOLIDAY. The Lay of a Boat-
ing Trip. With 17 Illustrations by HARRY
FURNISS. Demy 8vo. ... ... o 1 o

"This delightful *brochure* is exquisitely illustrated."—*Society.*

Mr. T. Fisher Unwin, 26, Paternoster Square.

THE TREASURE BOOK OF CON-
SOLATION: For all in Sorrow or Suffering.
Compiled and Edited by BENJAMIN ORME, M.A.,
Editor of "The Treasure Book of Devotional
Reading." Crown 8vo., cloth extra, gilt top ... o 3 6

BEAUTIES AND FRIGHTS, WITH
THE STORY OF BOBINETTE. By SARAH
TYTLER, Author of "Papers for Thoughtful Girls,"
"Footprints," &c. Illustrated by M. E.
EDWARDS. Second Edition. Small 8vo., cloth
extra, gilt edges ... ... o 2 6

"Miss Tytler is one of the few writers of modern times who know how to write girls' stories. It is impossible for her to be dull; her tales are always sprightly, easy, and clever, and while she does not condescend to preach, there are admirable life-lessons to be learned in all she writes."—*Literary World.*

THE SHIPWRECKED MARINER: A
Quarterly Maritime Magazine. Edited by W.
R. BUCK, Secretary of the Shipwrecked Mariners'
Society. Illustrated. Published in January, April,
July, and October ... ... o o 6
Yearly Volumes o 3 6

*** *Adopted by the London School Board.*
FIRST NATURAL HISTORY READER.
For Standard II. In accordance with the require-
ments of the Revised Code. Beautifully Illustrated.
Crown 8vo., cloth ... ... o o 9

"Written in a simple and pleasant style."—*School Guardian.*

"The woodcuts, which are to be found on every page, will make the lessons pleasant to the scholars, and the text is wisely put in a semi-conversational form, calculated to induce intelligent reading."—*Publisher's Circular.*

New and Recent Books.

MARGARET THE MOONBEAM: A
Tale for the Young. By CECILIA LUSHINGTON, Author of "Over the Seas and Far Away." With Illustrations by M. E. EDWARDS. Second Edition. Small 8vo., cloth extra, gilt edges 0 2 6

VERS DE SOCIÉTÉ & PARODY, with
other Essays. By H. A. PAGE, Author of "De Quincey," and "Thoreau." Crown 8vo., cloth extra 0 2 6

"We have been much interested in this amusing and instructive volume, the first half of which is devoted to 'Vers de Société and Parody.' . . . If published alone this essay itself would have deserved to have been placed alongside of the famous Rejected Addresses."—*Literary World.*

THE ILLUSTRATED POETRY BOOK
for Young Readers. Sm. Crown 8vo., cloth extra 0 2 6
Gilt edges 0 3 0

"It is the best book of the kind which has passed through our hands for some time."—*Bookseller.*

THE WAY TO FORTUNE: A Series of
Short Essays, with Illustrative Proverbs and Anecdotes from many sources. Third edition. Small 8vo., cloth extra 0 2 6

"Profusely illustrated with proverbs and anecdotes, which being throughout apt to the injunctions, are likely to act as useful memories, when the text of 'The Way to Fortune' is not at hand."—*The Inquirer.*

"The author is not only a man with a large outlook upon human affairs, but with a wide and varied knowledge of English literature. Any young man—or, for that matter, any young woman—who will lay the counsels of this book to heart, cannot fail to find the way to nobility, fruitfulness, and usefulness of life, if not to fortune. We could wish nothing better for this book than to see it in the hands of all who set any value on self-help."—*Literary World.*

"This is not a big book, but it contains no fewer than fifty essays. Each is necessarily brief, and yet there is not one that does not contain a large amount of wisdom, made more effective by the help of illustrative proverbs and anecdotes."—*Freeman.*

Mr. T. Fisher Unwin, 26, Paternoster Square.

PRINCIPLES TO START WITH. By ISAAC WATTS, D.D. Introduction by THOMAS BINNEY, D.D. Seventh Thousand. 32mo, red edges, cloth elegant, or in the new wood binding: maple, cedar, walnut, and sycamore 0 1 0

"A gem in the way of printing and binding, while the excellence of the short practical precepts offered by the writers can hardly be over-estimated."—*Rock.*

"Just the sort of book for a young man setting out in life. It can easily be carried in the waistcoat pocket, and we can conceive of no better *vade mecum*. It is seldom that we meet with so much good sense packed into so small a space."—*Congregationalist.*

THE CHILDREN'S BOUQUET OF Verse and Hymn. Gathered by AUNT SARAH and COUSIN GRACE. 32mo, red edges, cloth elegant, or wood : maple, cedar, walnut, or sycamore ... 0 1 0

"Love for the little ones has clearly been at work in the making of this selection; good taste as well, and a most catholic sympathy."—*Christian Leader.*

"Its little verses and hymns are selected with fine taste and appreciation of children's likings. Externally, the book is a little gem."—*Baptist.*

"One of the daintiest of dainty little books for little people. The selection of verses is admirable, containing, with some old favourites, many that will be fresh to most children."—*Christian.*

THE STARRY BLOSSOM, and OTHER STORIES. By M. BETHAM-EDWARDS, Author of "Minna's Holiday," &c. Illustrations by Miss JOANNA SAMWORTH. Small 8vo., cloth extra... 0 1 6

DAN STAPLETON'S LAST RACE. By Mrs. MILNE RAE, Author of "Morag," "Hartleigh Towers," &c. Small 8vo., cloth extra ... 0 1 6

WINMORE & CO. A Tale of the Great Bank Failure. Small 8vo., cloth extra 0 1 0

New and Recent Books.

HALF-HOLIDAY HANDBOOKS:

Guides to Rambles round London. With Maps, Illustrations, and Bicycle Routes. Crown 8vo.,

	s.	d.
sewed	0	9
Cloth	1	0

I. KINGSTON - ON - THAMES AND DISTRICT.
II. ROUND REIGATE.
III. DORKING AND DISTRICT.
IV. ROUND RICHMOND.
V. GEOLOGICAL RAMBLES ROUND LONDON: A Guide to Old-World London.
VI. ROUND TUNBRIDGE WELLS.
VII. GREENWICH, BLACKHEATH, AND DISTRICT.
VIII. FROM CROYDON TO THE NORTH DOWNS.
IX. ROUND BROMLEY, KESTON, AND DISTRICT.
X. ROUND SYDENHAM & NORWOOD.
XI. WIMBLEDON, PUTNEY, AND DISTRICT, including BARNES, ROEHAMPTON, MERTON, &c.
EPPING FOREST AND DISTRICT.
HAMPSTEAD, HIGHGATE, FINCHLEY, AND DISTRICT.
GUILDFORD, GODALMING, AND DISTRICT.

The last three are in preparation.

"We could not do better than consult one of these cheap Handbooks."—*Times.*

"Those 'Half-Holiday Handbooks' are very useful. But why not 'Whole Holiday Pocket Books,' showing where to go, when to go, and how to go it? If Mr. Fisher Unwin doesn't look sharp, we shall have this series out ourselves about Whitsuntide."—*Punch.*

"Will be a boon to the weary Londoner, anxious to commune with nature."—*The Inquirer.*

"Capital guides to walks in the districts."—*Daily Chronicle.*

"A pleasant and convenient series of books for the guidance of the pedestrian."—*Literary World.*

"An idea with which we and our fellow-naturalists heartily sympathise. The series is one marked by that feeling for nature which it is so desirable to extend."—H. W., in *Bayswater Chronicle.*

"The publishers have hit upon a good idea in their Half-Holiday Handbooks, which are likely to become popular favourites."—*Graphic.*

Mr. T. Fisher Unwin, 26, Paternoster Square.

A HANDBOOK TO
THE FERNERY AND AQUARIUM,
containing full directions how to make, stock, and maintain Ferneries and Freshwater Aquaria. By J. H. MARTIN and JAMES WESTON. With 43 Illustrations. Crown 8vo., cloth extra 0 1 0
Paper Covers... 0 0 9

*** Issued also in two parts, paper covers, 6d. each.

"We cordially recommend it as the best little *brochure* on ferns we have yet seen. Its merits far exceed those of much larger and more pretentious works."—*Science Gossip.*

ADULTERATIONS OF FOOD (How to
Detect the). By the Author of "Ferns and Ferneries." Numerous Illustrations. Crown 8vo., sewed 0 0 9

"The little work before us offers many useful hints to householders as to the detection of everyday adulteration."—*Pall Mall Gazette.*

THE BATH AND BATHING. By Dr. J.
FARRAR, F.R.C.P.E. Crown 8vo., limp cloth ... 0 0 9

"Dr. Farrar's manual is not only cheap, but it is so clear, concise, and practical that no one need fail to carry out his instructions, or in deriving wise counsel and direction from his pages."—*Literary World.*

GENESIS THE THIRD. History, not
Fable. Being the Merchants' Lecture for March, 1883. By EDWARD WHITE. Crown 8vo., Cloth extra 0 1 0
Sewed 0 0 6

SISTER EDITH'S PROBATION. By
E. CONDER GRAY, Author of "Wise Words." Small 8vo., cloth extra 0 1 0

"The three tales of which this volume is composed are not only well written, but cannot fail to strengthen those who read them, especially the young, in pure and holy living."—*Literary World.*

New and Recent Books.

EDUCATIONAL WORKS.
ARMY EXAMINATION SERIES.

I. GEOMETRICAL DRAWING: Containing General Hints to Candidates, Former Papers set at the Preliminary and Further Examinations, and Four Hundred Questions for Practice in Scales and General Problems. By C. H. OCTAVIUS CURTIS. Illustrated. Crown 8vo., cloth extra 0 2 6

II. A MANUAL OF FRENCH GRAMMAR. By LE COMPTE DE LA HOUSSAYE, Officier de la Légion d'Honneur, French Examiner for Military and Civil Appointments. Crown 8vo., cloth extra... 0 2 6

III. GEOGRAPHY QUESTIONS: Especially adapted for Candidates preparing for the Preliminary Examination. By R. H. ALLPRESS, M.A., Trin. Coll., Camb. Crown 8vo., cloth extra 0 2 6

EASY LESSONS IN BOTANY. By EDWARD STEP, Author of "Plant Life." With 120 Illustrations by the Author. Third Edition. Linen covers ... 0 0 7
Also in two parts, paper covers, 3d. each.

OPINIONS OF THE PRESS.

"Numerously illustrated, clearly written, with a good deal of matter packed with much dexterity into a small space."—*Science Gossip.*

"The arrangement is good; the illustrations are very numerous, there being three or four on almost every page; and the writer has done much to simplify the subject."—*School Guardian.*

POETICAL READER FOR THE USE OF SCHOOLS. Arranged on an entirely new principle, with Illustrations specially done for the work. In Two Parts, each 0 1 3
Or in sections separately.

"The editor of these two little volumes has managed to strike out an entirely new line for his pupils, and one which scarcely at any point crosses the beaten track."—*School Board Chronicle.*

AN ENGLISH GRAMMAR FOR SCHOOLS. Adapted to the Requirements of the Revised Code. In Three Parts. Price 2d. each, or complete in one cover 0 0 6

Mr. T. Fisher Unwin, 26, Paternoster Square.

TARANTELLA: A Romance. By MATHILDE BLIND, Author of "Life of George Eliot," "Saint Oran." Two vols. Crown 8vo. 1 1 0

ICHABOD: A Portrait. By BERTHA THOMAS, Author of "The Violin Player," "Life of Georges Sand," &c. Two vols. Crown 8vo. 1 1 0

WILBOURNE HALL. By Mrs. CAUMONT, Author of "Uncle Anthony's Note Book." Two vols. Crown 8vo. 1 1 0

THE CHANCELLOR OF THE TYROL. By HERMAN SCHMID. Translated by DOROTHEA ROBERTS. Two vols. Crown 8vo. [*Just Out* 1 1 0

CAMILLA'S GIRLHOOD. By LINDA VILLARI, Author of "On Tuscan Hills and Venetian Waters," "In Change Unchanged," &c. Two vols. Crown 8vo. ... ... [*In the Press* 1 1 0

A NOBLE KINSMAN: A Novel. By ANTON GIULIO BARRILI, Author of "Like a Dream," &c. Translated from the Italian by H. A. MARTIN. Two vols. Crown 8vo. [*Just Ready* 1 1 0

JEPHTHAH'S DAUGHTER: A Novel. By JANE H. SPETTIGUE, Author of "The Gregorys: A Cornish Story," "Love and Money too." Two vols. Crown 8vo. ... [*In Preparation* 1 1 0

MAJOR FRANK: A Novel. By A. L. G. BOSBOOM-TOUSSAINT, Author of "The English in Rome," "Raymond the Cabinet-Maker." Translated from the Dutch by JAMES AKEROYD. One vol. Crown 8vo., cloth ... ... [*Ready* 0 6 0

www.ingramcontent.com/pod-product-compliance
Lightning Source LLC
Chambersburg PA
CBHW030750230426
43667CB00007B/917